C000269959

"Never has the field of payments been more dynamic, nor more exciting. The sheer volume and pace of change and innovation across our industry, reflected in unprecedented levels of investment as well as M&A, is just extraordinary. *The PayTech Book* provides an excellent foundation to help the reader navigate everything that's going on worldwide, and to better understand the drivers for all of that activity."

Jim Wadsworth, SVP, Mastercard

"Technology and payments are yoked together. It is technology that is driving payments forward not only in developed markets but also in emerging markets where it is so important to have solutions that can enable the currently underbanked to have access to digital financial services. *The PayTech Book* provides a fascinating insight from industry thought leaders into how PayTech is powering the digital payments revolution."

John Chaplin, Chairman, Payments Innovation Jury

"Payment is the most fundamental building block of commerce, and technology has always been a part of it. The bronze age gave us tools to hammer out coins. The industrial revolution let us print bank notes en masse. And now, in the 21st Century, the way we pay is being revolutionised by digital technology.

From contactless cards to mobile wallets to cryptocurrencies, technology is making it easier, safer and more convenient to make payments. It's a trend that touches people at all levels of society, and it shows no sign of stopping. Which means there's no better time than now to understand how the world of payments technology works, how it's regulated, and how new innovations will change the way we all do business.

The PayTech Book has a lot to teach us about this payment revolution. More importantly, it will spark debates about the role PayTech plays in our global economy, and which future payment experiences can benefit businesses and customers alike."

Angela Yore, MD, SkyParlour

"Commerce is an essential requirem and families to thrive. Moreover, trus commerce and must perpetually ev users – or they're replaced. *The Pay* insights in areas such as complex a and products, technical considerati compliance and regulatory to enabl banks to thrive."

Gary Palmer, Co-founder, President, CEO, Chairman, First Performance, Chairman, TECS (tecs.at)

"*The PayTech Book* explains essential concepts of payments and current worldwide payment infrastructures for anyone to read and understand, offers a brilliant insight into the complex topic of regulation and compliance, including blockchain around the world, and finally provides possible responses to the most pressing payment questions and as how the future system could be shaped. It is a joy to read and I recommend it strongly."

Kamran Hedjri, Board Member, PXP Financial

"Keenly looking forward to *The PayTech Book*, the authors and contents suggest a formidable amount of brainpower and a fascinating read. This will be compulsory reading for the industry itself, but banks, retailers and large businesses ignore this revolution at their peril! I've worked closely with the editors and have the utmost respect for them. Enjoy!"

Mike Smith, Payments NED

"Few people understand the real influence and impact of payments and how they influence and promote economic growth. Few other consumer industries have adopted technology and innovated to the same extent as the payments space since the turn of the millennium and the pace of change over the last decade has been truly astonishing. From speed and ease of transaction and settlement to fraud detection and compliance there is no single discipline within payments that has not been materially and permanently changed for the better by the application of technology. Regulators consumers and merchants alike demand better, faster, more compliant, accountable, fraud-sure, frictionless and alternative payments. From watches and rings, to phones and fingerprints, the relentless application of technology and the willingness of both the established players and the burgeoning PayTech space to keep pushing the boundaries, the payments industry is undoubtedly answering all the questions posed of it. Who would have thought, just five short years ago that you would no longer need to buy a ticket to travel around London and always get the cheapest possible fare – as I say, astonishing."

Michael Harty, Founder MD, The Card and Payments Awards

"Payments has become a huge, global subject, with technology at its heart. So *The PayTech Book* is a 'must read' for all those involved in delivering or using payments. It very neatly takes the reader into this complex, evolving and interconnected world, drawing on insights from highly regarded industry experts, disruptive new market entrants and established players adopting digital transformation."

Paul Anning, Partner, Osborne Clarke LLP

"*The PayTech Book* provides context to the use of emergent, technology driven, financial service resources in each of many market sectors. Automated Fare Collection systems in the transport sector are rapidly developing into fully integrated environments leading on to MaaS and Smart Cities. PayTech excels in detailing how the financial services industry is keeping up with this progress."

Alan Leibert, Director, The ALCO Group Limited

"As we all know, 'PayTech' is well and truly embedded into the payments industry. 'FinTech' became ubiquitous when describing innovations within financial services, while PayTech encapsulates the specific technologies behind digital payment evolutions. It's these developments – plus the forward thinking companies behind them – that keep adding excitement to the payments ecosystem by innovating and pushing boundaries.

So, the key to staying on top is to keep expanding our knowledge and remain aware of industry issues. *The PayTech Book* offers just that opportunity – not only does it house a wealth of information on the infrastructure which supports payments, but clarifies and explores the regulation that ensures businesses and consumers are kept safe."

Tessa Unsworth, CCO at PrePay Solutions

The PayTech Book

A catalogue record for this book is available from the Library of Congress.

A catalogue record for this book is available from the British Library.

ISBN 978-1-119-55191-1 (paperback)   ISBN 978-1-119-55194-2 (ePDF)
ISBN 978-1-119-55195-9 (ePub)   ISBN 978-1-119-55197-3 (Obook)

10 9 8 7 6 5 4 3 2 1

Cover design: Wiley
Cover image: pkproject/Shutterstock

Set in 10/13pt Helvetica Lt Std by Aptara, New Delhi, India
Printed in Great Britain by TJ International Ltd, Padstow, Cornwall, UK

The PayTech Book

The Payment Technology Handbook for Investors, Entrepreneurs and FinTech Visionaries

Edited by
Susanne Chishti
Tony Craddock
Robert Courtneidge
Markos Zachariadis

Contents

5. Payments in Practice

6. Blueprint for Change

Preface

Join us on a journey through the fascinating world of payments. If you bring together consumers and businesses demanding change and a better customer experience, regulators enabling competition and technology making change possible, the future of payments is exciting, summarized in the term "PayTech". We will share our vision for how the digital world will unfold, what this means for cash, plastic cards, digital wallets and mobile money and the financially excluded, and how cooperation will allow the payments industry to satisfy consumers' and companies' growing needs for instant, convenient and secure payments.

We will explain the changing role of money in our lives, introduce the concept of programmable money and its adoption in a world of open banking, commonly accepted standards and digital identity. We also cover the impact of the network effect in payments, and how overlaying data-driven insights enables more effective marketing at the point of purchase. Cybersecurity and its importance in a world of increasingly sophisticated criminals is explained, and how data analytics and artificial intelligence can prevent fraud and money laundering.

McKinsey forecasts that **payments** will become a US$2 trillion business by 2020.[1] Payment transactions are increasing as economic activity grows, and the demand for payments is expected to rise globally as developing countries build their infrastructures and become more financially inclusive and as the emergence of the digital economy allows for more "on-demand" products and services driven by consumer demand. Investments in the sector have been strong – global PayTech investment reached US$18 billion across 123 deals in 2018. The record funding was due to Ant Financial's US$14 billion deal.[2]

In summary, the payments and PayTech sector is booming, with FinTech entrepreneurs and investors across the world working on the most cutting-edge solutions. In order to share with our readers the most valuable insights globally, we followed the same approach as with *The FinTech Book*, *The WealthTech Book* (focused on how new business models and technology innovation will change the global asset management and private banking sector) and *The InsurTech Book* (focused on the rapid changes in the global insurance market) – the first globally crowdsourced books on the financial technology revolution, published by Wiley, which have become global bestsellers.

The PayTech Book is the first crowdsourced book globally on the future of payments – a book that provides food for thought to FinTech newbies, pioneers and well-seasoned experts alike. The reason we decided to reach out to the global payment and FinTech community in sourcing the book's contributors lies in the inherently fragmented nature of the field of payments technology. There was no single author, group of authors or indeed region in the world that could cover all the facets and nuances of PayTech in an exhaustive manner. What is more, by being able to reach out to a truly global contributor base, we not only stayed true to the spirit of FinTech and PayTech – making use of technological channels of communication in reaching out to, selecting and reviewing our

---

[1] https://www.mckinsey.com/~/media/McKinsey/Industries/Financial%20 Services/Our%20Insights/Global%20payments%20Expansive%20 growth%20targeted%20opportunities/Global-payments-map-2018.ashx.

[2] https://fintech.global/global-paytech-investment-in-2018-set-a-new-record/.

would-be contributors – we also made sure that every corner of the globe had the chance to have its say. Thus, we aimed to fulfil one of the most important purposes of *The PayTech Book*, namely to give a voice to those who would remain unheard – those who did not belong to a true FinTech and PayTech community in their local areas – and spread that voice to an international audience. We have immensely enjoyed the journey of editing *The PayTech Book* and sincerely hope that you will enjoy reading it at least as much.

More than 148 authors from 30 countries submitted 168 abstracts to be part of the book. We asked our global FinTech and payment communities for their views regarding which abstracts they would like to have fully expanded for *The PayTech Book*. Out of all the contributors, we selected 74 authors who have been asked to write their full chapter, which has now been included in this book. We conducted a questionnaire among all our selected authors to further understand their background and expertise. In summary, our selected authors come from 20+ countries. The majority of our authors have postgraduate university degrees (60%, see Table 1),

Table 1: What is the highest educational qualification of our 74 authors?

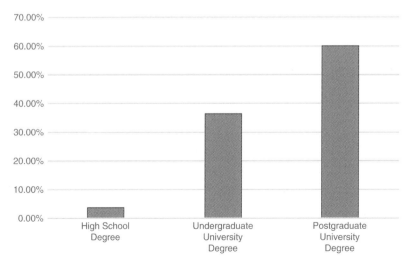

Table 2: List all areas in which our authors have domain expertise, multiple choices were possible

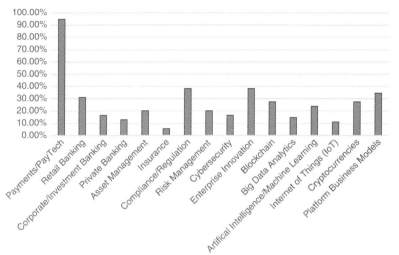

strong domain expertise across many fields (see Table 2) and over 87% of our finalist authors have had their articles published before.

Tables 3 and 4 show that almost half our finalist authors are entrepreneurs working for FinTech startups (many of them part of the founding team), a quarter come from established financial and technology companies and another quarter from service providers such as consulting firms or law firms servicing the FinTech and payments sectors.

A quarter of our authors work for startups with up to 10 people and another 40% for startups/small and medium enterprises (SMEs) of up to 100 people. A third of our authors are employed by a large organization of more than 100 employees.

We are very proud of our highly qualified authors, their strong expertise and passion for payments, PayTech and FinTech – either

Table 3: Authors selected the type of company they work in

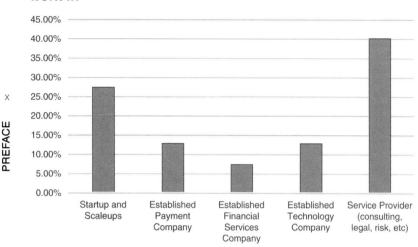

Table 4: Size of companies our authors work for

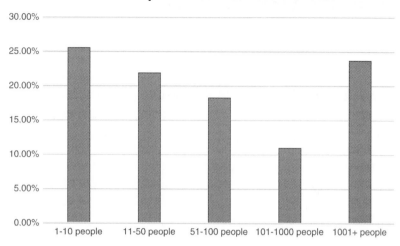

through being entrepreneurs or often "intrapreneurs" in large established organizations, all of whom are committed to playing a significant role in the global FinTech and PayTech revolution. These remarkable people are willing to share their insights with all of us over the next pages.

This book would not have been possible without the dedication and efforts of all contributors to *The PayTech Book* (both those who submitted their initial abstracts for consideration by the global FinTech community, as well as the final authors whose insights you will be reading shortly). In addition, we would like to thank our editors at Wiley, whose guidance and help made sure that what started off as an idea, you are now holding in your hands.

Finally, I would like to thank my fantastic co-editors Tony Craddock, Director General of the Emerging Payments Association, Robert Courtneidge, CEO Moorwand and Markos Zachariadis, Professor at Alliance Manchester Business School. Editing a crowdsourced book naturally takes several months and Tony, Robert and Markos were always a pleasure to work with, given their strong domain expertise and vision for the future of payments!

Susanne Chishti
Bestselling Co-Editor, The FINTECH Book Series
CEO FINTECH Circle & FINTECH Circle Institute

About the Editors

Susanne Chishti (Editor in Chief)

Susanne Chishti is the CEO of FINTECH Circle, Europe's first angel network focused on FinTech opportunities and founder of the FINTECH Circle Institute, the leading FinTech learning and innovation platform offering corporate innovation workshops to C-level executives and online FinTech courses. She is also the bestselling co-editor of *The FinTech Book*, *The WealthTech Book* and *The InsurTech Book* (published by Wiley). Awards:

- FinTech Champion of the Year 2019 (Women in Finance Awards)
- Social Media Influencer of the Year 2018 (*Investment Week*)
- Top 7 Crypto Experts Globally 2018 (*Inc Magazine*)
- City Innovator – Inspirational Woman in 2016
- European Digital Financial Services "Power 50", an independent ranking of the most influential people in digital financial services in Europe (2015)

After completing her MBA, she started her career working for a FinTech company (before the term "FinTech" had been invented) in Silicon Valley some 20 years ago. She then worked for more than 15 years across Deutsche Bank, Lloyds Banking Group, Morgan Stanley and Accenture in London and Hong Kong. Susanne is an award-winning entrepreneur and investor with strong FinTech expertise. She is a judge and coach at global FinTech events and competitions and a conference keynote speaker. Susanne leads a global community of more than 130,000 FinTech entrepreneurs, investors and financial services professionals globally (www.fintechcircle.com).

Tony Craddock

An enthusiastic leader of the world's most influential association in payments, a lively public speaker and avid networker, Tony is passionate about payments and the difference they can make to lives everywhere.

Tony shares his deep payments knowledge born from 15 years' experience, and his evangelical zeal for innovation, when speaking and chairing conferences; publishing books and white papers; or enrolling leaders to join the Emerging Payments Association (EPA)'s collaboration network.

His role at the EPA is also to help shape projects that drive lasting change. These cover areas such as financial exclusion, open banking, financial crime, diversity, international trade and banking access.

Tony conceived and launched the EPA in 2012 and is its Director General. The EPA promotes the UK as a global hub for payments innovation and the interests of the EPA's 150+ members, which include banks, card schemes, payments service providers, issuers, processors and acquirers, who all come together to drive collective industry change.

Tony also leads the communities of EPA Asia, EPA EU, EPA USA and EPA Africa. His vision is that this global network of interconnected capabilities, people and knowledge will prove to be truly transformational in how the world works, for the benefit of everyone.

Robert Courtneidge

Robert Courtneidge was appointed CEO of international payments specialist Moorwand in 2018, following a distinguished career in the card and payments industry dating back nearly 30 years. He has been named amongst the Payments Power 10, a highly competitive ranking of the most influential payments industry contributors, for six consecutive years and was voted No. 1 in 2015.

During his career working across the entire payments ecosystem, Robert has developed a deep expertise in e-money, having supported projects for major financial institutions and well known technology providers globally. Robert is highly skilled in all aspects of consumer finance issues, including consumer protection, banking regulation and compliance and data protection.

Previously, Robert achieved success as a senior legal professional specializing in matters related to the cards and payments industry, and has been recognized in the Legal 500 for Corporate and Commercial – Financial Services.

Robert is a frequent spokesperson on current issues facing the European payments industry, including the second Payment Services Directive, fourth Anti-Money Laundering Directive and the laws relating to blockchain, cryptocurrencies and initial coin offerings. He travels globally to speak about card payments and financial technology. He is a regular writer in a number of key payments industry publications, and co-presenter of the Fintech Unplugged podcast.

Markos Zachariadis

Markos Zachariadis is Professor and Chair in Financial Technology and Information Systems at the Alliance Manchester Business School, University of Manchester, and a FinTech Research Fellow at the University of Cambridge. Markos's research sits at the cross-section of economics and strategy of digital innovation, financial technology studies and network economics, and he has studied extensively the economic impact of information and communication technology adoption on bank performance, the diffusion of payment networks and the role of data and standards in financial infrastructures and markets. His research has been published in top academic journals and books, and he has been awarded the NET Institute award for his study on the economics of payment networks and the SWIFT Institute and GRI awards for his research on open application programming interfaces and digital transformation in banking.

A board advisor, mentor and international keynote speaker, Markos has been invited to present his research insights to various international conferences, governments and global organizations. He was also the organizer of an international PayTech conference at WBS, funded by the Gates Foundation and Mastercard.

In the past, Markos has been a Professor of Information Systems Management and Digital Innovation at Warwick Business School, a Visiting Professor in FinTech at Ivey Business School, Western University, a Research Associate at Judge Business School, University of Cambridge and a Visiting Scholar at London Business School. He holds an MSc and PhD from the London School of Economics.

Acknowledgements

After the global book launch events of *The FinTech Book*, *The WealthTech Book* and *The InsurTech Book*, we met thousands of FinTech entrepreneurs, investors and financial services and technology professionals who all loved the books and wanted to learn more about how payment technology will change not only financial services, but our world overall.

We came up with the idea for *The PayTech Book* and spoke to our payment friends globally. Payment entrepreneurs across all continents were eager to share their powerful insights. They wanted to explain the new business models and technologies they were working on to change the world of sending and receiving payments to individuals and organizations globally. FinTech investors, "intrapreneurs", innovation leaders at leading financial and technology institutions and thought leaders were keen to describe their embrace of the payment revolution. Payments are part of our lives, every day.

The global effort of crowdsourcing such insights was born with *The FinTech Book*, which became a global bestseller across 107 countries in 10 languages. We continued this success with *The WealthTech Book* and *The InsurTech Book*. We hope we can satisfy the appetite for knowledge and insights about the future of payments with this book.

We are aware that this would not have been possible without the global FINTECH Circle community, the Emerging Payment Association, the Fintech Unplugged Podcast and our own personal networks. We are very grateful to more than 130,000 members of FINTECH Circle for joining us daily across our website (www.FINTECHCircle.com) and our Twitter accounts and LinkedIn groups. Without the public support and engagement of our global FinTech and payment communities, this book would not have been possible.

The authors you will read have been chosen by our global payment community purely on merit: thus no matter how big or small their organization, no matter in which country they work, no matter if they are well known or still undiscovered, everybody had the same chance to apply and be part of *The PayTech Book*. We are proud of that, as we believe payments are at the centre of the world of finance. The global payment and PayTech communities are made up of the smartest, most innovative and nicest people we know. Thank you for being part of our journey. It is difficult to name you all here, but you are all listed in the directory at the end of the book.

Wiley, our publisher, has been a great partner for The FinTech Book Series and we are delighted that they will again publish

The PayTech Book in paperback and e-book formats globally. Special thanks go to our fantastic editor Gemma Valler. Thank you and your team – we could not have done it without your amazing support!

We look forward to hearing from you. Please visit our website (www.paytechbook.com) for additional bonus content from our global payment community! Please send us your comments on *The PayTech Book* and let us know how you wish to be engaged by dropping us a line at info@FINTECHCircle.com.

Susanne Chishti
Twitter: @SusanneChishti

Robert Courtneidge
Twitter: @PrepaidRobert

Twitter: @FINTECHCircle
@FTC_Institute
@FTCInnovate
@PayTechBook

Instagram: @FINTECHCircle
@PayTechBook

Tony Craddock
Twitter: @TonyCraddock

Prof. Markos Zachariadis
Twitter: @MarkosZach

ACKNOWLEDGEMENTS

Payments Explained

PAYMENTS 101

What are payments?
- How do they work?
- Where are they going?

How Automated Clearing House (ACH) and Real-time Cross Settlement (RTGS) systems work?

What is "payments as a service"?

 New emerging banks and their role in payments

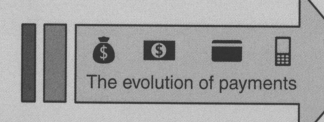 The evolution of payments

 Competing means of Payments: "The Race"

 "Payments are getting political again"

Payments regulation trends:
- Nationalism
- Compliant Innovation
- Interoperability
- Competition
- Cybersecurity

Executive Summary

From banknotes and coins, to plastic cards and mobile devices, payments have evolved over the centuries to include a number of instruments and means that help financial transactions to take place in the real economy. By nature, payment transactions are increasing as economic activity grows; the demand for payments is expected to rise globally as developing countries build their infrastructures and become more financially inclusive, and as the emergence of the digital economy allows for more "on-demand" products and services driven by consumer demand. But what exactly is in a payment and how are these cleared and settled in a modern financial system? What are the different technologies and infrastructures involved, and which elements are necessary in order to facilitate a payment?

This part looks at the broader question of *what's in a payment?* and provides explanations and descriptions of the various stages and elements of payment systems, as well as how automated clearing houses and real-time settlement systems work. It looks at these from historical as well as technological, procedural, socio-political and regulatory perspectives. It goes on to put this in the context of modern and emerging economies around the world. Special focus is put on the evolution of money and payments that look at the material representations of money, the establishment of electronic transactions and payment institutions, and the emergence of cashless societies. Case studies from emerging infrastructures and regulatory trends are used in order to illustrate progress in the field, and examples of new business model approaches – such as "payments as a service" – are highlighted to demonstrate how many of these technologies can introduce new business opportunities.

Payments are Getting Political Again

By Bill Maurer
Dean of the School of Social Sciences, University of California, Irvine, CA

In the USA, more and more retailers are adopting a "no cash" policy, only accepting payments by card or mobile phone. Sweden has long been touted as a country on an inexorable march towards becoming a "cashless society". In both countries, however, policy-makers are starting to worry about the impact of cashlessness on the public good. Some states and municipalities have even taken up the cause of cash, arguing that refusing cash unfairly excludes the un- and underbanked from everyday commerce, and disproportionately impacts the elderly and recent immigrants. Some of them even see Indian Prime Minister Narendra Modi's demonetization of high-denomination rupee notes as a cautionary tale. It sparked panic across the country during November and December of 2016, as people sought to exchange old notes for new, while the existing digital payment infrastructure was unprepared for an influx of new users.

Meanwhile, mobile app-based payments have swept through China. Alipay and WeChat Pay provide all-in-one suites of services, allowing users to purchase short-term bicycle rentals, order food delivery, buy movie tickets and even get fashion advice, and pay within the app or via QR codes scanned by the phone's camera. These companies have pioneered new ways to bridge the divide between the physical world and online or mobile interactions. Alipay can send near-instant push messages for shoppers in physical world stores containing digital offers and coupons, pegged to products customers have picked up and scanned with their phones while walking the aisles. WeChat and Alipay are going abroad, too, setting up across the world from the USA to Finland to provide payment options for Chinese tourists. Only those with Chinese bank accounts have access to these services, however, creating a sort of distributed, virtual zone of Chinese

state sovereignty created through payment, whether in Helsinki or Hanoi. In response, some countries have put restrictions on these companies, with Vietnamese authorities sanctioning store owners who set up WeChat and Alipay services without going through a Vietnamese intermediary.

Why Payments are Political

Payments are political in that they are a function of state sovereignty, and also an extension of it. This is old news, of course: money itself emanates from state sovereignty. But digital payments, obviating the anonymity of cash transactions and generating vast quantities of data in their wake, provide new opportunities for states to extend their reach. It goes without saying that the Chinese government is able to garner vast troves of information on its citizens in-country and overseas by tapping into the data streams of mobile payment services. Much is being made of the partnership between Alibaba, the parent company of Alipay, and the Chinese government around various "social credit" scoring schemes. But I think the more mundane practice of state surveillance via machine learning algorithms, which are learning to spot shopping behaviour in which the government believes it has an interest, is more chilling because it is so banal.

Payments in the World's Largest Economy

These politics of payments are not, of course, limited to authoritarian regimes. Payment providers have been enlisted into government service almost since their inception, whether in the tracking of cash to hamper criminal activities or in the regulations around customer due diligence and identification for cross-boundary payments of all kinds.

One of my colleagues once joked to me: "The [US] Bank Secrecy Act is the most moronically named law on the books.

It means the bank can keep no secrets from the government." When the card networks and PayPal froze donations via their networks to WikiLeaks in 2010, they inserted themselves into a debate over information security and freedom. They also created one of those moments when the politics of payments were made explicit: in the ability of payments infrastructure to serve political ends.

Operation Choke Point followed: the US Department of Justice in 2013 mandated that banks conduct additional scrutiny of transactions over the automated clearing house (ACH) marked with a set of codes for merchants deemed "high risk" for criminal activity and money laundering (firearms dealers, payday lenders, dating services and other businesses). This was suspended due to a political pushback from the right wing in 2017, which saw it as targeting businesses associated with their constituencies (such as the gun lobby). Most American legislators – to say nothing of the general public – probably didn't even know what the ACH was before this.

Payments Across a World in Turmoil

Recent geopolitical turmoil has put the spotlight on the politics of payments, too: it appears that Russian conspirators during the 2016 US Presidential election accepted payment in the cryptocurrency Bitcoin, in order to avoid the scrutiny of banking authorities. In February 2018, when there were rumours online that Chase Bank had been summarily closing the accounts of prominent figures of the white nationalist movement in the USA, there was renewed attention on Bitcoin among the far right. This underscored the origins of the cryptocurrency in libertarian philosophies about the relationship between so-called sound money and "liberty".

But this is also an old phenomenon. Payments are getting political, *again*.

In the USA, the abolition of interchange on cheques was one of the first important achievements of the Federal Reserve. It not only smoothed interstate commerce, but also represented a new extension of federal power over the states of the union. That the majority of non-par banking states were historically members of the Confederacy only underscores the politics of payment and, specifically, their inflection by histories of American racism. One can trace a lineage from those in Congress who argued against par clearance of cheques to today's white nationalists. At the time, the establishment of the Federal Reserve was seen as akin to the coming of the industrial railroads from the North: an affront to Southern sovereignty and to the hierarchies of race and value manifest, for Southern elites, in sound money and deposit banking.

Northern elites, it was argued, supported "greenbacks" (cash) and credit money, denaturing value in ways Southern elites likened to miscegenation (meaning "the interbreeding of people considered to be of different racial types").[1] Southern bankers established the National and State Bankers' Protective Association to fight the Fed's mandate of par clearance of cheques and Southern lawmakers fiercely defended non-par banks. As one pronounced on the floor of the US House of Representatives:

The country bank needs no eulogy, its money has cleared the forest, made the countryside livable, and the city possible. As a rule, its life has been honestly spent with one object in view, and that objective was the preservation of the physical values and character values of its community. It should not die, for with it will go the last bastion of States' rights, and freedom should shriek at its fall. (quoted in Miller 1949: 144)[2]

---

[1] M. O'Malley, *Face Value: The Entwined Histories of Money and Race in America* (Chicago, IL: University of Chicago Press, 2012).

[2] M.C. Miller, *The Par Check Collection and Absorption of Exchange Controversies* (Cambridge, MA: The Bankers Publishing Company, 1949).

Payments and their Relevance in Society

For physical values and character values, read whiteness. For State's rights, read segregation.

Federal Reserve agents travelling the country to enforce par clearance of cheques had to arm themselves (Medley 2014: 55).[3] The chairman of the National and State Bankers' Protective Association compared them to socialists (Medley 2014: 62). On the Great Plains, similarly situated with regard to monopoly country banks and driven by its agricultural sector (a sector enabled by federal extension of railroads, which were, nonetheless, resented as land grabs by an overreaching government), a local paper opined, in a column liberally laced with anti-Semitic reference: "The Federal Reserve System is the visible hand of the Invisible Empire picking the pockets of the producers of real wealth" (quoted in O'Malley 2012: 178).

We read this today as payments scholars and professionals and think "Wow! Really? Payments created *that* kind of passion?"

Again, though, this should not be a surprise. Dee Hock, the visionary behind Visa, proclaimed payments to be the business of the electronic transit of value. As transit systems, infrastructures or "rails" as those in the business call them, payments systems are agnostic about the source or origin of the value they carry. Know Your Customer policies demand that banks curate data on the individual or personal source of that value. But the state itself actually animates it in the first place: in today's world, states are still the dominant issuer and guarantor of the standard of value. The state sets the standard and literally makes the money. Even though bank credit expands the money supply and the world revolves around the hyper-financialization of everything, that the money is denominated by the state speaks volumes about the state's continued monopoly over the standard of value and the means of exchange.

Yet there are challenges to state dominance, not least because the state allows non-state providers to handle much of the business of payment. Historically, it has granted this licence to the banks. Today, the tech industry's interest in money and payments means there are countless non-bank parties coming onto the scene. The iPhone, M-Pesa and the 2008 financial crisis all fed into the hype and eventual traction of new FinTech startups promising new ways to pay and value-added services riding the rails of payment.

What this Means for the Future of Payments

All of this means that it's difficult to figure out exactly what payments might be becoming.

While some worry about payments as a means of state surveillance, more and more people are becoming conscious of the extent to which the most intimate details of their lives are known by Google, Amazon, Apple, Facebook and other such digital platforms.

These platforms themselves have variously dipped their toes into the payments industry, adding to the "Wild West" character that payments have taken on in the past 10 years. There are new entrants, new business models and often, frankly, imaginary business models built on dreams of data, or blockchain, or artificial intelligence, or a world of always-on, interconnected smart devices, which have to be able to transact with each other somehow…even dreams of payments in outer space, for if and when Earth becomes uninhabitable and people have to pay for stuff *somehow* out there in the solar system.

---

[3] B. Medley, *Highways of Commerce: Central Banking and the US Payments System* (Kansas City, KS: Federal Reserve Bank of Kansas City, 2014).

Several years ago it was common to imagine that payments would become a branch of marketing. By digitizing more and more payments and integrating payment data with physical world and online purchase data, as well as physical world geolocation, online browser, social media, text and voice, and even ambient sound monitoring via mobile phone, payments would become a piece in the puzzle allowing companies to anticipate or fill users' desires with just the right touch of personalization.

Payments Shaped for People, by People

What has always interested me, however, is those pesky users themselves. They have their own agendas, their own microlevel politics, as well as their own aspirational macropolitical relations too. Consider how Venmo and PayPal each generate unique constituencies or loyalties among groups of users, new social groups based on how, when and with whom you pay. For example, Venmo for friends sharing a dinner or renting an apartment, and PayPal for more distant relations or strangers over eBay, or in strictly online relationships.

With more attention to payments, and payment data, we can also hear the rumblings of another politics. Data activism has emerged as a potential social movement and political force. While users might haphazardly clear their browser histories or deny permission for mobile apps to access their digital photo collections or contact lists, signs of organized efforts to seize more control from platform companies over data are ever apparent:

- Information studies scholars point to and promote various efforts to obscure one's digital traces by generating more and more data rather than trying to embark on the hopeless task of cleansing one's data trails.[4]

- Sociologists and activists suggest alternative, cooperative data economies or means of data sharing or custodianship.[5]
- Some organized groups build new infrastructures by creatively adapting and rearranging the existing ones.[6]

One can discern in all this the rise of a new technological imaginary, one attuned to the centrality of data, its storage, ownership and use in everyday life. The EU's General Data Protection Regulation represents an obvious political response.

The Old Questions in Our New Digital World

What will all of this mean for payments? Leaving aside the scholars and industry professionals who work on and in payments and are probably hyperconscious about how they pay, it's difficult to say how intentional people's payment practices are outside of their quest for loyalty points or rewards. Will the politics of payments lead people to express political decisions in their choice of payment – that is, not in what they pay for, but in how they choose to complete the act of payment itself?

Again, though, these are in fact old questions. During prior periods of political upheaval around the world, people would overstamp state-issued banknotes or strike slogans on coins as an act of political assertion, and even the assertion of their own claim to sovereignty. What would be the latter-day analogue of this practice

[4] F. Brunton and H. Nissenbaum, *Obfuscation: A User's Guide for Privacy and Protest* (Cambridge, MA: MIT Press, 2015).

[5] Y. Milner, "An Open Letter to Facebook from the Data for Black Lives Movement" (2018), available at https://medium.com/@YESHICAN/an-open-letter-to-facebook-from-the-data-for-black-lives-movement-81e693c6b46c (accessed on 2 March 2019). N. Schneider, *Everything for Everyone: The Radical Tradition that is Shaping the Next Economy* (New York: Nation Books, 2018).

[6] T. Lehtiniemi and M. Ruckenstein, "The Social Imaginaries of Data Activism" (2019), *Big Data and Society*, Jan/Jun, 1–12.

where corporate-controlled data economies are concerned? How can we countermark our Facebook data in an effort to reground our relationship to it, whether that be a relationship of ownership or something else? How can payments themselves mobilize alternative imaginaries of these relationships, given that they are among the most intimate, and most frequent, and most consequential actions a contemporary human being makes that bridge the physical and digital worlds while connecting us to one another?

If payments have always been political, and if payment politics are coming to the fore again, how can the payment technologies and relationships we design point towards a new politics, adequate to this data-saturated, rapidly warming and politically unstable world?

Acknowledgements

Research on the payments industry has been supported by the US National Science Foundation, Law and Social Sciences programme (SES 1455859 and SES 0960423). Any opinions, findings and conclusions or recommendations expressed in this material are those of the author(s) and do not necessarily reflect the views of the National Science Foundation. I would like to thank the editors for the invitation to contribute this chapter. I would also like to thank my colleagues working on payments, particularly Quinn DuPont, Taylor Nelms and Lana Swartz. Special thanks to Jenny Fan, Farah Qureshi, Melissa Wrapp, Nathan Dobson and Nima Yolmo for research assistance along the way.

Money: A History of Gods and Codes

By Israel Cedillo Lazcano
The University of Edinburgh

The processes of innovation and diffusion unleashed by the introduction of distributed ledger technologies (DLT) in monetary matters have generated heated debates and new theories on the origin, nature and evolution of money. Some of them try to find the origins of this socioeconomic technology in the biology of exchange by which different organisms obtain reciprocal benefits, while others try to project it to the future, arguing that innovations like Bitcoin will eventually be adopted as an international single currency. However, to develop a sound argument that could transcend the theorization efforts above, first we need to discuss an old but fascinating question.

What is Money?

When one thinks of money, the first ideas that come to mind are structured around terms such as "dollars", "renminbis", "pounds" and even "Bitcoins". If one visits a collection of coins, the main objects that will be exhibited will reinforce these ideas; however, it is also possible to find other goods that people have used to conduct transactions, such as cowry shells, tea bricks and copper axes, among others. These collections show how money has evolved from one generation to the next, through a variety of different meanings and goods in different contexts, from sacred objects related to different banker gods to digital fictions ruled by codes.

Unfortunately, all the works on money that one can find around the orb evidence how the origins of this institution are lost in the mists of time, probably, as Keynes[1] noted, "in the Islands of the Hesperides or Atlantis or some Eden of Central Asia". Consequently, we tend to work with different ideas that assume spontaneous transitions between barter and the use of metallic coins based on a chaotic mingling of arguments on the history of particular monetary expressions and the history of money in general.

To face this challenge, and ease our understanding of these transitions, we take as our starting point the promissory texts found in different banknotes around the globe, which show promises to pay the bearer on demand certain amounts of money. What is fascinating about these instruments is that they offer us a window to the past, a past where proto-monetary forms acted as means of communication and instruments of hierarchization structured around social debts. These social debts probably worked like the *Vaygu'a* of the *Kula* ring and the gift schemes described by Bronislaw Malinowski[2] and Marcel Mauss,[3] respectively. Given that these first units emerged in pre-capitalist societies, transactions within a specific community depended on the spiritual power that was incorporated in each interaction, which underpinned the obligation to reciprocate. From the study of these proto-monetary forms, one can infer that the original source of liquidity was a sacred one.

From Barter to "Sacred" Money

Most of the hypotheses on the origin of money start with a basic barter model, which consists of chords among a wide variety of goods, one for each pair of goods representing an individual with a matching demand and supply on a single temporal line.[4]

---

[1] J.M. Keynes, *A Treatise on Money, Vol. I* (London: MacMillan & Co., 1914), at 13.

[2] B. Malinowski, *Argonauts of the Western Pacific. An Account of Native Enterprise and Adventure in the Archipelagos of Melanesian New Guinea* (New York: Dutton, 1961).

[3] M. Mauss, *The Gift* (London: Routledge Classics, 2002).

[4] R.M. Starr, "Why is There Money? Endogenous Derivation of 'Money' as the Most Liquid Asset: A Class of Examples" (2003) *Economic Theory* 21, 455–474, at 459.

Of course, it is possible to argue that barter was not a great system. For example, if you wanted to swap your fish for a loaf of bread, but the baker happened to want firewood for his stone oven, you were stuck with the task of finding someone with firewood who just happened to want your fish.

However, to avoid this problem, our counterpart could offer us a commodity that we probably did not desire, but that probably had a high cultural value with the aim of guaranteeing the fulfilment of his obligations. Accordingly, one of the parties would take the risk that he may not be able to obtain the bread he wanted, but once the commodity offered by the other party was linked to a "sacred" source of liquidity, gradually its general acceptance became self-reinforcing. From this example, it can be inferred that money emerged as a form of debt modelled as a multiplayer game of the Prisoner's Dilemma.

"Banker Gods" and Temples

The inception of the first "financial institutions" may be found in the sacred character of the practices developed in places such as Babylonia and Mesoamerica, where cults relating to deities such as Sămăs (the sun god and lord of justice and righteousness) at Sippar[5] and Yacatecuhtli (the Aztec god of trade and cacao)[6] emerged. Following these cults, temples and trade networks played a central role in what one could call the monetary system, given that they probably acted as regulators of the means of exchange in circulation,[7] which were designed around commodity standards.

---

[5] B. Bromberg, "The Origin of Banking: Religious Finance in Babylonia" (1942) *The Journal of Economic History* 2, 77–88, at 77.

[6] I. Cedillo, *Media of Exchange in Mesoamerica. The Case of the Aztec Empire* (Puebla: Unpublished Master's Thesis, Universidad de las Américas Puebla, 2012).

[7] C. Eagleton and J. Williams, *Money. A History* (London: The British Museum Press, 2013), at 19.

The Emergence of the Metallic Coin

Metals like gold and silver have been accepted as the ideal monetary raw materials, particularly after the traditionally accepted sovereign transition identified with the Lydian *electrum*, which was conceived in the late 7th or early 6th century BC. However, if one looks for evidence regarding the transition between the first forms of money and sovereign currencies, it is possible to find other sources – like the Sennacherib's claim[8] – whose content could make us conclude that, under the Western monetary tradition, the first metallic coin was probably created before the introduction of the Lydian coin, as an evolutionary expression of the practices developed by temples.

Sovereign Money

As seen in documents like the Gratinan's *decretum*, which pointed to the general rule that "*solidus, qui non habet charagma Caesaris, reprobus est*",[9] and the works of authors such as Jean Bodin,[10] eventually princes started to intervene in monetary matters, supported by the terms set by divine and natural law.[11] Only after the end of the Thirty Years' War, when monetary stability was considered as a public good, were the instruments to establish a stable monetary unit put in place through sovereign acts. These varied over time, from bimetallist and trimetallist standards to the Bretton Woods system. As the analysis of these efforts shows,

---

[8] P. Vargyas, "Sennacherib's Alleged Half-Shekel Coins" (2002) *Journal of Near Eastern Studies* 61, 111–115.

[9] "A solidus which does not have Caesar's stamp on it is false."

[10] J. Bodin, "Six Books of the Commonwealth" (2018), available at http://www.yorku.ca/comninel/courses/3020pdf/six_books.pdf (Oxford: Basil Blackwell) (accessed on 3 April 2018).

[11] A. Nussbaum, "A Note on the Idea of World Money" (1949) *Political Science Quarterly* 64, 420–427, at 423.

stability was not fully accomplished until the Classical Gold Standard (CGS) of the late 19th century.

Monetary Alchemy

Returning to our banknotes, one question emerges: "Can we exercise the rights contained in their promissory texts?" If we were living between the 16th and 17th century in trading centres like Amsterdam and London, the answer could be positive. In these cities, goldsmiths – who were often related to the Crown – issued receipts for gold or silver deposited with them.[12] Eventually, during the course of the 19th century, the evolution of our financial systems led to the monopolization of note issue and to the lender-of-last-resort function, both traditionally associated with central banking.[13]

Initially, some readers would be tempted to argue that bank notes are promissory notes within the meaning norms, like the Bills of Exchange Act 1882. However, it is important not to overlook the criteria set in cases such as *Suffel v Bank of England*,[14] which highlighted the fact that these notes are part of a system in which the state evolved to become the source of our "sacred" liquidity.

The Divinization of Code

In the context of the Fourth Industrial Revolution, technologies like artificial intelligence (AI) and DLT are contributing not only to our discussions on the evolution of the functions relating to money, but also to the way we interact with each other. Therefore, just as we can see throughout the content of this chapter regarding those contexts that saw the emergence of proto-monetary expressions and sovereign currencies, our "sacred" source of liquidity is evolving to adapt itself to a new digitalized environment, in which, for monetary matters, it is possible to state that code is the new god.

---

[12] H. Siekmann, "Deposit Banking and the Use of Monetary Instruments", in D. Fox and W. Ernst (eds), *Money in the Western Legal Tradition. Middle Ages to Bretton Woods* (Oxford: Oxford University Press, 2016), 489–531, at 494.

[13] R. Edvinsson, T. Jacobson and D. Waldenström, "Introduction", in R. Edvinsson, T. Jacobson and D. Waldenström (eds), *Sveriges Riksbank and the History of Central Banking* (Cambridge: Cambridge University Press, 2018), 1–25, at 14–15.

---

[14] [1882] 9 Q.B.D. (UK) 555, p. 563.

Payments Explained

By Tyler Anderson
Chief Operating Officer, FinTech Growth Syndicate

Introduction

Every day, billions of people transfer trillions of USD worth of value.

With only a small fraction of the world's currency as physical money, consumers are increasingly opting for a digital experience, which has promoted digital payments. Consumers and businesses are going through a behavioural change, seeking a more frictionless, personalized, efficient and economically feasible way of conducting their day-to-day transactions. The global PayTech ecosystem is evolving faster than ever before, greatly outrunning the local regulatory bodies and incumbents and legacy technologies. Regulatory bodies are enacting payments modernization efforts such as faster payments, ISO 20022 and data-richer payments and better ways to regulate such cashless societies.

For the average consumer, technology empowers us with the freedom and ability to pay for what we want, when we want and in the way we want. For businesses small and large, the way consumers pay is a significant part of the customer brand interaction. Throughout the past few years, the payments industry has experienced a significant amount of disruption – witnessing the conception of innovative and convenient payment technologies that transcend financial institutions' sovereignty within the payments space.

This disruption has been motivated by the increasing call from consumers for a more digital experience; one that is personalized, convenient, fast and secure. Despite this obvious growth, the payments industry tends to isolate those not native to the space; making it a complex industry that only a few understand. In the G7, large financial institutions have always been seen as the innate owners of the payment space, yet this has begun to change

(depending on region). In countries like China, technology has transformed the way that consumers pay and the relationships people have with organizations. As consumer expectations evolve, stakeholders within the payments space will continue to fight for a share of the consumer's wallet.

How do Payments Work?

Technology that enhances payments, or PayTech, can be understood as technology that is leveraged to enable the digital transfer of value. Within the payments space, there are three roles for payments: transacting, enabling and supporting.

For a credit card-enabled payment, the payment process begins when a consumer wishes to pay for a product or service. Once a payment is initiated by the consumer at the interface with the provider of value (retailer, online store or other point of contact with a value provider), both the amount of the transaction and the consumer's data is encrypted and authenticated by the processor and payment gateway. When the data about the transaction reaches the consumer's card issuer, the sale is either approved or declined. If approved, the consumer's card issuer will then proceed to send data about the value of the transaction to the merchant's bank to be deposited.

For each role that payments play in the customer journey, there are also a number of actors that are needed to perform each function. Most notably, there are three main actors involved in the payments process: the business, the consumer and the payment technology that completes the transaction. Traditionally, this process has been monopolized by large banks that have created and dictated the terms for both businesses and consumers.

But over the past few years, innovative solutions created by FinTechs have disrupted the relationship between these three actors significantly. Challenger banks have also begun to offer consumers alternative financial products and services, which threaten the autonomy of large banks within the payments industry. As consumers continuously opt for a more digital experience, FinTechs have been agile in simplifying processes through the creation and delivery of payment solutions that are reliable, transparent and secure, in a seamless and personalized user experience that consumers increasingly expect.

Where are Payments Going?

The way we pay can be considered a phenomenon in and of itself. This has been fuelled by consumers' universal acceptance of mobile payments, causing a behavioural change within our societies. Instead of going to pick up our food or hailing a cab, we can accomplish both through our phones. One of the biggest drivers for this notable change in consumer behaviour is the growing need for *convenient* and *frictionless* payment methods, and the proliferation of mobile phones worldwide.

As consumer behaviour and attitudes towards payments continue to evolve, transformation of financial markets is required in order to accommodate innovation. Presently, regulators around the world have begun to weigh the merits of adopting and embracing an open banking system. Open banking can be described as a collaborative model, in which consumer data is shared with third parties in order to deliver value, creating new capabilities and business models. The adoption of an open banking system will significantly change and transform payment technology. Through allowing FinTechs access to consumer data, challenger banks and many other new PayTech and non-PayTech entrants offering similar or adjacent products, would have a greater ability to create and deliver frictionless, secure and convenient experiences for consumers.

Platforms for Payments

The continued "platformization" of payment technology, for instance, is one of the most notable ways that FinTechs will deliver on the growing needs of consumers for efficient and personalized payment methods. Both financial and non-financial products will increasingly become accessible through mobile devices, competing with existing offerings from tech giants such as Alipay and WeChat Pay, companies that have begun to saturate financial economies.

Additionally, the need for stakeholders to create and deliver a complete digital experience has never been more pressing. As new generations enter the market and become increasingly empowered about their finances, the availability of an integrated digital experience will become more of a differentiator. Consequently, big banks will continue to collaborate with FinTechs for the use of their disruptive technology, and FinTechs will leverage the customer base and brand recognition that can be provided by incumbent banks and other players.

Here Today, Gone Tomorrow

Moving forward, payment technology will become increasingly invisible. Large technology companies such as Amazon have already begun to provide consumers with the option of an "invisible" payment experience. With the launch of Amazon Go, paying for everyday items has become as easy as downloading an app and picking up the desired items – without ever having to take out your phone or card to pay. Through leveraging recognition software and artificial intelligence, the future of payments will be centred around creating the ultimate user experience; one that is convenient, frictionless and fast. Uber is perhaps the most well-known example for what payments will become: invisible."

What Could Go Wrong?

Although the payments space has experienced a significant amount of disruption, many have argued that with innovation comes risk. In a financial ecosystem transformed by an open banking system, for instance, new opportunities for innovative payment technology could potentially equate to new opportunities for fraudulent activity. Particularly in recent years, many companies have failed to protect consumer data.

As large data breaches continue to victimize companies that consumers once trusted with their data, the issue of data breaches has grown to become more than just a potential public relations crisis. Stronger security procedures, as well as the introduction of controls on how companies store and use consumer data, comes as a response to governments implementing harsh legislation to regulate and punish companies that have failed to protect their customers from fraud and protect society from money laundering. However, as is the case in every economy and region on the globe, technology transformation is underway and unstoppable at this point. Regulations and government involvement to mitigate risk will be met with higher consumer expectations, availability of alternatives accessible globally, and adoption of new methods that will become the new norm. The one thing we know for certain is change is constant.

From Barter to App – How Payments Have Changed

By Markus Eichinger
Executive Vice President Group Strategy, Wirecard

The way people pay has changed enormously over the millennia – and continues to do so. Payment methods hugely influence economic, trade and purchasing behaviour. A payment can be the decisive factor behind customer satisfaction, tapping into new target groups or a retailer's success. One click and the purchase is complete. Above all, e-commerce merchants know how crucial it is to ensure that checkout processes are kept as simple and barrier-free as possible.

It is only in this way that their conversion rates can be increased over the long term and offer positive customer experiences – perhaps by ensuring that customers are no longer even aware of the payment, as their credit card data has already been stored in the background and the transaction is automatically processed, like in the case of Uber.

The Early Days of Payment: From Cowry Shells to Coin Counterfeiters

In order to understand the rapid developments in the field of payment, let's take a little look back through the ages.

While bartering has existed ever since human beings were capable of rational thought, the concept of "commodity money" came into being around 8,000 years ago. This included countable, rare objects such as cowry shells that could be transported and stored with ease. Commodity money laid the foundations of modern trade and facilitated the division of labour.

Trade was simpler and more dynamic when the first metal coins were used around 3,500 years ago. From the very beginning, coins had an innate, inherent value as they were forged from precious metals. However, this came hand-in-hand with a problem: counterfeiting and fraud, for example by filing down the edges of the coin.

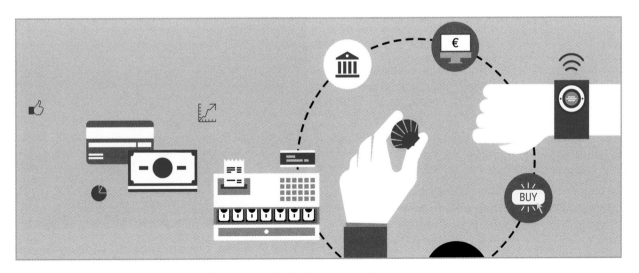

Figure 1: The evolution of payment: from barter to digital payment

The third major stage in the development of trade was the discovery of immaterial money – an early form of the demand deposit – on the back of cheque transactions in Italy in the 14th century. The basic idea behind demand deposits is to decouple the concept of nominal value from innate value. For the first time in history, it was possible to transport money in the form of "bank notes" over great distances, without having to carry the value asset in person. This marked the start of the development of the paper money that we are familiar with today: its value is guaranteed by the trust that society places in the solvency of the issuing economy.

Payments Today: Electronic and Varied

The modern form of the demand deposit is electronic (digital) or virtual money. This forms the basis of global trade and is what made e-commerce possible in the first place.

Digitization is changing so many areas of daily life, and this is particularly true when it comes to money. New payment methods can be developed more easily than ever before. This produces direct added value for the economy.

For example, a customer can choose from numerous different retailers when buying a new pair of trainers. These include online-only retailers as well as more conventional high-street stores. The quality of the product is identical at all merchants, with the price more or less the same as well. So what makes a crucial difference here? What is the unique selling point (USP)?

The answer is, the user experience. The central question for future retail will be quite simple: "*Are you able to provide a positive customer experience?*" Factors such as range and quality of advice will play a key role in deciding this, as well as consistent digitalization of processes – and payment will be a vital link in this chain.

China: Showing the World How it's Done

In order to get an idea of where this journey is heading, it is worth casting our eyes east towards China. Chinese consumers have made a direct leap to smartphone payments (i.e. without being diverted via physical payment cards beforehand) – and they are huge fans of all apps that make life easier. The "super apps" Alipay and WeChat Pay are used to make payments in all areas of modern day-to-day life in China – everything from a new suit to a taxi ride or even a quick polish from the shoeshine business on the corner. However, these apps can also be used to quickly order tonight's dinner, settle an energy bill, take out a loan, invest money and much, much more.

For retailers, Alipay and WeChat Pay offer a direct line to potential customers. They are able to address them individually; for example, a boutique fashion store can send a push notification to all women in a certain age bracket within 500 m alerting them that

Figure 2: Fast, uncomplicated mobile payment is just one of many features that Chinese "super-apps" like Alipay offer to users

silk scarves are now on offer, and customized vouchers can be issued to both new and existing, regular customers.

The Future of Payment: Seamless – and Invisible

What does the future of payment look like? Payment processes will become ever more invisible for customers, as they will increasingly fade automatically into the background.

The payment process will be fully digitized – although it will still take place in store. The greatest benefit for consumers will be that they can completely avoid queuing to pay. This is made possible by customers first registering – including uploading payment data – in order to then log in upon entering the store, for example using biometric technology such as facial recognition software or smartphone fingerprint technology. Smart shelves then track the items in the basket, allowing for a seamless checkout without the need to queue at the till.

While this may all sound far-fetched, the technology is, in fact, already up and running at some merchants, for example Amazon Go in the USA or the physical supermarket chain Hema, part of the Chinese e-commerce giant Alibaba.

Below are further practical examples of how "invisible payments" are already making life easier for customers and retailers:

IOT STORE – THE USER JOURNEY

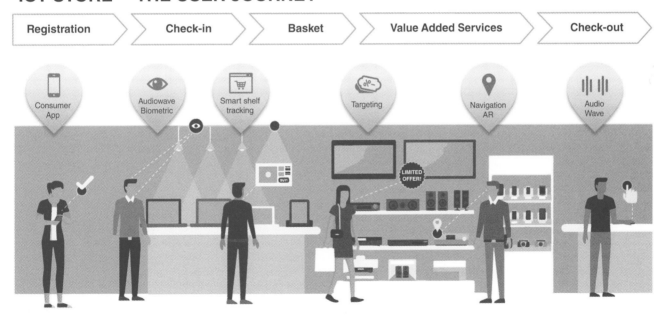

| Registration | Check-in | Basket | Value Added Services | Check-out |

Consumer App | Audiowave Biometric | Smart shelf tracking | Targeting | Navigation AR | Audio Wave

Figure 3: Connected Store: Internet of Things (IoT) technology, connected to smart data analytics tools and Artificial Intelligence, enable a cart-free and seamless shopping experience

- In Singapore, cars autonomously pay when leaving a car park – barriers at the entrance and exit or waiting to pay at the machine are a thing of the past. Drivers are conveniently charged via the ERP toll collection scheme.

- With Alexa or Google Assistant, voice command technology is being used to make payments.

- When using Uber, consumers are not just ordering a taxi to the location of their choice, they also pay for their journey on arrival in fully automated fashion.

What Does All this Mean for the Retail World?

Digitization has caused a paradigm shift in payments, opening up new possibilities for online and physical retailers alike. Therefore, those who embrace new technologies and digitization have a greater chance of offering their customers a positive purchase experience. Every retailer knows: *Happy customers are regular customers*. Data obtained from the purchase process and real-time processing also helps retailers to tailor their offering much more specifically to their customers and further personalize and optimize their purchase experience.

We are living in very exciting, dynamic times as far as payment is concerned – and retailers who are savvy enough to exploit the many new opportunities available will be able to leverage crucial competitive advantages.

Do We Still Need to Pay?

By Teresa Connors
Head of Market Engagement, RBS

With frictionless payments embedded into buying experiences, do we still need to pay?

We might say "Yes" without batting an eyelid. However, the response begs further questions. Namely, why do we still need to pay? And why does it matter? After all, we don't inherently receive pleasure from the act of making a payment. We hardly choose to spend our weekends making payments for the sake of it. The London Business School's Associate Professor of Organizational Behaviour, Niro Sivanathan, went as far as saying that "Parting with cash is psychologically painful".

The reality is that we make payments for exchange satisfaction. I give you money; you give me something to consume. From an employer's perspective, you give me labour; I pay you a salary which you can spend (or save, or both). As technology makes this dynamic more fluid, the significant question is, must we *feel* like we are paying? This chapter will explore how technology has changed the process of exchange satisfaction, asserting that trust determines the extent to which we can detach from the sensation of making or receiving a payment.

Payment Works

For many of us the way to pay was enshrined at an early age. Sweets in hand and £5/€5/$5 note poised, you marched towards the till to pay. Approaching the shopkeeper, you gave them your note, collected the appropriate change and received your receipt.

Intrinsic to those simple steps are the fundamental principles of a payment. Firstly, it was *secure*. There was no malicious third party who stole the money as you handed it over. Secondly, it was *authorized*. Upon being handed the note, the money belonged to the shopkeeper. Thirdly, the merchant was *identifiable*. There was no false shopkeeper standing behind a pretend till. Fourthly, it was *verifiable*. You received a receipt to prove you had made the transaction. Finally, the note was *valuable*. You and the shopkeeper existed in a society that accepted, albeit implicitly, the value of a currency note. These fundamental principles simultaneously enabled you to pay for the sweets and the shopkeeper to receive payment.

Technology Today Enables Greater Purchases

Fast forward to today and the payment experience is very different. Your payment is no longer restricted to the cash in your hand. In a largely cashless society, your limit is the amount available in your bank or payment account. On a shelf by the till, a brownie might coax you into spending more than you can truly afford. Granted, perhaps spending *all* of that currency note back in the day might also have stretched you beyond what was prudently affordable. But there was an objective physical limit. In today's society, frictionless card and mobile phone payments enable impulse purchases, and the lack of a physical limit facilitates an increase in spending.

Responsibility Lies with the Industry

Advancements in payment technology have undeniably changed our spending habits. Contactless cards and online shopping make consumption easier than ever, and losing track of spending can be a stressful consequence. As an industry we must not lose sight of this, taking responsibility to ensure our customers feel the benefits of frictionless payments while remaining in control.

Some businesses would also object to frictionless payments, although for different reasons. Take the corporate treasurer, responsible for making multi-million currency payments. With figures like these, security is prioritized over ease. If friction is required to ensure that errors are difficult to make and the payment is safe, then so be it. There is undoubtedly a demand for a degree of automation. But it is important to note that the more valuable the payment, the more caution is exercised. In this scenario, the frictional sensation of making a payment matters in order to ensure the correct due diligence has been applied in the process.

Powerful Technology Empowers

However, let us not forget the billions of people that benefit from frictionless payments. The vast majority of consumers are empowered by technology, having the liberty to spend what they *want* as supposed to what they physically *can* at that moment.

With prudent financial management and awareness of what makes you happy, buying what you want transposes into buying what you *should*. Moreover, online shopping means you can have the exchange satisfaction experience from almost anywhere. On the other side of the till, retailers also gain. Not searching for change means shopkeepers can serve more customers. For many mobile apps, application programming interfaces (APIs) have enabled payments to be so integrated into the customer journey that users do not even need to leave the app. In these cases, detachment from the sensation of payment leads to easier lives and economic prosperity.

Technology, Payments and Trust

In our digital world, how has technology impacted the fundamental principles of a payment? Payments remain indispensable, but digital has allowed us to make them with less time and effort.

The most significant driver of technology to emerge since our time in the shop of old is trust. Our payments are *authorized* because we trust our banks to have the technology to debit our account and credit the retailer. When paying via contactless card, we trust that the card terminal corresponds to the *identity* of the merchant. During an online shop, we trust that the retailer will email us the receipt to make that payment *verifiable*. Finally, as a society we implicitly consent that our mainstream digital currency will remain *valuable* and trust each other to maintain this status quo.

Given that the act of making a digital payment is more complex and hidden than exchanging cash, trust becomes crucial. As an everyday consumer, satisfying these fundamental principles probably won't keep you up at night. In the shoes of the corporate treasurer, they are essential.

Conclusion

Overall, the conclusion is unambiguous. Do we still need to pay? With the plethora of individuals and organizations, we must feel the sensation of making a payment insofar as the process gives us reason to trust that our money will be exchanged in return for what we desire to receive from a transaction. Therein lays the essence of a payment.

Sources:

https://www.london.edu/news-and-events/news/the-perils-of-contactless-payments-1271

file:///C:/Users/carewrb/Downloads/future-of-money-special-report-2018.pdf

https://www.clearscore.com/blog/shift-to-cashless-society-causes-three-in-five-brits-to-overspend

How ACH and Real-Time Payments Clearing and Settlement Works

By Imran Ali
Managing Principal, Answer Digital

Introduction

In the beginning, payments were processed individually and settled at the same time. This was reliable, but costly. As volumes grew, banks introduced the concept of an ACH (automated clearing house) as a more cost-effective way of processing payments. ACH payments soon became the new standard for clearing payments in most geographies. In the UK there are approximately 6 billion ACH payments processed each year.[1] In the USA, NACHA processes about 23 billion transactions a year.[2] By and large, ACHs still represent the cheapest way of processing non-urgent payments.

However, a few years ago a revolution began with the introduction of real-time payments (RTPs). As societies moved to a digital age where services are available in an instant on the end of a computer or mobile phone, customer expectations moved accordingly. Three-day or even next-day clearing systems started to be perceived as slow. Customers couldn't understand that goods ordered online could arrive the same day yet payments made between two banks would take two days. RTP addressed that problem by delivering a payments capability that processed

---

[1] For more details see https://www.bacs.co.uk/NewsCentre/PressReleases/Pages/PayUKPostsRecordVolumesAndValuesAsIndustryRevampRampsUp.aspx.

[2] https://www.nacha.org/news/ach-network-moves-23-billion-payments-and-51-trillion-2018.

payments in seconds. This chapter describes how ACH payments are processed, how RTPs function, the differences between them and the issues that still exist.

ACH Payments

ACH payments are processed in bulk and often on an overnight basis, although some take longer and some are done the same day. They are typically non-urgent payments that can be scheduled, such as bill payments or salary. Being able to submit and receive payments in batches makes it easier for corporates and banks to process the transactions.

ACH payments typically go through the following process:

1. **Payment submission**
   The payment is first submitted to the bank by the consumer or the corporate/merchant. This is done either online or at the bank. The bank has a daily cut-off time each day, at which point it will batch all the payments submitted that day and send them to the ACH. The bank will also include any warehoused payments that were submitted by a customer on a previous date but are due for processing now. The bank will have to format the payments in accordance with specific messaging standards as set out by the ACH. Standardized message formats ensure that each player in the ecosystem is sending the right information and payment processing is kept as efficient as possible. ACH message formats tend to be very limited, as the main benefit of ACH is the ability to process large volumes in a few hours. Recent clearing systems have started to adopt XML (largely based on the ISO 20022 format) as the ACH payments standard (e.g. SEPA clearing houses), which can hold more information but invariably requires greater processing power.

2. **Processing**
   Once the ACH receives the file of payments, it carries out structural and business validation ensuring the file is constructed as per the standards, and contains all the correct information.

The ACH will have standard rules that it follows to validate the submitted payments. Exceptions raised at this point are either automatically corrected or flagged to the bank for correction. Where a file cannot be corrected, it is rejected and sent back to the submitting bank. Duplicates are also flagged with the bank to prevent payments being made twice.

3. Routing

Once payments have been successfully validated, they are reformatted and constructed into new output files. The files are batched per destination bank and are then sent out at an agreed time. This is typically overnight, so the receiving bank can ensure payments are credited to customer accounts first thing in the morning.

4. Settlement

ACHs operate on a deferred net settlement basis. This means that settlement takes place after the payments have been processed and routed to the beneficiary bank. It is also done on a "net" basis, which means that the amount owed between any two banks is netted off. The ACH will total up the value of the payments sent and received by each bank during that clearing window. It will then send a settlement report to the settlement agent, typically the central bank, who will then transfer the relevant funds in and out of the accounts held by each bank participating in the clearing.

Settlement Risk

Operating on a deferred settlement basis creates a level of settlement risk. Payments could be sent from one bank to another, but the bank may not have sufficient funds to honour those payments. A bank may fail completely, or struggle to have sufficient liquidity.

Settlement risk mitigation is therefore a critical component of clearing systems. The central bank will insist that banks hold a certain value of funds in their accounts, at the central bank, to safeguard against settlement risk. These funds are used for

settlement should the bank struggle to do so for any reason. In some countries, such as the UK, the clearing system also places a cap on the maximum debit position a given bank can hold, limiting its settlement exposure. Central banks also take a firm regulatory position on banks, ensuring policies are in place to mitigate settlement risk; and regular reviews are held with banks to monitor their settlement patterns.

Real-Time Payments

RTPs operate in a slightly different way to ACH payments. The primary difference is that the payments are not processed in a batch. They are processed as single payments, thereby allowing them to be cleared in real time. Banks can submit files, but tend to submit single payments into clearing. The clearing system then undertakes the same process as for ACH payments, except it is condensed into micro-seconds and exceptions are not flagged or corrected, they are simply rejected. Payments are also not batched for routing to the beneficiary bank, but rather sent out as soon as they are successfully processed. This enables RTP clearing systems to receive, process and output payments in seconds.

Settlement for RTP is done in the same way as ACH payments, on a deferred net settlement basis. Hence the same settlement risk exists with RTP, and so the same mitigation is required.

Closing Issues/Recommendations

Clearing systems have come a long way in terms of processing speed and risk mitigation. However, some issues still exist that need to be tackled by the industry:

- *End-to-end real time.* RTPs are processed in seconds, but often the bank processing time is longer. This can dilute the benefits of RTP and dampen the customer experience. In order to deliver true real-time payments, banks need to implement real-time processing capabilities.

- *Risk mitigation.* Although risk will never be mitigated completely, there is always more that can be done. Clearing systems need to be smarter at spotting fraud, errors and hacks; and the provisions against settlement risk need to continue to be reviewed and enhanced.

- *Enhanced data.* ACH payments have historically been limited in the information they hold to ensure quicker processing.

However, with the advancement of modern technology, ACH payments should now be able to hold more information and still be processed quickly. Corporates should be able to send invoice information with payments; consumers should be able to send photos of meter readings with their bill payments. Clearing systems can become smarter and more useful parties to transactions.

Payments as a Service

By Julian Sawyer
Co-Founder and former COO, Starling Bank

It was the economic historian Tim Harford, in his excellent book (and BBC Podcast) *50 Things That Made the Modern Economy*,[1] who outlined how the electric dynamo transformed the way factories, over 100 years ago, powered their industrial output. Before that, if you owned a factory you also had to create your own power, typically with coal power/steam generation which turned turbines that powered the plant via massive shafts running through the factory floor. Then came the electric dynamo, but this still required generation. Moving forward to today, we have specialists who create electricity in the most efficient ways (coal, nuclear, wind) and are able to distribute it anywhere in the country – in a consistent manner (i.e. at 240 V), not hampered by surges in demand and all with a predictable price point.

This was a fundamental disruptive shift in manufacturing, enabling factories to focus on their value-added activities of making things and let others worry about some of the inputs such as electric power.

Has the time come for a similar change in payments? In this chapter I propose that the answer is yes, it is time for a change that will shift how people consume payments, opening access to payments to organizations that would struggle to gain access to consistent and immediate payments with a known and consistent pricing.

Let's look back at the UK payments infrastructure over the last 10 years. The Faster Payments Service was developed by the top 10 UK banks, wanting to provide an infrastructure for immediate payments to complement the two existing payment schemes – CHAPS (which is typically for larger transactions) and BACS

(which is a three-day processing cycle for direct debits and direct credits). When created, the UK was leading this global movement to provide a payment scheme for real-time payments – and even today it is held up as a case study to replicate.

If you were not one of those 10 banks you would need to be "sponsored" to gain access. Typically, one of the four largest retail banks would offer this service to the 400-odd banks and building societies in the UK. This service was slow, typically cleared and settled in batches, and expensive. It was also slow to on-board, creating a two-speed payments world between those directly connected and those sponsored in an indirect model which has been tolerated for the last decade.

To address this, the payments industry, with pressure from the regulator, started the Faster Payments Access Programme to make it easier for banks and more recently payment service providers to on-board. Since this was started in 2016, approximately 15 organizations have joined as direct participants of the Faster Payments Service, including Starling Bank, one of the UK's challenger banks.

At the other end of the spectrum, the UK has been the dominant player in the global FinTech space, with over 1,500 e-money institutions and payment institutions. Almost every day we hear about an amazing new company challenging the status quo, creating a new user experience and helping consumers or business. However, these companies are still constrained by the underlying payments infrastructure and the slow mainframes residing in the incumbent bank's data centres.

Starling Bank was the first challenger to see this and decided to open up the payments infrastructure and disrupt the market. Providing real-time access to faster payments, in the indirect model, via a set of application programming interfaces (APIs), transforms the market because instead of batching up payments and sending them to a bank, you can fire off each payment instruction in real time and it gets executed, there and then.

[1] T. Harford, *50 Things That Made the Modern Economy* (London: Little, Brown, 2017).

Providing access to sort codes and virtual accounts complements this proposition, delivered in a few weeks rather than months.

So why is this transformational? Let us look at a few use cases.

1. SME bank

You're a mid-tier small to medium enterprise (SME) bank making loans and taking deposits for the business market. You need access to payments but it's not really core to you; it's expensive to join the Scheme and to remain compliant and you have a lot of infrastructure to manage and maintain. You could remove this burden and use software-as-a-service, enabling payments via an API. You only consume the services you need and the complexity is managed by the service provider. Costs are reduced, life is simplified and you deliver a better service to your customers.

2. e-Money institution

Maybe you're an e-money institution, someone with a great idea, one that will change the world, but you then need to deal with the old-style banks, and even then you're not able to offer real-time payments. By using payments-as-a-service, this takes the payment integration off the critical path and allows your firm to focus on the customer experience and doing something different and exciting while still providing real-time payments.

3. Company paying salaries

However, by far the most exciting area is when people are looking at challenging the status quo and seeing new opportunities that real-time payments present. This includes paying suppliers in real time to align with their just-in-time deliveries, and paying staff more frequently or enabling them to draw down their salary, immediately, before the typical month end pay day. In the next two years a large proportion of UK employees will be paid differently than they are today using this service.

Conclusion

Real-time payments is an exciting field. It opens up new opportunities for both traditional financial institutions and new entrants. This technology and the software-as-a-service approach will change how payments are consumed. This is similar to moving to have coal-powered generators sitting outside factories, creating their own power – consuming a critical service from a specialized provider who has optimized the service, quality, security and price. The game of real-time payments is about to change forever.

The New Emerging Banks and Their Role in Payments

By John Ryan
Director General, Emerging Payments Association Asia

We live in a world where payments are becoming increasingly frictionless, where spending happens with greater ease and money is being moved even more frequently. We see payment transactions rising in 2019 at a rate of 32% p.a.[1] in emerging economies in Asia. The tangible world of bricks-and-mortar institutions and physical cash is transitioning into a virtual world of digital data and tokens.

The role played by banks in this new world of payments must change. This chapter describes the drivers behind such changes, outlining them and concluding with some big questions facing the banking industry.

Traditional Retail Banks

Retail banks have been around since the 15th century, a timeframe which speaks to their reputation for security and reliability. Originally, banks were simply a repository for money. Today, the services on offer are far more comprehensive, offering a one-stop shop for all banking and payment services. Mutual or community banks have also grown organically during this time, offering more localized banking services. These "mutuals" offer cost competition in selected services, even if their offering is often limited compared to the large banks.

In the last decade, just as high street retailers have suffered at the hands of online merchants, so there has been a migration of customer banking relationships online. These days most consumers rarely visit a bank branch more than once a year. Yet in the face of changing consumer trends, many of the traditional banks have been slow to adapt to the wider consumer demands for better online service delivery. Enter a new type of banking entity: the neo bank.

So What is a Neo Bank?

These new banks, dubbed neo or challenger banks, are wholly focused on leveraging the latest technology advances to gain efficiencies and also to provide greater transparency to the customer.

Monzo, N26, Starling and Revolut are some of the best known, but new entrants are arriving on the market every month. According to Infiniti Research in 2019, customers are looking for multi-channel buying experiences and impeccable customer service. Since the global financial crisis, customers have also become increasingly weary of their existing banking service providers. Governments have been adapting legacy banking rules to cater for the orderly and safe entry to market of these new "virtual banking" entrants.

Neo banks can get to market within a matter of months and be fully operational within two to three years. It's also relatively easy to plug in to the credit card companies via rails service providers. They can also layer on regulatory reporting thanks to recently developed artificial intelligence (AI) systems. They most likely use Cloud Computing.

There is no doubt that neo banks are typically perceived as having better technology that provides better access and better services than the established players. Neo banks also tend to speak to their customers with greater clarity providing transparency and better incentives or deals. They can also offer faster client onboarding.

In their response to neo banks, traditional banks have been held back by outdated legacy systems, ill-equipped to cope with the challenges

---

[1] Deloitte Banking Trends Report 2018.

of the modern consumer banking market. Many of these legacy systems also creak under the heavy burden of regulatory compliance, and outages occur with remarkable frequency as a result.

Traditional banks seek to maintain sufficient controls to avoid large-scale fraud or overcharging errors to customers. This is partly driven by the increased tendency to fine banks for such failures, along with high-profile public inquiries. An example is the recent Australia Royal Commission into banking, which issued 76 recommendations for change in banking in Australia in the final report issued in January 2019.[2] Inquiries like these, combined with regular reports of process failures and service breakdowns, have further damaged the public's perception of the traditional banks. It has fed the growing interest among consumers in the neo banks.

On the upside, the traditional banks have large balance sheets and large customer bases. Both of these were historically significant barriers to entry for new entrants. That's no longer the case, and has led some of the traditional banking players to consider acquiring a neo bank as a way to catch the market trend.

Post Neo Banks

However, there is another trend emerging in the banking world: payment app providers are now becoming the new one-stop service provider for a wide range of services. These app providers were initially focused on payment transactions, but are rapidly expanding their offerings. While the payment apps typically have banking relationships backing their service, customers seem happy with these providers' front-end app service experience and are no longer concerned about who is providing the back-end facilities. It is turning banks into service suppliers to the app providers.

---

[2] https://financialservices.royalcommission.gov.au/Pages/reports.aspx.

Neo Banks, Where to From Here?

So what is life like inside a neo bank? The ethos is similar to any other modern tech startup. It's high-energy, enthusiastic and fast-paced. Risk and regulation quickly factor in the business model planning, while regulatory reporting around compliance is very much a focal point.

Neo banks have learned valuable lessons from the mistakes made by the incumbent banks. They also have the advantage of being able to make IT decisions quickly. It's the pace of adoption that gives them a significant advantage over traditional banks, which have been comparatively slow to adopt new consumer-focused online services. Neo banks can be Open Banking enablers.

So, what will the success threshold look like for the neo banks? This comes down to the funding (the larger the balance sheet the better), and the speed of getting the latest services to market. Can the neo banks meet all the banking criteria set by regional regulators?

Where in the World?

Neo banks have set the pace of change in Europe, whereas in Asia the payment apps and digital wallets are leading the changes.

Adherence to regulation can be challenging for neo banks anywhere, because of their relative lack of experience and weak relationships with regulators. The compliance requirements of the country of incorporation are relevant too. Neo banks are often attracted by locating their business in a sovereign region which is more favourable to assisting the growth of the business and less traditional in its approach to compliance.

The risk of failure for neo banks is high, like any startup. The effect of failure of some of the leading neo banks remains to be seen, should it happen. It is an area of concern with the regulators and one they continue to monitor closely.

A Positive but Uncertain Future

Ultimately this is a long-term play, and there are several trends to watch. Will some of the traditional banks be tempted to take over a neo bank in the hope that it will change their internal culture to meet the new consumer tastes and speed up their adoption of new technology? Or are the traditional banks too stuck in their old ways to make such radical changes? And on the global market, will it be the neo bank model in Europe or the payment apps model, popular in Asia, that wins the day? These are the questions being addressed by bankers everywhere, whether in traditional banks or those of the neo variety.

The Payments Race

By Ali Paterson
Editor in Chief, Fintech Finance

The Payments Race is a challenge that has taken place over the last two years, where a group of "racers" head as fast as they can between two cities while trying to complete a series of challenges on the way. The catch? They are only allowed to use **one** method of payment for the entire trip.

Highlight #5

Race III: Hong Kong to Singapore – March 2018

The market wants what the market wants:

Amelie Arras, using only Bitcoin, had managed to travel south through Vietnam. The incredible thing was that, unknown to her, Bitcoin is illegal in Vietnam. This only came to light while standing in front of a Bitcoin ATM, when a local Hanoi resident informed her that asking to buy food in Bitcoin was illegal.

One of the great appeals (or downfalls) of Bitcoin is that it can be sent person-to-person without any government being made aware of it. In Vietnam, despite being banned, Amelie managed to pay for food, board and transport using a payment method that was technically illegal…and found it easier than other countries where it was still legal.

Highlight #4

Race V: New York to Vegas – October 2018

Financial inclusion of crypto across the ages:

Maximilien Meilleur, using only a variety of cryptocurrencies, found himself in the city centre of Denver, CO, in desperate need of a bus ticket. After spotting a large chap with a big beard, glasses and a Star Wars T-shirt, he weighed up his options and headed over to speak with him. He wanted to see if he would help him out by buying a bus ticket in exchange for a couple of segments of Bitcoin.

Max gave his spiel of how to download a Bitcoin wallet, and how he would send some Bitcoin to him. The chap needed Max to explain to him what Bitcoin was (by which time any curiosity he may have had, had evaporated), before telling Max he was not interested.

The next thing you know, an elderly lady, sat a few tables across from Max, called out "You selling Bitcoin? I'd have me some of that? What is it?"

Max headed over and explained how to download a wallet, and what he needed in exchange for him sending some Bitcoin to her newly created wallet, on what turned out to be the first app that she had installed on her phone without the help of her granddaughter.

Crypto wallets are typically aimed at the tech savvy, but that doesn't mean they are restricted to the tech savvy. Indeed, it turns out that even people with no interest in seeking out new payment methods can be fast adopters when presented with the option in an out-of-context situation.

Highlight #3

Race IV: Istanbul to Amsterdam – June 2018

Choice wins out:

On the fourth race, each racer had a companion camera person with them, filming their (almost) every move. They were given the same budget as the racer, but as they were there in a "behind-the-scenes" capacity, they didn't have to adhere to the payment rules (i.e. the camera people were able to use whatever method they wanted).

It was during this race that one of the biggest nightmares turned out to have little effect in Europe, when Visa went down with an outage. This had no effect on the racers for Team Crypto, or Team Cash, but it was a worry for those racers using cards, either plastic or virtual…and **all** the camera people.

It was during this very brief window that the camera person from Team Cash had to be helped out by his racer, as his wallet only had Visa cards. The only effect that the Visa outage had…was on Team Cash (!)

With Europe having so much choice in types of card payment alone, it proved to cause no slowdown for the racers, as they swapped out to use Mastercard or Amex, or even JCB.

Highlight #2

Race I: London to Copenhagen – June 2017

People, people, people:

For the very first race, no one expected much from the more abstract, less widely recognized payment methods such as Bitcoin, gold or pennies (!) So it came as a surprise when, a few hours after eight racers left Trafalgar Square, Ash Cooper (using gold) posted a selfie outside the Bella Centre in Copenhagen.

It came as even more of a surprise later that in exchange for a gold ⅛ ounce maple leaf, various residents in the Verterbro were hearing about this strange Englishman swapping gold in exchange for room and board. Over the next two days, Ash found himself being taken on boat tours, to golf courses and to the Tivoli theme park, as well as being put up in various penthouses. The incredible thing was that none of Ash's hosts even planned on cashing in the gold for hard currency, but instead opted to keep it as a memento.

The experience was what was being traded, not the actual value of the gold itself. Ash had some concerns before the race around having a formal certificate testifying to the value of the gold, something Neha also requested during the third race, but no one even questioned whether or not the gold was real. What they saw, what they bought into, was the story and the charisma, but also the general human urge to help other people out if they can.

Highlight #1

Race II: Toronto to Vegas – October 2017

Race V: New York to Vegas – October 2018

What a difference a year makes:

Jordan Drew, using only Near Field Communication (NFC) payments, had no problem on his journey across Canada, managing to use a mixture of a K-ring, Apple Pay and tap on his card to make it all the way from Toronto across the US border, with a lot of pre-planned buses all arranged. However, once in the USA, the game changed completely, with almost every payment terminal, every vending machine, every checkout, even those displaying the EMV contactless symbol "not turned on" or "*Oh I know it says that but I don't know how to work it*". The exceptions were the titans of the retail space – Starbucks and Subway.

12 months later, this time starting in the USA, Megan Hayes was armed with just NFC devices. She found herself in a Greyhound bus terminal, with exactly the same vending machine as a year before. This time, the machine worked with Apple Pay.

Within 12 months, the only payment method to have to forfeit in 2017 managed not only to make it across the USA, but to thrive. All it took was the technology that was already in place to be either enabled, or the people setting it up to be made aware of how to bring the hardware to its full potential.

Seeing your business from your customers' point of view sometimes requires us to become consumers. The Payments Race has taught us many lessons about the reality of next-generation payments, and how the experience of the payer varies so much around the world, depending on which technology is used.

PayTech Regulation Trends

By Bruna Jachemet Esin
Lawyer, Brazilian Bar Association

Payment innovation and related technologies have the potential to make electronic payments faster and globally more accessible. However, the flip side of this is that there is an increase in the already inherent risks in the payments ecosystem. Historically, the primary objective of payments' regulation has been to ensure systemic stability, which has multiple facets, the most prevalent being security and efficiency. More recently, the entry of non-financial players and non-fiat currencies into the payments ecosystem has created new or enhanced threats to the stability of the financial system. As a result, regulators tend to address the risks that are growing in line with innovation in payments. In an attempt to foresee potential future regulation, this chapter focuses on five identified trends.

1. Nationalism

Nationalism promotes the interests of a particular nation, favouring self-governance over outside interference. As far as regulation of e-payments is concerned, nationalism manifests itself by restricting participation of foreign entities and protecting national currencies.

Some jurisdictions have regarded it as necessary to impose rules to protect particular local interests, such as in India, where the Reserve Bank of India's rules since 2018 require that data relating to Indian transactions be stored locally. Other jurisdictions require domestic payments to be processed locally. This local approach tends to reflect one jurisdiction's politics; an example is China, which, despite removing restrictions on foreign payment processors years ago, has yet to assess foreign applications to enter China's domestic market. Most jurisdictions are basing discussions around how to regulate cryptocurrencies and protect their sovereign currencies.

The tendency is to see each jurisdiction defining its rules for PayTechs according to its local values. With nationalism, the global regulatory landscape tends to be more fragmented, with each jurisdiction giving its own local flavour to PayTech rules.

2. Compliant Innovation

Innovation assumes investment in developing new technologies, improving products, services, processes and business models. Regulators need to strike the right balance in order to address new risks without hindering innovation.

Innovative solutions bring digitization to all processes within the payments ecosystem, for instance by replacing outdated paper-based tasks. In order to foster innovation, regulation should drop barriers by updating rules where necessary to recognize electronic verification and other new technologies. Regulators can support enabling digitization by, for example, recognizing digital identity proof in know your customer (KYC) processes. Take the example of Brazil, where in 2016 the Brazilian Central Bank allowed banks to open digital accounts relying on remote identity verification.

Whilst PayTechs will have more autonomy to adopt innovation, they will also be required to set up enhanced controls to ensure compliance. Greater levels of compliance are required in a highly interconnected environment, particularly towards prepaid anonymous cards and cryptocurrency payment instruments. FinTechs and PayTechs are expected to develop tools to ensure KYC systems mitigate the enhanced fraud risk and comply with anti-money laundering (AML) requirements.

3. Interoperability

The e-payments ecosystem has been highly interoperable since its origins, connecting schemes, financial institutions, merchants and consumers in a collaborative way. More recently, FinTechs,

PayTechs and tech giants have integrated the e-payments ecosystem, thereby multiplying the possibility of connections between all players within it.

The key feature of such interoperable systems is the adoption of standards to allow semantic interoperability (i.e. that data is readable and understood by all components of the payments network). The integration of new players into the ecosystem, the use of more application programming interfaces, artificial intelligence and distributed ledger technology demands the development of new standards.

Payment schemes rely on the standards established by the industry itself, such as specifications developed by EMVCo to address QR Code payments. Regulators may also establish standards, such as the Regulatory Technical Standards in Europe, that set out the technical standards for strong customer authentication (SCA) under the second Payment Services Directive (PSD2).

Standardization most likely will not come from the regulators, but from the players, associations and standardization bodies, but regulators are expected to welcome standardization from the industry. The adoption of standards is crucial to facilitate the interoperation within the payments ecosystem, but can also improve cost and time, favour competition and improve the user experience.

4. Competition

Regulators in general aim to create markets with more competition and hence greater efficiency. To achieve this goal, regulators may decrease entry barriers and competition agencies will act against unfair practices.

The payments schemes are multisided platforms, having on one side the payers and on the other side the payees. In the interest of having more payers, in general, merchants bear most of the costs of e-payment, which means the merchants subsidize the payments. Having an adequate balance when distributing the cost of payment by means of pricing is essential for the sustainability of electronic systems.

The Interchange Fee Regulation capped the interchange fees in Europe, but it has not capped the fees that merchants pay to acquirers. The Payment Systems Regulator has undertaken a UK market review into card-acquiring services regarding entry barriers. One of the reasons for the market review is that acquirers may not have passed on their savings from the interchange fee caps to smaller merchants.

While most regulators understand that merchants are the subsidy side of the payments platform, the trend is to have more control over the fees charged to merchants by acquirers. Additionally, to promote competition, regulators are expected to support open banking by mandating access to third-party providers as required by PSD2. So, the trend is to have more regulation to guarantee no discrimination and more surveillance against anti-competitive practices.

5. Cybersecurity

Electronic means of payment are convenient and fast, but they can only be a preferred payment method if they are reliable. The use of tokenized devices, combined with biometrics, can bring more trust to electronic payments. Cybersecurity is one of the biggest concerns regarding e-payments, mostly in times when there is more interconnectivity and interdependency between systems.

Cybersecurity requires a high level of security in transactions, namely for card-not-present transactions. SCA requires two-factor authentication for online transactions (a combination of two or more elements categorized as something only the user knows, something only the user possesses or something the user is). SCA will be obligatory across the European Union as of

September 2019, requiring all card issuers to perform enhanced authentication processes.

With stronger authentication methods, more biometric and behavioural information enters the payment system, which results in risks growing exponentially. The conundrum is that the more data that enters the systems to ensure more security, the higher the levels of security that are required.

In general, the trend is that consumers can have more control over their data. From both new players and traditional ones, the tendency is to enhance security controls and reduce exposure to data breaches. Regulators will require more transparent, ethical and non-discriminatory processes to collect and use data, therefore cybersecurity practices are expected to be intrinsically embedded into payments services.

The Right Framework to Enable Innovation

The aforementioned trends are the major ones driving the regulatory environment and they can be affected by changes in technologies. The goal of this chapter is not to dictate pathways or predict future regulation, but to identify a number of trends based on recent experiences in different jurisdictions. The undeniable trend, however, is for a fluid environment, with an elastic regulatory framework that does not constrain innovation.

An Innovative Local Payments Method in an Ancient Land

By Havva Canibek
Vice President Product Management, Card Payments at
Bankalararası Kart Merkezi (Interbank Card Center of Turkey)

Payments have been part of our lives in different forms since olden times.

Anatolia, at the crossroads between modern-day Europe and Asia, was one of the early adopters of money and at the centre of significant trade activity. Lydians minted their first coins as early as 600 BC, and the *macellum* – a round Roman indoor market at the ancient Hellenistic city of Aizanoi – was founded before 200 AD and was one of the first organized stock exchanges in the region (in the modern-day province of Kütahya in Turkey).[1]

In short, the region of Anatolia has played an important role in the history of money and payments. In today's global payments industry, the Turkish payments market – the largest in Europe in terms of number of cards – has made significant leaps towards the adoption of new technologies such as Chip & PIN, contactless and mobile payments. Yet, it has only been recently (since 2016) that the Turkish payments market has introduced its own payment method, TROY.

So, what drives the need for local payment methods even in developed payments markets such as Turkey? What is their value proposition and how do they contribute to the payments industry?

---

[1] Permanent Delegation of Turkey to UNESCO: https://whc.unesco.org/en/tentativelists/5724/. The ancient town of Aizanoi (Ancient Greek: Αἰζανοί) reached political and economic significance during the Hellenistic period and became "a cradle of trade" under Roman control when the local market, the *macellum*, was established and the "Price Edict of Diocletian" was introduced as an attempt to limit inflation of the price of goods.

What are the critical success factors for local payment methods and the lessons learned from cases such as TROY?

What Drives the Rise of Local Payment Methods?

To many, local payment methods are not a new phenomenon. Soon after cards were introduced as a means of payment, the world witnessed the arrival of several local card payment schemes, especially in Europe and Asia during the 1970s and 1980s. Later though, in the 1990s, local card payment schemes entered a period of stagnation, as they could not keep up with the wave of globalization.

The turnaround for the local card payment schemes was the establishment and fast growth of the Chinese scheme UnionPay in the 2000s. UnionPay took over the global card schemes in terms of number of cards only 10 years after it was first introduced.

Today, there are many local card payment schemes with different levels of market penetration. According to different sources, they had more than 2 billion cards issued by 2017 and are bigger than some global card schemes in total. Moreover, they scored a total 12–15% share in the global payment market of US$26 trillion, this share being as high as 30–40% in Western Europe, Australia and New Zealand.[2]

There are three drivers behind the rise of local payment methods around the world:

1. *Geopolitical and strategic considerations.* Some countries consider having a local payment scheme as a strategic advantage, reducing their dependency on other countries and keeping the locally produced technology in the home market.

---

[2] McKinsey on Payments (October 2017); RBR Global Payments Card Data 2018; Turkish Card Payment Market Report by TROY, August 2018.

2. *Agility and innovation.* For today's consumers or businesses, the speed at which companies respond to their needs is very important. Local payment methods have proven more agile than global players, since the local market is central to their businesses. Hence, they drive innovation in many markets, such as Dankort and Multibanco, that are seen as pioneers of digital payments in their region.

3. *Cost-effectiveness.* Local schemes help their local members reduce their costs with more affordable pricing; the saving rate ranges from 25% to 75%.[3]

Local payment methods are instrumental for those with "cashless" or "less-cash" visions, especially through helping the unbanked population access the financial system. India's RuPay, for example, has helped increase the banked population from 48% to 80% in three years.[4] In addition, local payment methods also contribute to the economy by generating an ecosystem around them.

TROY: A Unique Local Payment Solution

Turkey, the largest European card payment market (with 213 million cards in 2018) stands as a unique case as far as local payment methods are concerned.[5] The country has a demographic background that attracted global payment players to the market as early as 1968. It has a large population of over 80 million, with half the people under 32 years old and almost 40% belonging to "Generation Z".[6] Moreover, it is a tech-savvy population, as evidenced by the high mobile ownership (113% population penetration)[7] and smartphone penetration (69%).[8]

The Turkish payments market has been quite advanced in terms of product features, with banks as the main players in issuing and acquiring. The diversification in the market has increased recently, with new players such as electronic money institutions and payment service providers (PSPs) entering the market. Switch and clearing have been done domestically by the Interbank Card Center since 1990, which has helped accumulate know-how.

As advanced as the market is, there is still a sizeable population (~17 million as of 2017) with no or limited access to the financial system.[9] Hence, the Turkish payments market needs innovative solutions to embrace different segments in a fast and cost-effective way to help address this problem.

TROY stands as the most recent example of a local technological payment solution to serve this purpose. Prior to TROY, the Turkish market had been dominated by the international card schemes. TROY was established to meet a growing demand for a local solution that better addresses the local needs while shortening time-to-market for innovative solutions in a cost-effective way.

The case of TROY, which was established only recently, proves that even in developed payments markets such as Turkey, local payment methods can succeed in not only penetrating the current segments, but also finding new avenues of growth.

---

[3] For more information, see "National Payments Schemes: Drivers of Economic and Social Benefits?" by J. Chaplin, A. Veitch and J. Bott.

[4] Interview with Abhaya Prasad Hota, *Capital Turkey*, December 2017 Issue.

[5] Interbank Card Center Data, European Central Bank Payments Statistics (2017).

[6] Turkish Statistical Institute.

---

[7] Mobile phone penetration shows the ratio of number of mobile subscribers to population size over 9 years old.

[8] Turkish Information and Communication Technologies Authority (www.btk.gov.tr); Statista.

[9] According to the World Bank, 31% of the total population (age 15+) is unbanked.

Understanding the Success of TROY

Launched for consumers in May 2017, TROY has quickly penetrated the market. 31 financial institutions constituting nearly 100% market share are already members. As of July 2019, TROY cards reached the 9 million mark. This number translates into a 3.9% market share in total number of cards. In addition, TROY has achieved a market share of ~30% in newly issued cards between 2017 year end and July 2019.[10]

TROY's success helps us identify the critical success factors behind successful local payment methods.

1. Local acceptance

First, the readiness of the acceptance network is the most critical factor for fast market penetration. TROY has ensured 100% acceptance in the country before its launch. This has helped TROY be welcomed by the card users in a market where full acceptance is a hygiene factor.

2. International acceptance

In the same way, international acceptance is a central part of any payment method's value proposition in today's world. Local payment methods should find ways to ensure international acceptance. TROY has leveraged innovative models (such as partnership with global PSPs) for online acceptance and ensured physical acceptance by partnering with other networks.[11]

3. Rapid, cost-effective innovation

The most crucial success factor for local payment methods, though, is the ability to develop innovative products and services to meet un- or undermet demands in the market in a fast and cost-effective way by leveraging new technologies. This is an area where local payment methods have proven to be more successful than their global counterparts.

In TROY's case this has been evidenced by its mobile and QR payment solutions. TROY had introduced its mobile contactless payment solution (HCE) for Android devices only one year after it was launched. It has recently announced a new solution enabling iOS devices to make in-store mobile payments through Bluetooth technology, which is a first in the market and a benchmark for the global payments industry.

TROY has also launched its QR payment solution to enable electronic payments in micropayments. Considering the share of micropayments within the economy (67% of household payments and 11% of household consumption), and the fact that cash dominates micropayments (67% of micropayments are in cash), TROY's QR solution is expected to be instrumental in penetrating this area.[12]

4. Transportation enabled

Transportation is expected to open the door to many other areas for local payment methods. Hence, TROY's transportation solution in the form of cards, mobile devices and wearables has been an important avenue of growth for TROY.

5. Low cost

Last but not least, staying true to their value proposition, local payment methods should reduce the cost of operation for their members. In TROY's case, this has been the most critical value for issuers and acquirers in Turkey. Its fee structure has enabled issuers and acquirers to reduce their scheme fees significantly.

Going forward, penetrating public payments such as social aid and public procurements, which are mainly in the form of cash or

---

[10] Interbank Card Center Data, Press Releases by TROY.

[11] During 2016–2018, 89% of the cards were used only domestically and 98% of transactions were domestic; 50% of the international transactions were e-commerce transactions.

[12] Interbank Card Center Research "Payment Behaviors at Points-of-Sale", TUIK data.

bank transfers, will be vital for the payments ecosystem and TROY. One of TROY's strategic targets is to increase financial inclusion among Turkey's unbanked population and improve the financial literacy of the Turkish population.

TROY also aims to create value for the Turkish economy, which would in turn increase per capita GDP and standard of living. It has already succeeded in this mission, as it has created a large ecosystem around itself.

Conclusion

Even though the world is a global marketplace, there has been increasing demand for local payment methods that would better address local market needs. There are many local payment solutions around the world which have managed to penetrate the market in a short time. They have been vital for driving healthy competition and enabling sustainable growth of the local economy. TROY proves that this is true even for advanced payment markets such as Turkey.

Payment System Infrastructures and Money Transfer Technologies

2

PAYMENT SYSTEMS INFRASTRUCTURE AND MONEY TRANSFER TECHNOLOGIES

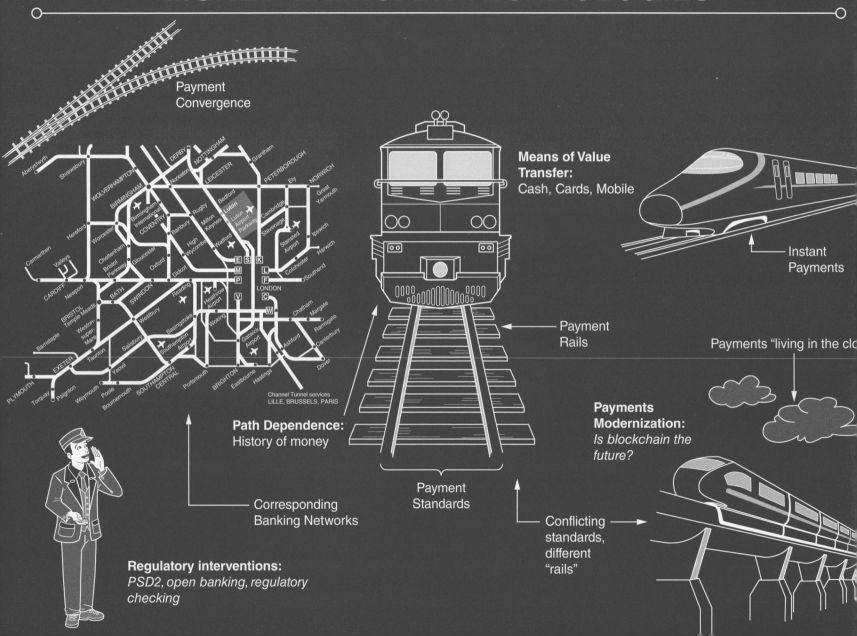

Payment Convergence

Means of Value Transfer:
Cash, Cards, Mobile

Instant Payments

Payment Rails

Payments "living in the clo[ud]

Payments Modernization:
Is blockchain the future?

Path Dependence:
History of money

Corresponding Banking Networks

Payment Standards

Conflicting standards, different "rails"

Regulatory interventions:
PSD2, open banking, regulatory checking

Executive Summary

Financial infrastructures, such as payment systems, financial telecommunication networks, clearing houses and settlement engines, are critical "institutions" that facilitate value transfer. These are the rails upon which money and data flow, making possible the exchange of goods and services in the economy. How these systems originate and evolve over time, as well as the impact of technology, standards and governance in this context, are matters of great interest both for practitioners and scholars in this space.

This part aims to examine the latest developments in payment system infrastructures and how these will shape the future of money transfer. In more detail, we explore:

1. What are the technologies transforming the field of payments?
2. How do the different stakeholders that utilize the payment rails, such as merchants, consumers and national market infrastructures, respond and influence payments modernization in the global market?
3. What is the role of financial messaging standards in this space?
4. How does geopolitical uncertainty contribute to the shaping of these infrastructures?
5. How does new regulation help (or not) to push innovation in payments?

This part also provides insights on the factors that affect the adoption and diffusion of payment technologies and the conditions under which they can achieve greater acceptance.

The Convergence of Card Payments and Bank Payments

By Mark McMurtrie
Director, Payments Consultancy Ltd

Current Position

For the last 50 years, card and bank payments have been managed as if they existed in parallel universes. It is as if card payments are from Mars and bank payments are from Venus. There is little dialogue between these two worlds, even within the same financial institution; they talk different languages, have limited understanding of their parallel universe and run their own payment systems. Terms such as "payment service provider" and "mobile payments" have very different meanings depending on which tribe you are speaking with.

But things are starting to change, mainly due to technological advances, regulatory action, competitive pressure, standards and consumer preferences. Bank payments tend to be used for large-value transactions, and scheduled bill payments to regular payees which are processed as batches. Card payments, in contrast, offer payment in real time for goods purchased at shops, when travelling and for e-commerce purchases, and have lower average transaction values, particularly since the introduction of contactless cards.

Types of Payment Systems

Historically, three types of payment systems have been operated in most countries:

- *Large-value payment systems (LVPSs) and real-time gross settlement (RTGSs) systems*. Used by corporations, small and medium enterprises, governments, central banks and individuals to handle very high transaction values, these require fast and guaranteed funds transfers and higher levels of security.

- *Retail payment systems (RPSs)*. Operated by banks to handle lower-value transactions, including regular scheduled payments for retail banking customers (not to be confused with retail merchants). RPSs are now moving to real-time processing and away from batch, with around 50 countries introducing instant bank payment services. The SEPA Credit Transfer (SCT) Inst service is now available across Europe. And with limits of up to £250,000 in the UK, these real-time RPSs are no longer just for low-value transactions.

- *The card payment network*. In many countries these are now operated by an international payments brand like Visa or Mastercard rather than by a national processor. And much to the European regulator's disappointment, there is no European card payment network anymore.

Market Drivers of Change

High levels of Internet and mobile phone adoption have dramatically transformed consumer lives and business practices. Millennials and Gen Z expect to be able to use their smartphones for everything they want to do. We live in an instant $24 \times 7 \times 365$ world and payments are viewed as "mission critical".

Regulatory action is also dramatically changing the payments industry. New regulations such as the second Payment Services Directive (PSD2) and the Interchange Fee Regulation, alongside the creation of electronic money institutions and payment institutions, are helping increase competition, accelerate innovation and transform the market.

Customers increasingly want to manage all aspects of their payments and accounts electronically and/or remotely. Continued criminal attention and escalating levels of financial fraud have to be acknowledged and tackled. In addition, one of the factors driving the convergence from card to bank payments is the increasing number of card transactions now taking place in a digitized format, whether that is for e/m-commerce or from within a digital wallet/app like Apple Pay or Google Pay.

The introduction of real-time bank payment systems is also acting as a catalyst for payments convergence. The pan-European SCT Inst scheme brings the advantages of irrevocability and instant funds transfer to retail payments. When coupled with lower fees, many merchants will find it appealing to transition away from cards to real-time bank payments. Sectors like airlines, hotels and professional service providers with high average transaction values will be early movers. However, new services like confirmation of payee and request to pay, and stronger consumer protection rights, will need to be added to bank payment schemes. The PSD2 requirement for strong customer authentication in Europe is a further driver towards bank payments.

Timescales

Nothing happens quickly in the payments industry, despite the high levels of investment and the many clever people and great companies working in the sector. We are already starting to see the convergence of card and bank payments. But we are only at the start of that convergence. Industry analysts and commentators agree that convergence will happen. The key questions are where this will be seen first, the rate of convergence and when the cross-over point will be reached. Convergence is expected by 2030, with significant cannibalization before 2027. One analyst firm forecasts that instant bank payments will have overtaken card payments for European e-commerce transactions by 2025.

Depending on your perspective, these timescales may seem too aggressive or conservative, but I would point out that history has shown new payment technology adoption (Chip & PIN, contactless, Faster Payments Service, SEPA, 3DSecure,

PSD2) has typically taken between five and seven years before becoming mainstream.

Early Adopters

Many factors will determine who will be the early adopters. Some of these are cultural, such as attitude to cash or credit, whilst others are around availability of infrastructure and standards. The UK market is expected to be one of the first countries to see this convergence from card to bank payments. Within continental Europe, Germany, the Netherlands, Poland and Hungary are expected to be early adopters. e-Commerce payments are expected to be the first to transition to bank payments, with face-to-face merchant payments following. The availability of instant bank payment schemes is a key factor influencing convergence rates. In the Netherlands, for instance, we can expect transition from the current iDeal system to the new national instant payments scheme. New standards being developed by GS1 will help accelerate merchant adoption of SEPA instant bank payments.

Winners and Losers

The international payment networks, including Visa and Mastercard, probably have the most to lose from this payments convergence. However, they have recognized the changing market dynamics and are busy preparing for the future. Mastercard's acquisition of Vocalink and the real-time payments division of NETS is a clear sign of this, and we should expect further merger and acquisition activity. Mastercard is also launching new real-time payment products that utilize their global debit card infrastructure and relationships. We can also expect to hear more about Mastercard's PaybyBank app as part of this convergence.

Acquirers risk being disintermediated if merchants and consumers switch from card to bank payments. They will need to consider connecting to the real-time bank payment rails or becoming a payment initiation service provider (PISP), or introducing a

Visa Direct or Mastercard Send proposition. Acquirers who do nothing will be the losers, as they will see payments transition, resulting in lower merchant service revenues and less profit as interchange++pricing becomes the norm.

Role of Standards

International standards have a critical role to play. Bank payment systems and card systems have so far relied on their own set of standards. But now one international standard, ISO 20022, has emerged and is being adopted globally by financial institutions for both bank and card payments. This has defined message formats for bank, card, ATM, clearing and settlement. GS1 HIPPOS standards will also be helpful.

Conclusion

Many card-based payments will transition to real-time bank payments. This will initially be seen in e-commerce and for high-value transactions. The rate of convergence will vary, but it will definitely happen. In the future, both card and bank payments should be able to be processed on the same payment system. ISO 20022 will help enable systems convergence. Millennials and Gen Z will be the early adopters, and smartphone adoption is a catalyst.

Instant Payments: A New Deal for the Payments Market?

By Andréa Toucinho
Head of Studies, Prospective and Training, Partelya Consulting

Instant payments represent a huge evolution for the payments market. This innovation symbolizes the evolution from a conservative and national market to a real globalized and modern sector. How it has and will evolve around the world is the question.

Background

Instant payment was born in the post-SEPA context, thanks to institutional initiatives from the European Central Bank (ECB) and the European Payments Council (EPC). In certain countries, like France, many professionals had already targeted the creation of a fast SEPA credit transfer (SCT) as a huge goal to modernize the payments market. The technological process of instant payment – SCT Inst. – was recently guaranteed by an ECB initiative: the creation of target instant payment settlement (TIPS), officially launched on 30 November 2018 to foster European connectivity.

The ECB is positioned as a technological provider to foster instant payments. This is a position that the market can understand when it analyses the idea that instant payments represent a huge challenge for European sovereignty. In fact, confronted with American and Asian solutions like Apple Pay, or even Alipay, it seems logical that Europe should develop its own payment scheme.

An Institutional and Geopolitical Initiative

More than a technological evolution, instant payments are a huge challenge at a geopolitical level. In fact, the goals of international solutions like Alipay, for instance, reinforce the necessity for European actors to develop their own payment scheme. In recent years, Alipay has signed agreements with several French banks, retail Spanish actor El Corte Inglés, Portuguese bank Millennium BCP and, above all, obtained a European payments licence, confirming that Alipay has huge goals in the European payments sector. Confronted with this global strategy, European payments companies that operate in a very fragmented context should work towards creating a real European payment scheme to foster competition between American, Asian and European actors.

Despite this evident goal, it remains, even today, difficult to create a common position on instant payment in Europe. In fact, like the UK with its Faster Payments Service, certain countries are very proactive on this new means of payment, unlike others who are adopting a "wait-and-see" attitude. The position depends on national markets, uses and strategies, which remain very different across Europe – even if regulators and actors are linked with the same goal of the harmonization of payments.

A Strategic Issue for European Banks

As in the UK with the Faster Payments Service, a lot of European countries welcome instant payments to their markets. Examples include: the Netherlands, where consumers are already users of iDeal and thus already prepared to use instant payment; Italy, where banks are prepared for a new means of payment which symbolizes acceleration of payments and huge benefits, above all for small companies; Spain, where banks are prepared, fostered by the national context of the Spanish banking community.

Between the eight European banks that have announced the adoption of the new TIPS scheme in November 2018, five are Spanish (Abanca Corporacion Bancaria, BBVA, Banco de Credito Social Cooperativo, Caja Laboral Popular Cooperativa de Credito, La Caixa), two are German (Berlin Hyp, Teambank) and one is French (Natixis Payments).

In relation to "wait-and-see" attitudes, many factors explain the situation. First, a specific national context. In Portugal, the payments market is already developed thanks to the initiatives of the national scheme SIBS (Sociedade Interbancaria de Serviços), which has more or less a monopolistic position in the country, complexifying new initiatives. Nevertheless, the situation is changing thanks to the adoption of the second Payment Services Directive (PSD2), which opens up the market. The symbol of this new deal can be seen in the evolution of the position of the national regulator Banco de Portugal, previously conservative but now open to innovation and new actors with, for instance, the creation of a "lab" dedicated to FinTech to drive market evolutions. Second, a strategic national issue linked with existing payments methods. The example of France is very interesting. Despite a real interest in instant payments, French banks set out to define business models and uses before launching a solution. Natixis Payments was the first French bank to announce the launch of instant payments in July 2018. The uses for this are largely person-to-person (P2P) payment, refund or insurance payments. More generally, many actors in the French payments market expect that the launch of instant payments will begin with P2P payments through the banking solution Paylib, and will later continue in remote payments (Internet, mobile) and, finally, in proximity payments, with the use of Iban to pay by mobile phone. In many cases, and above all for retailers and corporates, instant payments are welcomed and seen as a huge step towards a real modern market.

A Step Towards Modern Payments in a Global Market

If instant payments represent a huge step towards modernization, it is also because of the evolution of the back office of banks. In fact, this new means of payment represents the necessity, for banking actors, to realize an evolution from batch processing to unitary processing. It implies the necessity of updating security solutions faced with the reality of instant payments. This is a situation that represents significant costs for banking actors, but also many opportunities – such as using new security technologies and artificial intelligence. This behaviour is a priority when the payments market is living through a process of globalization thanks to new actors like Internet giants, new cross-border technologies such as blockchain or even crypto-assets, and new uses created by new generations that are very well positioned in mobility and digital.

More than just an evolution of the payments market, instant payments can also be seen as an answer to these social evolutions. Europe is not the only region to work in this field: Australia, Hong Kong and the USA are also promoting instant payments and the well known actor SWIFT is already working on a globalized instant payments solution. Defining a European scheme for instant payments appears, consequently, not just a goal for Europe – even if it is very important for European sovereignty – but above all a huge step towards a modern and totally globalized payments market.

PIN on Mobile – A Pivotal Moment for Payments

By Nigel Dean
Head of Marketing, MYPINPAD

In this chapter, we introduce a new technology which removes barriers to entry for smaller merchants wishing to accept card payments that fully satisfy today's increasingly mobile consumers, while also providing a platform for larger merchants to enrich the purchasing experience.

The Transforming Payments Landscape

2018 was a tumultuous year for the UK payments industry, with new regulations such as the second Payment Services Directive (PSD2) driving innovation and changing the way we pay for goods and services. Customers' search for a seamless, personalized, yet secure payment experience has been a dominant feature of the payments scene over the last few years, and it is certain to drive a significant transformation in how the check-outs in bricks-and-mortar shops across the UK work in the future.

A good example of this is the boom in the use of contactless payments in the UK since their launch by Barclaycard in 2007. Some 63% of consumers across the country used contactless as their preferred payment method in 2018 – attracted, no doubt, by a seamless, convenient and fast experience. The adoption of this method of payment shows no sign of slowing down any time soon – in fact, in-store contactless payments are projected to reach US$2 trillion by 2020.

The rise of contactless has also led to a breakthrough for alternative payments like mobile wallets. More and more younger consumers are adopting them in place of cards – attracted by the convenience of only having to carry their smartphone instead of a bulky wallet or purse. Cryptocurrencies are also being used more for in-store transactions, although these have some way to go before they reach the kind of popularity enjoyed by cards and e-wallets.

Regardless of the type of cashless payment, consumer demand for convenience and seamlessness has profound implications for the make-up of shop check-outs. It's already driven an increase in the number of self-serve "cashier-less" tills at mainstream supermarkets across the world. Modern consumers want the payment process to be as fast as possible, whereas merchants desire a more powerful point of interaction to encourage loyalty and increased sales. Self-service tills are more efficient compared to the traditional purchasing experience, but fall far short of what is potentially possible.

The Impact on Merchants

This revolution in payments has repercussions on all merchant sectors. As an example, over five million small retailers across the UK are still unable to accept card payments. This is because the cost and functionality of traditional point of sale (POS) terminals render card acceptance costly and impractical, particularly for small and medium enterprises. For larger retailers the challenge is slightly different, with the continuous drive to deliver an engaging and seamless in-store and omni-channel purchasing experience.

The accelerating diversification of payment methods – from e-wallets to cryptocurrencies – is exacerbating this issue. In order to meet diverging consumer demands, POS terminals increasingly need to be compatible with an ever-growing number of payment types, while also meeting ever-evolving security requirements. This is a huge challenge in the traditional payments landscape, since there is an ongoing requirement to upgrade ageing POS terminals to meet these demands. As such, it is a never-ending cycle and the result is a significant cost of ownership for all involved.

Regardless of the retailer's size, failure to invest in new technologies will see a decline in sales. This is reflected in the growing trend in the popularity of non-cash-based payments, which overtook cash in the UK for the first time in 2018, with 13.2 billion debit card purchases made compared with 13.1 billion cash transactions.[1] With so many consumers preferring to pay by card and demanding an ever more seamless purchasing experience, merchants risk losing sales to cashless consumers, whereas larger retailers miss the opportunity to promote additional sales. This, of course, can have a significant negative impact on their revenue and profits.

New Technology for Tomorrow's Consumers

Taking this into account, a new technology is entering the scene which removes barriers to entry for smaller merchants to accept card payments, while also providing a platform for larger merchants to enrich the purchasing experience.

The technology is called PIN on Mobile (PoM), which allows PIN-based card transactions to be securely accepted on readily available commercial-off-the-shelf (COTS) devices such as mobile phones and tablets. In principle this may sound simple, but there are significant challenges that need to be overcome in order for PoM to be delivered to the market. The biggest of these is security – ensuring that transactions processed via this method are every bit as secure as those on traditional POS devices.

Isolation Can Save the Day

"Isolation" is not a word we hear every day in an industry as collaborative and dedicated to knowledge sharing as payments. But it is key to ensuring optimum payment security. Simply, any PoM system must be able to securely isolate a customer's PIN and card data from the unsecure environment in which they are entered.

There is considerable work being done by the ground-breaking businesses and the card schemes to make this a reality, with a number of crucial developments over the last year. The most important of these was the introduction of the new standard from the Payment Card Industry Security Standards Council (PCI SSC) for software-based PIN entry on COTS (SPoC) devices. This is a significant milestone for the payments industry. The standard provides a software-based approach for specifically protecting PIN entry on the wide variety of COTS devices in the market today.

The standard is made up of several core principles in a solution made of three components:

1. A secure PIN entry application residing on the COTS device.

2. A secure card reader for PIN (SCRP), which connects to the COTS device via Bluetooth.

3. An extremely powerful remote monitoring system.

The overriding principle is to ensure that all components are secure at all times and the isolation of the PIN from other account data.

This isolation of components is critical to counteract correlation attacks. A correlation attack occurs when a fraudster obtains payment data elements, such as track 2 data, from one part of the payment ecosystem (e.g. skimming of a payment card) and another data element, such as a PIN, from a separate attack, and then manages to link these data elements to enable a fraudulent transaction.

Software security has a crucial role to play in achieving this goal. As such, the standard emphasizes secure software development and release practices as well as many software protections to maintain integrity against attack.

[1] https://www.independent.co.uk/money/card-payments-cash-overtakes-shopping-purchases-high-street-a8403346.html.

Laying the Foundations for a Payments Revolution

With the new standard in place, developers of PoM solutions now have a set of rules and principles they can fully align to help keep consumers' payment information safe. This paves the way for a revolution in how millions of merchants across the globe accept card payments. These changes include:

- Merchants can inexpensively use a COTS device to take payment compared to purchasing or leasing an expensive single-purpose POS terminal.

- The very fact that all COTS devices are connected to the Internet allows additional value-added services to be downloaded from openly available app stores. This provides a powerful platform to promote customer loyalty while also enabling up- and cross-selling.

- The implementation of an omni-channel experience lends itself perfectly to this approach, since all COTS devices are connected to the Internet.

- A host of business development tools can also be hosted on the COTS device to help merchants manage their business and customer base.

Thanks to all of this, solid foundations have been laid to deliver mobile-based in-store payment solutions, helping to maximize the number of payment acceptance points globally and promote sales for all merchant sectors.

One such solution is set to boost sales in merchants of all sizes in the very near future, enabling merchants, acquirers and payment service providers to deploy PoM technologies without applying for their own PCI SPoC certification, thereby removing complexity and saving time and money when deploying a payments solution.

A Brighter Payments Future

PoM will transform the payments ecosystem beyond comprehension. Combining consumer familiarity with entering their PIN and the established market penetration of acceptance points (smartphones and tablets), the barriers to adoption previously experienced with technologies have been removed. Consumers will enjoy a brighter, better payments experience as a result and retailers will have access to a host of enhanced technologies to support their business success.

PayTech in the Cloud

By Rami AlHasan

Senior Manager Digital Commerce Solutions, Etisalat

Startups in the FinTech/PayTech space need to run a lean operating model with very low initial investments, allowing them to test and try and pay as they grow. To do this they need to live or precisely host their services on one of the shared public clouds offered by the main players in the market – Amazon Web Services, Microsoft Azure and Google Cloud.

But in the financial space there are many challenges facing financial services: stringent regulation and compliance requirements, security risks, fraud risks, customer data protection, to name but a few. How can the PayTech leaders guarantee security of their financial service, protect the privacy of their customers and comply with regulations while being fully hosted on a shared public cloud?

Cloud Security Best Practices

This can be achieved by conforming to the following "Best Practices in Cloud" security, to make sure the service and its customers are safe and secure.

- **Secure applications**
  It all starts with a focus on security during requirements analysis and design. Technical teams are under pressure to deliver innovations quickly, yet they need to be supported by getting the same focus on designing applications that are secure and safe, protecting data and guarding them from potential fraud. This is especially important for PayTechs, because trust is everything in this business.

  Important business design aspects are effective identity registration and verification for customers, secure access controls (e.g. two-factor authentications where relevant, with strong password policies), anti-money laundering and sanctions screening.

Secure code is a key factor in protecting the business from future data breaches too. Developers need to focus on handling passwords securely, strict input validations, rigorous authentication of users on all application resources and verifications of privileges – validating that users only access what they are privileged to access.

User sessions should be protected through proper encryption, so hackers cannot take control of users' sessions through phishing. All user and system actions should be traceable and auditable through detailed encrypted logging. No confidential data is presented as clear text anywhere, and confidential data should be encrypted at rest and on the move. Also, the importance of proper handling of application exceptions cannot be overemphasized.

- **Secure DevOps**
  DevOps manage the application releases across various stages of the development lifecycle, driven by the agile concepts of continuous integration and continuous delivery (CI/CD). They must have a process for the automation of security tests to discover any vulnerabilities in the release early on in the process. Automated testing tools should also be able to discover security issues in application design, coding, integrations, deployment configuration, cloud infrastructure configuration or any missing patches.

Similar to applications, automation should be used to provision cloud nodes with the right security controls as per the required compliance and best practices for the industry. Cloud service providers provide tools and templates to help automate the configuration of security policies, the discovery of any missing patches and to scan infrastructure for any vulnerability covering the network, operating systems and some application servers needed to host the application.

- **Secure APIs**

  In the payment industry, integrations amongst the players are key for value creation, and many business models would not have materialized without the ecosystem's diverse integrations. Application programming interfaces (APIs) make such integrations possible, bringing improved agility and dynamic exposure of business capabilities that can foster innovation in a service or product offering.

  With all the benefits comes the high risk of exposing insecure APIs or integrating with insecure APIs of other ecosystem players, especially under the pressure of time to market. Securing network access is critical, requiring the use of IP Sec VPNs and other secure tunnel technologies, limiting reachability through IPs whitelisting and mandating the digital certificates for client authentication over SSL and VPNs. Moreover, all API layers should be properly hardened, and assigned privileges should be narrowed down to roles that are needed by the integrating party.

  Of course, APIs should also follow the strict code security aspects discussed earlier, especially as we are deploying on a public cloud environment. Similar to any core software component, APIs should apply all the security provisioning scripts needed and should pass all security testing requirements before any release to production. This is where a proper security governance is key to success and security should become part of the culture, enforced at all levels to guarantee long-term customer trust.

- **Secure cloud infrastructure**

  The cloud infrastructure has to be designed and configured to address the security risks targeting financial service providers.

Every organization may have its own security policies, but operating in a certain domain, industry or region may mandate compliance with certain industry security standards.

This is especially true for the payments card industry, where card schemes (e.g. Visa/Mastercard) and partner banks mandate being audited by third-party certified security auditors for compliance with the latest version of PCI-DSS. Cloud solution providers (CSPs) provide useful frameworks and shared infrastructure components to speed up compliance. PCI-DSS touches every aspect of infrastructure management and operation, starting from network configurations (such as virtual LAN segregations and access control lists) to network components (such as DNS, switches, firewalls, web access firewalls, intrusion detection & protection and load balancers, etc.). PCI-DSS focuses on the route of card data while being transmitted or stored in any layer, operating system, virtualization layer, database storage or key vault (i.e. secure key management for encryption and decryption of confidential data).

Card data protection is the target, and such confidential data should always be transferred in a secure encrypted tunnel. Data should not be stored in memory, file or database in clear text. Card data needs to always be stored encrypted.

This is why strong identity and access management (IAM) is a key component in selecting the CSP. IAM takes care of the policies and access controls to ensure that the right people have the appropriate access to service resources, whether this is for the consumer or the administrators and the business users.

The Rise of a Super-Correspondent Banking Network

By Anders la Cour
Co-Founder and Chief Executive Officer, Banking Circle

Financial exclusion is no longer limited to vulnerable consumers; it is fast becoming an increasing concern for businesses too. Post-recession business lending is a challenging market, and small and medium enterprises (SMEs) often face a tough battle for finance. With banks closing branches across the country, businesses are more restricted in their access to financial experts and this is having an impact on their ability to borrow.

When we spoke to over 500 heads of finance for SMEs in 2018, we found that almost all (92.5%) have needed to access additional finance within the past five years, and just 13.5% had a positive experience when doing so.

Without additional funding, 24.6% of the SMEs we surveyed would have to let employees go, and 13.3% believe this would ultimately lead to the failure of the business. With SMEs making up 99.9% of private businesses and employing 60% of the UK workforce,[1] this is a dangerous situation. If these businesses cannot access the necessary finance, over 16 million people are at risk of unemployment if their company struggles or becomes one of the 90% of startups that don't make it to their fourth anniversary.[2]

The importance of financial inclusion, and the size of financial exclusion as a global problem, cannot and must not be underestimated. The banking and payments industries must work together to improve the prospects for SMEs and those who rely on their continued success.

Tough Terrain for SME Lending

Business lending has been a challenge since the beginning of the financial crash. Banks have struggled to lend to any company, let alone startups and SMEs which are often perceived as higher risk.

The biggest challenges faced by our SME interviewees were rates, fees and speed. 35% said their bank didn't offer the best rate; 28% found the fees too high; and for 23.4% and 21.4%, respectively, the speed of facilitation of the finance – and even speed of response from the bank – were a problem. 18.8% found that their bank didn't offer the length of loan they wanted, demonstrating the inflexibility of traditional banking systems.

Each of these specific issues can exclude a company from fair and affordable access to the finance required for business prosperity or expansion. SMEs are being financially excluded and are at real risk of failure.

Big banks remain the largest business lending providers, yet they cannot meet the changing needs of businesses today. Their inflexibility due to legacy infrastructure holds them back from offering the flexibility SMEs need – not to mention the rapid arrangement of funds that a fast-paced business requires to help it remain competitive.

However, new providers are stepping in to fill the gap left between what banks can do and what businesses need their bank to do.

The End of Banks?

Traditional banks may no longer be best-placed to offer small business loans, but they do remain vital to the global economy for other core banking functions such as deposits. It is not the relevance of banks which is changing, but the position they hold in the market.

---

[1] "Business Population Estimates for the UK and Regions 2017", November 2017.

[2] http://www.cityam.com/280376/forget-embracing-failure-startups-deserve-best-possible.

Gone are the days of banks owning the entire value chain. Gone are the days of business and consumer banking customers having to make do with limited, expensive, inflexible options.

The role of banks may be undergoing its most significant change in generations, but banks will not disappear. Financial utilities can give banks and FinTech businesses the ability to provide their business customers with better borrowing solutions.

Working together with third parties, in the increasingly popular ecosystem model, allows financial institutions to deliver transparent, easy-to-manage, flexible and low-cost lending solutions. For the first time, this can be done without the significant investment it would require for banks to develop and deliver innovative solutions in-house.

The agility of alternative providers, such as financial utilities, means they can build and deploy the most efficient and cost-effective solutions far more quickly than a larger, more traditional provider is able. As such, they are more capable of meeting the ever-changing needs of SMEs in today's market, allowing them to stay far ahead of the competition.

With lenders able to provide better and more accessible solutions, they are improving financial inclusion and therefore the long-term prospects for SMEs of all sizes.

Beyond Lending

As the world becomes a smaller place in terms of trade, cross border payments become increasingly important – and current solutions become increasingly problematic. The traditional cross border transaction solution of the correspondent banking network is too slow and too expensive, having not changed in decades. The network no longer serves the market efficiently. Added to this, many banks are pulling out of their correspondent relationships due to increased regulation and the high costs involved in processing international payments.

Delays in payments can cause significant problems for businesses, as we saw in our research with SMEs. Slow, expensive cross border payments can halt business expansion into new markets and stop companies from achieving their global potential.

As the correspondent banking network model begins to break down, we are seeing the creation of a new, super-correspondent banking network. This network is built on the ecosystem model, which holds potential benefits reaching far beyond better lending solutions for SMEs.

Future Banking

In these early stages of the digital economy, large institutions will continue to dominate the payments space, but FinTechs threaten banks' ongoing profitability and success. Working with a third-party financial utility, able to do the pipes and plumbing more efficiently and at lower cost, banks of all sizes can focus resources on the client relationship and growing their client base. At the same time, they continue to bring fresh solutions to market quickly, enabling them to compete more effectively.

A few short years ago, the idea of large or small banks working with external partners to deliver banking services was unfathomable to most. However, in today's market, with the complexities of legacy systems – together with the rapidly increasing competition from FinTechs – banks are ready for such a collaborative approach. Embracing the ecosystem model is the only way for financial institutions to prosper long-term.

We are already seeing banks and FinTechs accepting a move towards the ecosystem model, working in partnership with third-party allies able to deploy tailored solutions on their behalf and in their name. This super-correspondent banking network brings huge benefits to bank and FinTech customers without the usual significant investment required to build and deploy these solutions in-house.

Conclusion

With a financial utility handling the tech side, without it being a burden on bank resources, banks can offer credit, foreign exchange and both local and cross border payments to all customer segments. Working with financial utilities within the super-correspondent banking network to deliver better banking, lending and payment services will ensure business and consumer customers have affordable access to the best financial solutions in the market, which is good for the entire global economy.

Why Distinctions Within Mobile Wallets and Tokenization Matter

By Mark Gerban
Payment Industry Expert

Card tokenization in the payments industry has been around for almost 20 years. While most of us may have been exposed to using the technology without being aware of it, it has now started to become mainstream due to merchant data breaches and the need for increased security. That same security burden is where card schemes, such as Mastercard and Visa, have pieced together the concept of network tokenization, where card networks are looking to take over the responsibility of securing card numbers, as opposed to outsourcing to traditional acquirers.

Tokenization – The First Steps

When not considering the multiple complexities of card networks, acquirers, payment or token service providers, tokenization itself is a rather simple concept. The general purpose for the creation of tokenization was online security, whereby first-time-entered credit card numbers were moved from a receiving merchant platform to a secure "vault". After storage of the actual card number in a vault, a representation of that card number (e.g. a token) would be sent back to the merchant platform and associated with a user account. This entire process was defined and set up to prevent the theft of credit card numbers.

Thereafter, anytime an existing user wanted to initiate a purchase, the merchant platform would query their vault with the stored token to reference the actual user credit card number. Upon successful matching of the token and the card number, a transaction request for processing the actual card number (not the token) would be passed on to the merchant acquirer for payment.

With the basic details of tokenization now explained, we can look at the underlying wallet technologies.

Mobile NFC Wallets

Big tech companies such as Apple, Google and Samsung have adopted network tokenization technology across the board, and this has created a wide variation in how network tokens are applied. Each type of individual phone wallet use case has a varying degree of problems or limitations to consider, and it is not that these issues are unsolvable in the future, but they do pose some real-world problems today that most of us may not be aware of.

Secure Element (SE) Tokenization

To comprehend the basic differences in wallet technologies, first to be discussed is SE tokenization. On a simplified level, this form of tokenization involves storing static PAN token credentials inside physical hardware, or secure chips. The provisioning of these static tokens normally occurs within a secure onboarding process between the issuer and wallet technology.

After multi-factor authentication, these static tokens are then repeatedly used and queried in SE environments with the use of issuer-specific cryptographic keys. This type of tokenization is commonly seen within the Apple ecosystem for use in NFC or web-based purchases, while mobile network operators may also use SIM SE on Android and other devices.

The credentials stored within SE hardware environments are generally accessible via NFC applications that can query the SE hardware itself, but the details on the SE are controlled by internal applications that generally cannot be accessed or breached by external parties.

Host-Card Emulation (HCE)

HCE is the core basis for most wallets outside of the Apple ecosystem. The onboarding process with issuers may be similar to what is done with SE wallets, but the overall security and NFC functionality behaves differently in the background.

HCE was created to remove the dependency on SE hardware, specifically SIM SE environments, mainly due to the politics of mobile network operator (MNO) fragmentation. HCE is a full cloud-based software solution, where unlike SE (which stores static tokens on chips), HCE must download a new card payment token for each transaction and save the token(s) in the system software for use on an NFC or web interface. Depending on the issuer, more tokens may be downloaded per device to prevent inaccessible fund scenarios (e.g. no Internet connectivity for the user) from occurring.

Generally, HCE also serves a larger purpose as it is a more scalable workaround when having to deal with hundreds of different mobile devices in the Android ecosystem for enabling NFC, rather than having to set up SE configurations for each device.

What are the Differences?

It is clear that SE tokenization is driven more as a hardware-based solution, while HCE utilizes the cloud. Understanding this basic difference, there are some finite details in each service which should be considered.

With an SE scenario, if a device or SIM card is stolen, the funds can potentially be used with a longer open time window. Apple has done a fantastic job using FaceID and TouchID as authentication methods, but it is still possible to enable payment via PIN, and this is still considered a vulnerability. While a cloud shutdown of Apple credentials is possible, it is much easier to enable shut-off

to payment accessibility with HCE, since the infrastructure is built around the cloud and can be shut off more easily on a remote basis by the user.

HCE requires downloads of tokens on devices, and this in itself is a potential security issue. As tokens are stored locally via software on the device, these tokens have the potential to be skimmed and used elsewhere under certain, although unlikely, conditions. This type of cloud skimming is not possible with SE hardware, as the payment tokens are static and remain on a device in a chip.

SE payments will be accessible at all times, even while a phone has no Internet connectivity or is in flight mode after the card token has been provisioned. This means that the user experience and accessibility for cash will be much more dependable. HCE requires downloading of tokens, which could be very problematic when in low Internet connectivity areas or travelling abroad. This reduces the dependability of the wallet, and accounts for perhaps the largest reason of failed transactions with Google Wallet.

Conclusion

While the differences between HCE and SE tokenization seem finite, there are some viewpoints to consider from a payment perspective. Cash has been a dependable system for thousands of years, and while it is ripe for disruption, it is always able to work when needed most.

The convergence of mobile and wallet technologies has proven that there is room for payment disruption, but finite differences can reduce user adaption to a crawl, especially if the technologies are not always dependable and accessible.

Wallets always need to be accessible when users need them most, and while network tokenization has offered a strong security aspect, there are more improvements needed in wallet infrastructure to transition into a stronger adoption growth phase.

The Future is Already Here; It is Just Not Evenly Distributed

By Ali Sohani
Founder and Chief Technology Advisor, Optimizia

Rafi Ullah Khan
Head of Data-Science, Optimizia

and Suneel Kumar Rathod
Head of Blockchain, Optimizia

Introduction

At present, payment infrastructures at the national as well as the international level are mostly in the form of messages and rely on the exchange of files amongst parties. If the deployment of distributed ledger technology were to be adopted on a large scale for payments, it would provide significant benefits for both payment and money transfer mechanisms.

Payments would no longer require heavy clearing and settlement systems, while companies would have a real-time accounting ledger in their enterprise resource planning (ERP) or treasury management systems. This would also enhance security of payment systems significantly. The best option is to introduce crypto-tokens, that will be part of a peer-to-peer cryptocurrency whose value would also arise from the market. Pricing would be according to how much it is worth to consumers; a basic supply and demand model. People would purchase tokens from exchanges at market value and use these tokens instead of paper money. All the transactions would be logged using distributed ledger technology (DLT).

By adopting such a DLT system, several transparency and security benefits could be realized.

The Process of Exchanging Value

Generally speaking, a payment refers to the process of transferring value or assets from one individual or organization to another in exchange for services, goods or the fulfilment of globally accepted standards of a legal obligation.

Global payments are an extension of this concept, in which payments can be made across geographical boundaries through multiple legal currencies. The current payments infrastructure mostly relies on the exchange of financial messaging between multiple payment parties. A typical payment lifecycle includes many steps and multiple parties to process the payments, which takes hours and days to complete transactions, and can result in delays in the process.

To minimize such delays and time-consuming processes, DLT disruption could be highly transformative. Banks, organizations and clients can cash in on the advantages of DLT in terms of higher levels of security, speed and low cost. DLT, however, is not only a source of attention for new financial companies, but also for traditional players to convert their processes from traditional systems to advanced emerging technologies. For example, processing an international money transfer using DLT could provide settlement in real time and reduce the operating costs, enabling new business models like micropayments with new models of regulatory oversight. DLT will have the strongest impact on financial business models when it has reached its peak.

Payment System Over DLT Transaction Flow

When payment systems are deployed using DLT, what will be the flow of the system? Detailed processing steps in the resulting system could be as follows:

- Banks will provide interfaces to their customers/users. Forms will be submitted to the banking networks in processed, encoded and DLT format. For transactions processing and settlement, it will be forwarded to systems.

- Transactions will be recorded and updated in all the ledgers of connected nodes once the transaction is initiated.

- The transaction state will be change from "confirmed" state to "unconfirmed" state once validations and verifications are complete. All the details will be logged. If the required nodes cannot be confirmed, it will be in the unconfirmed state.

- Upon successful transaction, the account of the issuing bank/institution/entity is debited and the receiving bank/institution/entity is credited with the value of the transaction. Permission to authorize the transaction(s) will be made by all nodes or a majority of the nodes taking part in the payment system, although the transaction will be peer-to-peer.

- Each of the participants can see the entire transactions history. The history will be in encrypted form but can be accessed with special permission by each participant.

- As the transactions are processed on an end-to-end basis, in case any one of the activities/processes relating to that specific transaction is unsuccessful, this will result in transaction rejection by the system and the originating centre will be notified accordingly.

Some of the requirements that should be fulfilled to implement or shift traditional payment systems over a DLT architecture would relate to:

1. The system's relevance to open source software.

2. Its standard protocol (token) and how universally accepted it is.

3. Its transaction openness (shared in cryptographically encrypted access levels).

4. How disturbed it is (to enhance security and trust levels amongst participants).

5. Its traceability (keep trails of all records for analysis purposes).

6. Its digital account and addresses (enhanced system security by keeping all transaction addresses unique).

7. If it employs a universal currency.

8. Its global community rate fix.

Reasons DLT Technology Will Change Real-Time Payments

Real-time payments are a top-of-mind goal and may be the need in today's era for both DLT technology firms/institutions and legacy payment processors. Here are the three main reasons that address the question: "why it is so?"

1. **Consumer expectations.** A customer wants to make a transaction (payment) between two accounts (let's say PayPal) or two Bitcoin accounts, but in real time. If the two accounts are at the same bank, the transaction should be instant and free. But what if he/she wants to make a transaction (payment) across two different banks or transfer money to an overseas account? The expectation is that it will take up to five business days and will often require additional charges. Customers now expect more user-friendly, simpler and more efficient payment products.

2. **Payment technology powering.** DLT can enable faster transactions across different payment networks in a way that doesn't generate a significant amount of risk and additional costs, but ultimately requires an updated infrastructure. There is still a challenge that payment systems to be used in the future must be capable of seamlessly handling multiple currencies (used at different geographical locations across different countries) across different networks in a cost-efficient manner.

3. **No more silos.** Confirming settlement without relying on a central counterparty and possibly in real time is against the trust levels of individuals and institutions. This is considered one of the most important pieces of the puzzle that must be solved to implement settlement. Better and more efficient business logic will help coordinate large-scale and complex systems of diverse

parties to manage associated risk, liquidity, transparency and speed. There will be a fundamental change in real-time payments and the way money is handled.

Conclusion

However the DLT succeeds in different areas, the discovery and acceptance of technology is only a matter of time. End users will benefit from advances in DLT because it represents a catalyst that can better simplify the global capital transfer industry.

If DLT technology can be deployed on a large scale for payments, it will bring significant benefits to banks and companies. Banks will no longer require significant investment in clearing and settlement systems, and the company can have a real-time accounting ledger in their ERP and financial management systems. This will greatly enhance the security of payments.

PSD2 Open Banking: The Challenges of Third-Party Provider Identity and Regulatory Checking

By David Parker
CEO, Polymath Consulting

When considering the changes brought forward by the second Payment Services Directive (PSD2) regulatory framework, one of the first questions that needs to be addressed is: "Who has the responsibility to check on third-party providers' identity and regulatory status?" The answer is largely: "Any company that delivers PSD2 open banking access and offering a transactional account", as stated in PSD2. In the UK, the Financial Conduct Authority (FCA) defines a transactional account, in the FCA handbook, as a "payment account". And the FCA Regulation 2 definition of a payment account is:

an account held in the name of one or more payment service users which is used for the execution of payment transactions.[1]

The definition of a transaction account is thus far wider than just bank accounts. In fact, based on some research published by Konsentus, it is estimated that there could be around 9,000+ ASPSPs (account servicing payment service providers, often just called financial institutions or FIs) in Europe to which the regulation will apply (see Table 1 for relevant figures).

The regulations are not just relevant to consumer products. PSD2's open banking requirements also apply to business payment accounts where the relationship is based on standard terms and conditions between the FI and the business. Whilst many companies will consider themselves not to be banks, or offering "accounts", many products such as e-money wallets and credit cards will be covered by PSD2 open banking.

When a third-party provider (TPP) seeks access from an FI that has to deliver PSD2 open banking, the FI needs to check who is seeking access and if the TPP has the correct regulatory status to receive the data they are requesting; they may be requesting access as either an AISP (account information service provider) or a PISP (payment initiation service provider), providing their services. If an FI provides data to someone they should not

Table 1: Number of ASPSPs across the UK and the EU[2]

ASPSPs – types of FI	Number of institutions
Banks	4,800+ across EU Member States
Building societies	UK: 44
Credit unions	1,548 across EU Member States
Electronic money and payment institutions	UK: 5,500+/EU: 8,800+
Prepaid programme managers (obligations passed down from BIN sponsors)	EU: 50+

---

[1] FCA Handbook PERG 15 Guidance on the Scope of the Payment Services Regulations 2009. Accessed at https://www.handbook.fca.org.uk/handbook/PERG/15/3.html.

[2] Sources can be accessed at https://www.ecb.europa.eu/stats/ecb_statistics/escb/html/table.en.html?id=JDF_MFI_MFI_LIST (excluding the UK); https://www.bsa.org.uk/statistics/sector-info-performance/sector-information; http://www.creditunionnetwork.eu/cus_in_europe; https://paymentinstitutions.eu/about-epif/the-payment-institutions-sector/about; http://www.telegraph.co.uk/business/2016/09/20/almost-5500-finance-firms-use-passports-to-access-single-market/; Polymath Consulting Analysis.

have, then they are potentially in breach of both PSD2 and GDPR (General Data Protection Regulation).

Under PSD2, all TPPs will be required to obtain regulated/approved status with their home country national competent authority (NCA) in accordance with Article 5 of Directive (EU) 2015/2366. On obtaining approval from an NCA, all TPPs, other than those in the UK, are issued with an eIDAS certificate from a qualified trust service provider (QTSP).

In the UK, the PSD2 Stakeholder Group, managed by the New Payment System Operator, has written to the Department of Business, Energy and Industrial Strategy (BEIS) stating that the UK needs to create a QTSP that will issue qualified certificates in order to comply with EU law post 2019 and thus will issue eIDAS certificates to UK regulated/approved companies.

There are, however, several challenges in this process.

1. eIDAS certificates

There have been discussions around whether FIs can use the eIDAS certificates presented to an FI as proof that they are approved by their NCA, and thus have access to end users' data. This issue has been documented and described in the ERPB report of November 2017.[3] The key section states:

Considering that the NCA is not obliged to inform the QTSP, and the QTSP is not obliged to check the NCA register, it is clear that although we can trust the certificates for identification, in the case that an NCA has withdrawn a license and the certificate has not yet been revoked, there is a period when the roles in the certificate will not be accurate. In the case that anybody wishes to check the up to date role of an ASPSP, then they must look at the Home NCA of that entity.

---

[3] The report can be downloaded from the following link: https://www.ecb.europa.eu/paym/retpaym/euro/html/index.en.html.

In summary, whilst an eIDAS certificate confirms who a TPP is at the moment they were granted regulated/approved regulatory status, it does not prove that they are still approved on the relevant NCA database at the time of use and have not been revoked or suspended at some point after the issuance of the eIDAS certificate.

2. Scheme regulatory databases

Scheme regulatory databases such as UK Open Banking, etc. have made it clear that they will offer machine-readable databases for FIs to connect to and verify that a TPP is approved by an NCA.

The purpose, though, of Open Banking's database is to bind API providers (i.e. ASPSPs and TPPs) to the arbitration rules necessary to achieve a self-regulating industry. UK Open Banking has been designated by the FCA, so the question is: "Do all TPPs have to register with a scheme regulatory database like UK Open Banking for the market they wish to access APIs in?" If we look at the UK and the UK Open Banking group it appears not, as the Operational Governance Rules and Guidelines for March 2017 Open Data state, and specifically paragraph 4.3.2:

d) A User does not have to be registered to access Provider APIs, but will still be required to accept the Participation Conditions on the Open Banking website prior to access through Open Banking.

… and paragraph 5.2:

5.2 API User – Validation and Registration

a) The Registration process will be optional for Users who will in all cases be required to accept the Participation Conditions via a tick box on the OBS website.

b) Any User that does not register will be required to accept the Participation Conditions via a tick box on the OBS website, but will not be able to take advantage of any support services offered by Open Banking as defined in these rules and guidelines. This includes disputes resolution, complaints handling and application and security monitoring.

… and paragraph 5.3.3 Withdrawal from the Central Register:

d) API Users will be permitted to withdraw from the OBS at any point following the withdrawal process via their access to the Central Register (refer to Service Levels).

e) Where an API Provider or an API User has withdrawn from the OBS, the Central Register must be updated (refer to Service Levels).

In summary, there is no legal obligation on a TPP once regulated or approved by their home country NCA, and passported to another NCA for the market they wish to operate in, to then be registered with a local scheme regulatory database. Further, there is no legal obligation once a home country NCA revokes a TPP for them to notify a scheme regulatory database.

3. National competent authorities

Home country NCAs will be the source data on whether a TPP is regulated/approved to carry out activities at the time it is making the request. The challenges with NCA databases are that they:

- Present data in different formats/structures.
- Present data in different languages.
- Present different data sets.
- Are generally currently not machine readable.
- Publish updates in different methods and at different times of the day.

Thus, whilst NCA databases will be definitive in the data they hold, they will not be easily accessible or usable by FIs. If an NCA revokes a TPP, there is an obligation to advise the NCA where it has passported into, but no SLA on the speed of this has been published.

So, what is the role of an NCA here? In the UK the FCA states that its role in regulating AIS and PIS providers is:

We are responsible for ensuring AISPs and PISPs are registered or authorised. For businesses that only carry on account information services, there is an option to become a "registered account information service provider". These providers have no capital requirements and need to meet fewer conditions than authorised firms. Businesses that provide payment initiation services must be authorised and must have a minimum of €50,000 in initial capital (or higher if they provide certain other payment services). Both AISPs and PISPs have to hold professional indemnity insurance (PII). The EBA has developed Guidelines on PII (link is external).

In summary, home country NCAs hold the source data, but it is not accessible via APIs in a machine-readable form.

4. EBA database

In theory the EBA database is the logical solution to check on the regulatory status of a TPP, but there are challenges:

- It is not accessible on a real-time basis to check TPP transactions.

- It publishes updates twice a day with NCAs providing data once a day, although not all at the same time each day giving an issue around how up to date it is.

- The EBA in fact explicitly takes no liability for the information in the register

EBA Disclaimer: "*The present Register has been set up by the EBA solely on the basis of information provided by national competent authorities of the EEA Member States. Therefore, unlike national registers under PSD2, this Register has no legal significance and confers no rights in law. If an unauthorised institution is inadvertently included in the Register, its legal status is in no way altered; similarly, if an institution has inadvertently been omitted from the Register, the validity of its authorisation will not be affected."*

- ASPSPs are thus fully liable for fraudulent transactions – not the EBA when using the EBA registry to check on TPP status.

- Further Credit Institutions who are allowed to act as TPPs without further registration with the relevant National Competent Authority are not covered by the EBA TPP registry. They are covered on the "The EBA Credit Institution Register", but again this only allows manual searches (there is NO downloadable version) and is only updated 'regularly'.

- The EBA registers also do not contain any information on eIDAS certificates or their status.

Conclusion

Overall, the challenges of TPP identity and regulatory status approval are:

1. eIDAS certificates prove who a TPP is, but not whether they are approved and there are over 70 QTSPs that an FI needs to reference.

2. Scheme regulatory databases offer lists of approved TPPs, but TPPs do not have to register on them.

3. National competent authorities hold lists of approved and registered TPPs, but generally not in a machine-readable form.

4. The EBA registry does not offer a real time, machine readable TPP identity and regulatory checking solution covering all TPPs and Credit Institutions in a single place. It is not the system of legal record, and therefore takes no liability for the information contained therein.

Taking PayTech to the Villages of India

By Vishal Gupta
Business Architect, Tata Consultancy Services

India is a great market for PayTech, with several players like PAYTM, BHIM, Google Pay and Phone-Pe present and thriving. In cities, people are adopting digital means of payment and digital payments are carving a niche in people's lives.

I live in Gurugram, a city close to India's national capital. I can go out without cash and manage all my expenses like travel, food, movies, grocery and medicines using payment apps. However, the real penetration of PayTech in India has a long way to go as these modes of payment are not readily available once you step out of the cities; 95% of the Indian economy is still cash-based, and 90% of merchants only accept cash payments. With over 600,000 villages across India, creating a cashless economy presents both a great opportunity and a significant challenge.

In November 2016, the Indian government carried out "demonetization", banning 500 and 1,000 rupee notes in an attempt to curb the black market and encourage a cashless economy. This resulted in an initial push towards digital payments, but cash soon took over from digital again. The volume of digital transactions, which had increased in November and December 2016, declined by 20% in February 2017. The Reserve Bank of India (RBI) annual report released in August 2018 confirmed that 99.3% of demonetized notes were returned to the banking system.

With a large part of India's population living in villages, there are many reasons why the digital mode of payment has not penetrated. These include:

- trust;
- education around apps and smartphones;
- physical infrastructure;
- Internet speed; and
- language.

People have not yet developed *trust* in digital payments, especially in villages, where the main household spender is generally aged between 40 and 60. They completed their education 15 years ago, well before the smartphone revolution in India, and digital payments did not exist when they were younger.

They have not become familiar with digital payments because they are still using cash. Where digital payments are required, such as for completing forms, booking trains and making bus reservations online, they go to the Internet shop where they pay a little extra in cash and someone does it for them. People trust the person sitting in the shop, but not the mobile app. Taking advice from elders is part of the Indian culture, and this hampers the adoption of digital payment techniques. Where elders have no familiarity or personal experience with digital payments, and thus have not developed trust in it, they cannot pass this on to youngsters. Instead, the elders need to learn from the youngsters.

People are comfortable using Facebook and YouTube as they know that no money is involved. But when it comes to banks and payment apps on smartphones, they are very concerned and do not want to take the risk. My parents are postgraduates but are still not confident about withdrawing money from ATMs, let alone using payment apps. People lack a basic understanding of smartphones and how payment apps work, and are not accessing the *education* that is available. Let's take an example. A person who has a basic understanding of a payment app goes shopping and uses digital payment to buy a mobile phone. The payment fails due to connectivity issues but the money has gone from the account and this will give him a sleepless night. Someone familiar with digital payments will understand that the money will be refunded to the account after two to three working days, but a person who has dealt in cash for 40 years will find it hard to understand and will probably feel more secure returning to cash for future transactions.

We have a deep-rooted familiarity with the bank branches and individuals who have been taking care of our money for decades. But digital payments have no *physical infrastructure* in the villages. People still want to talk to a person face-to-face if they have any money-related issues. An issue with a cash payment at a retailer where the shopkeeper speaks their language can be resolved then and there. But if a problem follows a digital payment, you need to call a helpline and wait for customer support to help.

Another factor contributing to the poor penetration of digital payments is *Internet speed*. Mobile data services have improved in recent years, but the Internet speed in India lags far behind the rest of the world. According to speedtest.net's December 2018 Speed Test Global Index, India was ranked 109th out of 125 countries for average mobile Internet speed. This problem with Internet speed, even present in metros in India, means that payment apps do not work the way they should and it does not provide a streamlined experience. Most digital payment apps in India use a one-time password (OTP) for authorization however due to poor Internet connectivity people do not receive the OTP in real time and consequently the payment fails, people have to resort to an alternative mode of payment such as cash. The repeated experience of a person in a village trying – but failing – to pay digitally is likely to result in frustration and they will find it more reliable to pay by cash in future.

Language is also a critical factor, English is not the first language in Indian villages and most of the digital payment apps in India are in English. Localization is something which some innovators are trying to address by offering digital apps in local languages. This is, however, a complex challenge, since there are 22 major languages in India, written in 13 different scripts, with over 720 dialects. Just imagine the potential chaos caused by a single update of a single payment app handling this amount of complexity. If we want to replace cash with digital payments, we need to replicate the customer experience which people have in a local retail shop where shopkeepers interact in their language.

What Can be Done?

Changing the payment landscape in Indian villages is clearly a mammoth task and will take time. The move from paper to digital provides a useful learning experience. Around 20 years ago, people knew they had to stand in bank queues to update their paper passbooks to show transactions which would mirror their deposits and withdrawals. As computers and the Internet have penetrated our lives, we have grown to trust them and you can now find bank passbooks with no entries. People now know that the notification they receive when money is deposited in or taken from their bank account can be used in future if some issue occurs. Similarly, I anticipate that cash will be replaced slowly by digital payments, but it will be a time-consuming process.

Digital payments cannot be forced, as we saw from the experience of the Indian government through demonetization, and any big corporate looking to create disruption should be aware of this.

Payments Regulation and Compliance

3

PAYMENT REGULATION AND COMPLIANCE

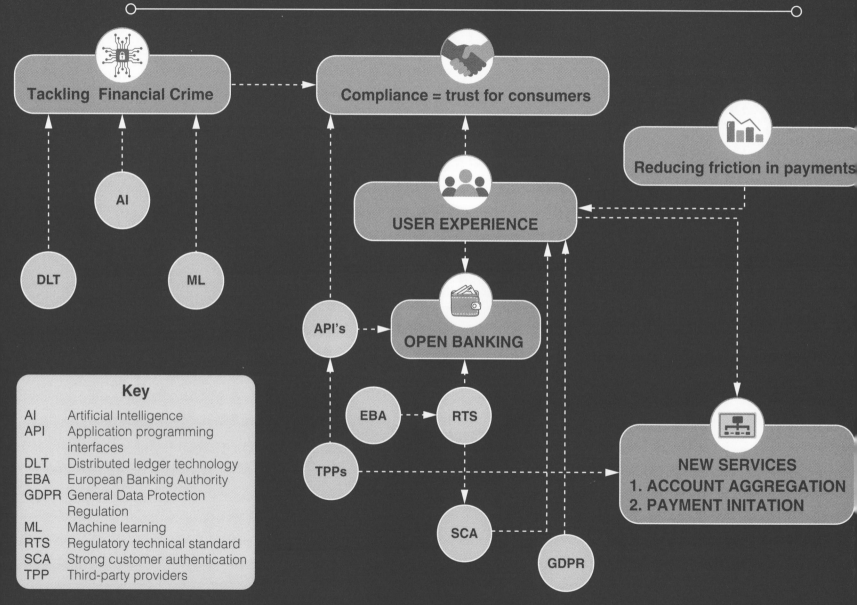

Tackling Financial Crime

Compliance = trust for consumers

Reducing friction in payments

USER EXPERIENCE

AI

DLT

ML

OPEN BANKING

API's

EBA

RTS

TPPs

SCA

GDPR

NEW SERVICES
1. ACCOUNT AGGREGATION
2. PAYMENT INITATION

Key

AI	Artificial Intelligence
API	Application programming interfaces
DLT	Distributed ledger technology
EBA	European Banking Authority
GDPR	General Data Protection Regulation
ML	Machine learning
RTS	Regulatory technical standard
SCA	Strong customer authentication
TPP	Third-party providers

Executive Summary

In this part we look at the role compliance and regulation are taking in the PayTech space.

We see the way in which collaboration is the key to collective responsibility in redefining the model of tackling financial crime. How compliance is creating trust in the marketplace. But it needs to be proportional, balancing the need to reduce red tape and regulatory burden with a less frictionful payment experience for the end users of the systems. Consumers want security but not at the expense of utility so, to this end, the winners will always be the PayTech companies with the best operational agility to take into account the compliance requirements without affecting the user experience!

The advent of the application programming interface (API) has revolutionized the way open banking is being achieved. Now under the second Payment Services Directive (PSD2), third-party providers are being given bank APIs to enable them to offer account aggregation services, giving consumers the ability to view all their payment accounts in one app, or payment initiation services, enabling customers to make direct payments from their bank accounts for online merchant purchases. Alongside this there have been a number of attempts to create enhanced interoperability using open standards on these APIs. This has been led by the European Banking Authority (EBA), whose obligations under PSD2 have led them to produce regulatory technical standards (RTSs) for these APIs. In both Australia and Hong Kong, they first used a proportional approach based on bigger financial institutions. Many believe that Europe should have followed suit, rather than going for a one-size-fits-all approach.

In addition to APIs, the EBA has been tasked with producing RTSs for secure customer authentication. This, in conjunction with the latest change in data protection – the General Data Protection Regulation – has created a new era of trust in consumers using banking services.

The latest tech solutions here rely on artificial intelligence, distributed ledger technology and machine learning. Companies in this space are swift and very nimble, and want to win customers using their tech experience. Finally, we see how to use technology to deal with Ponzi schemes.

How Payments Regulation and Compliance Can Create a Better Future

By Robert Courtneidge
CEO, Moorwand Ltd

Commencing my career as a young lawyer in Citibank Consumer Bank and Diners Club in 1990, I have lived the past 28 years as a payments lawyer navigating the ever-changing world of regulation and compliance. In the past year, as CEO of a regulated electronic money issuer with primary membership of Visa, Mastercard and UnionPay for issuing and acquiring and direct access to accounts at the Bank of England, Faster Payments and SWIFT pending, I can honestly say that the world today is so much more complex and challenging, but also more exciting and rewarding. In the past, regulation was led by the regulators who created a set of rules for the banks to follow and if you wanted to become part of the payments ecosystem, you either had to be a bank or work with a bank. This has changed significantly and the whole era of open banking[1] is here.

The first indication of change came in the early 1990s, when Tim Jones and Graham Higgins at National Westminster Bank conceived Mondex.[2] This was the first iteration of money stored on a chip on a card and was the forerunner of electronic money and electronic wallets as we know them today. It was in parallel with this that, in May 1994, the European Monetary Institute, now the European Central Bank, published its first report on "Prepaid Cards".[3] It looked at the advent of electronic wallets as developed

initially in the prepaid phone vertical but soon to gain wider use and acceptance. It started:

Prepaid cards have developed first as a single-purpose payment instrument for which the card issuer and the goods or service provider have been one and the same (e.g. telephone cards). Such cards have not raised central banks' concerns because the value embedded in them did not have a wide range of uses and, therefore, did not have the characteristics of money. Drawing on the experience of single-purpose prepaid cards, and on recent technical developments (in particular the invention of the chip card), a new payment instrument is under development in many countries: the multi-purpose prepaid card, also known as the 'electronic purse'.

Its conclusions, set out below, laid the foundations for the amazing changes in law and regulation to follow and formed the basis of the transformations we today refer to as FinTech, PayTech and RegTech.

POLICY CONCLUSIONS

- Only credit institutions should be allowed to issue electronic purses.

- EU central banks should continue to monitor developments in the field of prepaid cards, possibly in cooperation with other central banks outside the EU.

- In this context, EU central banks should be kept informed, if possible at an early stage, of any major prepaid cards schemes involving more than one good or service provider, and decide whether they should be considered as 'limited-purpose' or as 'multi-purpose'; in the latter case, the provisions of this report will apply.

- Central banks may wish to examine carefully the security features of proposed prepaid cards schemes. In some cases, they may wish to discourage some initiatives in order to protect the integrity of the retail payment system.

---

[1] https://www.openbanking.org.uk.

[2] https://www.chyp.com/it-was-twenty-years-ago-today/.

[3] https://www.ecb.europa.eu/pub/pdf/other/prepaidcards1994en.pdf?9fc7b56c72b0b1a42eb60ad5f97fb7d3.

The first Electronic Money Directive (EMD1)[4] was adopted in September 2000 and with it a new kind of credit institution first saw the light of day, the Electronic Money Institution. It had a high bar to entry with a minimum capital requirement of €1 million but, unlike today, there were no safeguarded accounts required nor many of the other protections that have since developed.

Around that time, the EU started to look at something they then called the new legal framework for payments, which in 2007 became the Payment Services Directive (PSD1).[5] This came about because the European Payments Council (EPC), who were working on SEPA[6] and the creation of an industry-led initiative for payments, needed the power of an EU directive to manage a lot of the key areas that an industry body, however powerful, could not achieve. PSD1 created that framework and then the real work started in understanding how electronic money fitted into this new framework. It clearly needed to be updated from the very short EMD1 and work began on the second Electronic Money Directive (EMD2).[7] This caused some conflict within the Commission as there was growing confusion as to how electronic money differed from a deposit and what a payment account was when it was neither a deposit nor electronic money.

Some members of the Commission would have preferred a merger between electronic money and payment accounts but this never happened, which many believed was a wasted opportunity. EMD2 was adopted in 2009 and this considerably lowered the initial capital needed to set up an electronic money-issuing business (dropping it to €350,000). It also widened the scope of services that an electronic money issuer could undertake to include all payment services. There was a further opportunity to merge electronic money and payment accounts when the second Payment Services Directive (PSD2)[8] was proposed, but unfortunately the merger still did not occur, so we must wait for EMD/PSD3 to see whether this will finally happen. In the EPC's paper on the SEPA political, legal and regulatory framework,[9] in relation to the need for further development of the payment services regime, it states:

> The digitalisation of the European economy has steadily progressed since the implementation of PSD, creating new players who offer new services for online payments (the fintech start-ups). These were outside the scope of the PSD and not regulated at EU level. In order to take into account this new state of play, the Commission proposed a revised Payment Services Directive, widely known today as PSD2. Its objectives are to make payments safer, increase consumer protection and foster innovation while ensuring a level playing field for all, including newcomers.

PSD2 was finally published on 23 December 2015 and was required to be transposed into national laws in the EU on 13 January 2018 (which the UK duly achieved). The implementation of PSD2 relies on the six regulatory technical standards (RTSs)[10] and five sets of guidelines related to PSD2 that the European Banking Authority has been mandated to develop, which were finally delivered on 13 March 2018.[11] All this regulation and the standards have given rise to a growing RegTech industry,[12] supplying the ability for the new PayTechs to comply with this growing plethora of

[4] https://eur-lex.europa.eu/legal-content/en/TXT/?uri=CELEX%3A32000L0046.

[5] https://eur-lex.europa.eu/legal-content/en/ALL/?uri=CELEX%3A32007L0064.

[6] https://ec.europa.eu/info/business-economy-euro/banking-and-finance/consumer-finance-and-payments/payment-services/single-euro-payments-area-sepa_en.

[7] https://eur-lex.europa.eu/legal-content/en/ALL/?uri=CELEX%3A32009L0110.

[8] https://eur-lex.europa.eu/legal-content/EN/TXT/?uri=celex%3A32015L2366.

[9] https://www.europeanpaymentscouncil.eu/about-sepa/sepa-political-legal-and-regulatory-framework.

[10] https://eur-lex.europa.eu/legal-content/EN/TXT/?uri=CELEX%3A32018R0389.

[11] https://www.europeanpaymentscouncil.eu/news-insights/news/european-commissions-final-rts-are-official-journal.

[12] https://en.wikipedia.org/wiki/Regulatory_technology.

compliance. Being able to outsource many of the functions to third parties is a great enabler for the PayTechs, as it means they can keep staffing numbers low and focus on delivery of their services. This also enables them to stay nimble and keep moving to the latest and best-of-breed service providers. A modular approach is enabling greater flexibility, which, when coupled with the use of cloud-based servers, can offer massive scalability.

No discussion on PayTech and its regulation could be complete without talking about the elephant in the room, distributed ledger technology (including blockchain – people often confuse these as the same thing, but the latter is a subset of the former)[13] and cryptocurrencies. Bitcoin was the first and most widely recognized cryptocurrency and was well described in the article by Bernard Marr entitled "A Short History of Bitcoin and Crypto Currency Everyone Should Read".[14] The subsequent rise in price of Bitcoin is well documented, but it was not part of the plan of the Cypherpunks,[15] who are believed to have been the original architects of it. It was seen as a utopic vision of taking power away from governments and banks and moving the power of holding and moving value to the individuals. Bitcoin is a utility token and has no actual value, except that which individuals are willing to trade it for. The only thing they didn't foresee in their plans was the greed that these tokens could create as they started to gain higher values. This resulted in the race for "blocks" and a whole industry created around building the tools to mine blocks. This went crazy, with faster and faster processors being built, requiring more and more power to crack the solution to the next block.

This resulted in the mad situation of businesses looking at places with the lowest cost of electricity to power their block-mining processors. With the current stabilization of Bitcoin, this race for processing power and electricity is finally slowing down. In addition, there has been a growth of new tokens/coins coming to market, with the majority being built on the Ethereum network using ERC20 tokens.[16] As at March 2019, there were 2,525 cryptocurrencies listed[17] with a market cap of US\$134,605,974,815 and still growing, but they are hardly traded below number 30. The regulation of these currencies around the world is an ever-changing picture, with some countries banning them and others embracing them and creating laws and regulations to encourage such businesses to establish in their territories. Some of the most forward-thinking countries are the smallest; Malta, Gibraltar and Switzerland all saw the advent of the new tradeable tokens as a potential source of new income to their countries, enabling a new economy to grow. However, until there is more widespread acceptance of these regulations and proper interoperability is established with international standards, they will never grow to their full potential. At the moment it is best to monitor the laws of the jurisdictions in which you are doing business and work out how best to work with these new payment methods.

Cryptocurrencies are nothing to be scared of but should be embraced and dealt with sensibly – by creating a policy for how you deal with cryptocurrencies and then sharing it. Banks should embrace them, and the new laws coming out through the 5th Anti-Money Laundering Directive should enable more comfort,

[13] For further explanation, see M. Zachariadis, S.V. Scott and G. Hileman (2019), "Governance and control in distributed ledgers: Understanding the challenges facing blockchain technology in financial services", *Information & Organization* (forthcoming) and the Tradeix paper on "The Difference Between Blockchain & Distributed Ledger Technology", https://tradeix.com/distributed-ledger-technology/.

[14] https://www.forbes.com/sites/bernardmarr/2017/12/06/a-short-history-of-bitcoin-and-crypto-currency-everyone-should-read/#765a06063f27.

[15] https://medium.com/swlh/the-untold-history-of-bitcoin-enter-the-cypherpunks-f764dee962a1.

[16] https://www.investinblockchain.com/what-are-ethereum-tokens/.

[17] https://www.investing.com/crypto/currencies.

with proper AML processes around everyone who touches cryptocurrencies.

Alongside cryptocurrencies and these changes to the law and the regulation of payments that moves them out of the exclusivity of the banks into this PayTech revolution, we have seen many changes to the related laws on AML, data protection and cyber security. This has helped Europe and specifically London – within Europe the place for PayTech – to grow and thrive. The speed of technology growth is only matched by the innovation and boundless thinking of the people in this industry.

As a lawyer, I met these new entrepreneurs on a regular basis to help them deliver their dreams in a legal and regulated way. Now, as CEO of a payments business, I am not only giving them the route to a minimum viable product that is compliant but am able to put many of the pieces in place to deliver the solution they have come up with. What excites me is that many of the more established companies, including the major banks and the payment schemes, are embracing this change. Together, with effective payments regulation and compliance, we can create a new payments landscape that makes the world a better place.

Refining the Collective Responsibility for Compliance

By Nicolette Brown
Marketing Manager, Napier

and Julian Dixon
CEO, Napier

The Rise of the FinTech Revolution

Technology, and in particular smartphones, have revolutionized our day-to-day lives in ways that were unimaginable as little as 10 years ago. The speed with which the digital and mobile wallet industry is changing is exponential. By 2022, it's estimated that the transaction value of mobile payment apps will reach nearly US$14 trillion – up from just over US$4 trillion in 2018.[1]

Over 42% of digitally active adults now use the services of at least one FinTech firm, and more than 20 million people in the UK make use of banking apps as a more convenient way of managing their finances.[2]

Publishing the Fintech Strategy Report in 2018, the UK government stands firmly behind the FinTech revolution and is keen to incentivize innovation. The report highlights that the government and regulators have an important role to play in removing barriers to entry and growth and, as a result, it has created a host of initiatives, which include:[3]

- The Financial Conduct Authority's (FCA's) Regulatory Sandbox and Innovation Hub testing environment for new FinTechs.

- The FinTech Accelerator facilitated by the Bank of England.

- Legislation so that non-bank payment service providers will be able to directly access payment systems, creating a level playing field with incumbent financial services firms.

- Creating a new Payments Systems Regulator to ensure that challenger banks and FinTechs can gain access to the payments systems on fair terms, and that the payments systems embrace innovation in the interests of consumers and businesses.

In addition, in 2016 the Competition and Markets Authority ordered the nine largest banks in the UK to deliver "open banking".[4] This allows consumers and small and medium enterprises to access a range of new and innovative products that better meet their needs, by providing third-party providers with secure access to their current accounts. This could include, for example, products that enable consumers to access cheaper overdraft facilities without switching current account provider.

Compliance Challenges

The flipside of FinTech is that there are potentially new ways for criminals to exploit the financial system. Money laundering and fraud are two of the world's oldest crimes. Despite the existence of 25 regulatory bodies to tackle money laundering and the financing of terrorism, financial crime continues to be a big problem which is evolving and exploiting new technology for bigger gains.[5] Just 0.2% of the US$2–4 trillion of illicit funds in circulation is ever recovered.[6]

[1] https://merchantmachine.co.uk/digital-wallet/.

[2] https://assets.publishing.service.gov.uk/government/uploads/system/uploads/attachment_data/file/692874/Fintech_Sector_Strategy_print.pdf.

[3] https://assets.publishing.service.gov.uk/government/uploads/system/uploads/attachment_data/file/692874/Fintech_Sector_Strategy_print.pdf.

[4] https://www.gov.uk/government/news/cma-paves-the-way-for-open-banking-revolution.

[5] https://assets.publishing.service.gov.uk/government/uploads/system/uploads/attachment_data/file/655198/National_risk_assessment_of_money_laundering_and_terrorist_financing_2017_pdf_web.pdf.

[6] https://www.ey.com/en_gl/banking-capital-markets/how-to-maintain-trust-in-global-banking-digital-ecosystem.

Even the biggest banks find fighting the relentless, highly sophisticated nature of financial crime a significant challenge. Five of the UK's top banks have been found responsible for money laundering offences or violating sanctions in the past decade. Each bank has had to bear substantial fines,[7] as well as difficult-to-quantify damage to hard-earned reputations and customer trust.

While you might expect banks to be better placed than any to understand the financial services regulatory landscape, FinTechs are very often new to the industry and find it a challenge to both engage regulatory requirements and bear the considerable costs of compliance.[8] The concern at the moment is that while banks are more experienced at putting transaction monitoring and client screening processes into place, they are still falling short with regulatory compliance.

The reasons banks fall foul of regulators are many, from the consequences of relying on inadequate legacy systems and governance processes, to not having sufficiently trained anti-money laundering (AML) specialists on the job. Many British banks still run on legacy systems that were never designed to monitor transactions in the way they need to today.[9] This means it can take banks days to process what FinTech systems can do in hours. The larger volumes of transactions associated with digital banking, contactless cards and changing consumer purchasing and payment behaviours require modern systems capable of processing billions of transactions using new and varied payment methods and cutting-edge technology. While banks recognize that legacy systems are not keeping pace with the way the world is changing, and are trying to enhance systems to cater for new requirements, there is no quick fix.

The Various Ways of Preventing Money Laundering

As banks vie to keep up with regulatory compliance, the violation of AML regulations could also be a result of the lack of structured regulatory advice and stipulation. One look at the FCA's *Financial Crime Guide: A Firm's Guide to Countering Financial Crime Risks* and it is clear that the job of interpreting the guidelines and establishing suitable systems and processes to meet regulatory requirements is left entirely to the bank.[10] As a result, every bank has its own way of handling AML and managing the related data and risk.

Perhaps the biggest problem in the industry is that each bank is completely different. Every bank varies from the client, product and service portfolios to the markets and countries' risk appetite and capital base. With different asset classes, funding structures, weightings and operational styles, there is no single AML system that would be the same for any two banks.

Inexperience Exacerbates the Problem

The compliance challenge is heightened when you consider the relative inexperience in financial compliance that FinTechs, especially the startups, may bring to the industry. There are also the FCA's special measures for FinTechs to take into account.[11] In return for providing crucial infrastructure in support of new FinTech business models, banks can insist on reasonable standards being established by FinTechs, and bring value and experience in financial crime compliance. Currently, banks are assuming that regulators will be satisfied with their approach to compliance and

---

[7] https://www.theweek.co.uk/97000/europe-s-biggest-banks-fined-for-money-laundering.

[8] https://assets.publishing.service.gov.uk/government/uploads/system/uploads/attachment_data/file/692874/Fintech_Sector_Strategy_print.pdf.

[9] https://www.fnlondon.com/articles/banks-face-spiraling-costs-from-archaic-it-20170912.

---

[10] https://www.handbook.fca.org.uk/handbook/FCG.pdf.

[11] https://assets.publishing.service.gov.uk/government/uploads/system/uploads/attachment_data/file/692874/Fintech_Sector_Strategy_print.pdf.

diligence in the event of controls at FinTechs and new payment providers being insufficient to prevent money laundering or terrorism finance.[12]

Above all, there is a very fragmented industry approach to battling financial crime. This produces a distinct grey area of responsibility for regulatory requirements and compliance between banks, new payment providers and FinTechs.

How to Handle AML and the Digital Revolution

Financial institutions often find themselves managing their financial crime programmes in silos for many reasons. In fighting financial crime though, the case for sharing data is gaining more traction.[13] If we consider that, beyond compliance, the ultimate aim of AML is to shut down criminal activity, it makes sense that any intelligence is shared with other banks, regulators and the authorities.

One way to do this is through introducing technology to enable data sharing in a secure and GDPR-compliant way. Such sharing not only makes financial institutions' AML programmes more effective and efficient, but also assists in focusing their resources on important matters. In such a collaborative framework, there is also potential to see the perception of compliance evolving from a checklist of costly regulatory requirements to a competitive value proposition for FinTechs and new payment providers. If, for instance, AML and sanction screening compliance processes are built into products and services, some of the work will be lifted from banks.

Setting the Standard

Going forward, there needs to be a well-defined and globally accepted set of standards defining how banks, FinTechs and new payment providers ought to share the collective responsibility for tackling financial crime and achieving regulatory compliance within a clear collaborative framework.

[12] https://www.sc.com/en/feature/the-digital-revolution-managing-the-emerging-aml-and-regulatory-risks-of-new-payment-methods/.

[13] https://www.complianceweek.com/news/news-article/data-sharing-ai-may-be-antidote-to-failing-aml-efforts.

Can Operational Agility Grow Payments in the New Online Platform Marketplaces?

By Anna Tsyupko
CEO, Paybase

The importance of stringent regulation and compliance is arguably more crucial in payments than in any other industry. Of course, that is how it should be. Compliance equates to an agreed set of standards being followed to ensure as much protection as possible for both customers and businesses. Without that level of protection, people would be unable to put their faith in non-cash payments. Quite simply, financial services rely on trust, and that trust is achieved through a strong set of rules which prevent payments from being manipulated, misdirected or mismanaged.

There is, however, a downside to such tight regulation surrounding payments. Regulation can, at times, act as an inhibitor to innovation – stifling creativity and creating obstacles for businesses attempting to get to market. For many modern businesses, it is not necessarily the risk associated with their offerings which is the problem, but having unique needs that are not being served by current payment solutions and regulatory frameworks. This means that, in many cases, the more innovative their offering, the more difficult it is for them to build their business.

Online marketplaces, gig/sharing economy platforms, cryptocurrency exchanges and FinTechs are examples of relatively new businesses with particular payment challenges. These businesses often require a different approach to due diligence, risk management, product setup and more. There is a growing need, therefore, for operational agility which is flexible enough to meet more refined demands, whilst at the same time not sacrificing the necessary security that comes with strong compliance. We look at three examples in these areas.

Issue 1 – Goods Rental on a Platform

All rental services have one inherent concern. When the rental price of a good is so much lower than its sale price, and it is so easily available, how do you prevent it from being stolen or damaged? The answer to this question has always been relatively straightforward – insure the assets and charge a sizeable deposit to the buyer. This is still the case for the majority of rental services, and works well if your buyers are able to cover a large fee. But if your buyers are not able to do so – tough luck. This is what the sharing economy attempts to address. It connects those that have with those that need/want. As such, platforms that allow their users to rent cars, camera equipment and accommodation have begun to appear. However, many of these platforms have faced the same challenge.

Let's examine the camera equipment renting example. The owner of the equipment cannot benefit from the safety net of a high deposit fee, as this will not work on a sharing economy platform. As for assets being insured, this is far more difficult on a platform, as the platform is not the owner of the assets. The only way of having these assets insured is to perform due diligence on both sellers (those owning the equipment) and buyers (or "renters"). The issue here is that the vast majority of payment service providers do not perform due diligence on buyers, as it is not a regulatory requirement. This has seen many rental platforms either struggle to get off the ground, or rely on an unrealistic level of trust between its buyers and sellers.

Here is a clear example of how operational agility can encourage innovation. Instead of having such a narrow view on how due diligence is performed, a payment service provider could assign "roles" to each party in the transaction process. A varying level of due diligence can then be performed on any of these roles, depending on what is relevant to the business – in this case, an equivalent level of due diligence on both sellers and buyers.

This flexible approach to due diligence would enable many more innovative platforms to reach market, with the advantages of the sharing economy benefiting all.

Issue 2 – Rationalizing Due Diligence for Cryptocurrency Exchanges

Most would argue that there is still much to be established regarding cryptocurrency – the industry is still in its infancy. What *is* becoming more accepted is that cryptocurrency is not a fad. Investment continues to pour in, with varying crypto businesses appearing on a regular basis. One of the most common business types is the cryptocurrency exchange platform. Millions of pounds are being transferred every day as investors assess the fluctuating values of different cryptocurrencies. The challenge many of these businesses face is that their customer base is, in a way, too varied. There are those who wish to trade with £100, seeing where it might lead them, and those looking to move upwards of £1m. How can due diligence be performed on users operating with such varying sums of money without negatively impacting the user experience (UX)?

Due to the operational rigidity of most payment providers, these businesses are presented with two choices. They either perform a level of due diligence strong enough to accommodate users that want to transfer such high volumes, meaning that those simply wishing to trade with £100 may still have to provide several proofs of address and an image of their passport, or they restrict users from trading with more than a certain amount of money. Both are undesirable for the platform. A far wiser approach would be to create a tiered system of due diligence. This would instantly request higher levels of information from a user as the values they operate with increase, with the user being moved to the next "tier" when the information has been submitted and accepted. Innovative payment providers can create a tiered system that reflects the normal transaction flows – it can even be modified over time. This alleviates the need to sacrifice good UX to provide strong due diligence, just for the sake of a handful of users.

Issue 3 – "Trust Us" Guarantees in a Marketplace

In recent years we have seen a sharp increase in the number of platform businesses. Whilst giants such as eBay and Amazon are far from newcomers, many smaller, more product/service-specific platforms have begun to appear. All new platform businesses face one core challenge – trust. For marketplaces, how can a buyer trust that they will be able to easily get their money back if they purchase an item that never arrives or if the item arrives in an unsatisfactory condition? For gig/sharing economy platforms, trust can be an issue for both sides, depending on when funds are transferred. On a platform that connects freelance designers to businesses, for example, designers risk doing work that is not paid for and businesses risk paying for designs which are not completed.

Whilst buyer protection does exist, it can only go so far in terms of trust. Users do not know how long it will take to get their money back or what that process will entail. What many of these businesses require is an escrow service, allowing funds to be held between parties until an event is agreed upon, then automatically released. High levels of operational agility can not only provide this, but also tailor escrow solutions to each business. A marketplace may prefer to route payments between buyers and sellers instantly, with only transactions of a certain value being held in escrow. A platform business of tradesmen may choose to offer the buyer a certain percentage of the fee back if the task is not completed in an agreed time.

These features are not yet commonplace, but in the near future buyers and sellers will come to expect them. Taking an operationally agile approach, these expectations can be met and exceeded.

Conclusion

Despite the legacy technology and legacy thinking within the industry, payments have proved that the industry has the ability to change. It has begun supporting and streamlining more intricate payment flows and helped innovative businesses reach market.

However, there is still a considerable way to go. Regulated businesses continue to be punished, not due to their business carrying unnecessary levels of risk, but because their requirements do not fit the norms in relation to regulation and compliance. The more operationally agile payment providers can become, the more innovative and dynamic businesses we will see in the market.

The Hidden Value of Greater Standardization for the EU-Wide FinTech Market

By Mihaela Breg
Advisor – Risk and Regulatory Compliance, SmartBill FinTech Startup (Smarter Financial Ltd)

The major EU regulation, Europe's second Payment Services Directive (PSD2) that came into force in January 2018, is an interesting test case for promoting an open and collaborative payments ecosystem. According to the PSD2 framework, banks are required to open appropriate communication channels for third-party providers (TPPs) and share customer data upon approval from the customer.

The main benefits of the PSD2 open environment were expected to come via the application programming interface (API)-based solutions of TPPs. The API-enabled environment has indeed opened doors to stakeholders to play roles such as account information service providers (AISPs) and payment initiation service providers (PISPs), eventually improving the collaboration between incumbents and new players at local level. However, there is still an important challenge to be addressed. There are clear concerns regarding the lack of harmonization due to the absence of common global API standards and a centralized API infrastructure. This may lead to joint API infrastructures developed in silos by local banking communities.

The Journey from API to Open API and Open Banking

To make sense of this, it's essential to understand that the newly introduced PSD2 framework is not in any way a set of technical standards, and the regulatory paper is much less prescriptive when it comes to defining what the APIs should look like. The

European Banking Authority (EBA) has specified regulatory technical standards (RTSs) for PSD2 separately, but these primarily cover strong customer authentication (SCA) and secure communication. These major principles drafted by the EBA will become effective in September 2019. In other words, the EBA is not seen as the 'Implementation Entity' for PSD2 as the EBA has not been given the task to oversee the creation of an industry-wide standard API for the EU-wide financial market.

The Characteristics of APIs

APIs are mainly built on globally accepted technical standards (a set of rules, instructions and specifications), which allow two computer programmes to communicate with each other (send and receive data) and create connections. In a never-ending world of information, it is almost impossible for humans to understand the kind of connections that a computer can easily see. There are many successful cases outside the financial industry, from well known market participants, that clearly evidence how society benefits from open API strategies. A good example is the social media platform Twitter, which created a mutually beneficial relationship between third-party developers through open API usage in order to enable more functionality and facilitate convenience for consumers.

It goes without saying that technical interfacing alone is not sufficient when we start talking about collaboration across organizations that operate in the financial market. Our relationship with our money is definitely more sensitive than our daily consumption of media. Where funds and sensitive data are involved, building trust is essential. We all want error-free and frictionless payments, safely stored savings and abundant credit so that people can afford to buy and companies can fund new and original projects. In such a critical and strategic sector for the real economy, how do we safeguard something as fragile as trust?

This is where banking regulation comes into play. Thanks to EU-driven regulation for open APIs around payments (PSD2), previously unchanged banking businesses started to think out-of-the-box. We now experience a financial environment where the power balance appears to have shifted in favour of the consumer over the banking institution.

The UK has gold-plated the EU regulations into open banking, aiming to adopt common standards around data sharing across the banking industry. However, at the time of writing, only a handful of banks in the UK are using the same API and the proposed standards leave a lot of room for improvement. If open banking is to reach its full potential, now is the right time for greater standardization and a truly "open" banking environment.

Banking Industry Should Put a Premium on Openness

To address these problems, the top EU banks should jointly fund the creation of a common global API standard and a centralized API infrastructure. By adopting joint standards across the wider banking industry (outside the local market), existing frictions associated with data sharing can finally be reduced. Furthermore, the development of standardized APIs could create a level playing field to enable innovative products and services in a truly open environment, while still maintaining high standards of personal data and consumer protection.

In Europe, the Commission aims to respond to the requests addressed by both the European Parliament and the European Council for a more future-oriented regulatory framework in order to foster competition and innovation in the market. A new PSD3 regulatory paper is perhaps a somewhat optimistic expectation. However, Open Banking Europe (a wholly owned subsidiary of EBA Clearing) could probably be tasked with the creation of an industry-wide API and a harmonized environment where innovative FinTech solutions can be rolled out rapidly across the EU (benefiting from the single market economies of scale).

Conclusion

Open banking will not reach its full potential without the development of open standards that increase competition, enhance interoperability between systems, encourage an open and collaborative payments ecosystem and simplify the exchange of, and access to, data between market players. Furthermore, if such standards are created and adopted, a solid foundation will be created for building great FinTech applications that benefit all parties involved.

Is Europe a Good Example of Open Banking?

By Rachel Gauci
Head of Legal & Compliance, Truevo Payments Ltd

At the time of writing, most account servicing payment service providers (ASPSPs) in Europe are scrambling to ensure that their application programming interfaces (APIs) are ready for testing by the deadline, in accordance with the EBA's Regulatory Technical Standards (RTSs) on Strong Customer Authentication and Common & Secure Communication. Despite the fact that the second Payment Services Directive (PSD2) sought to harmonize the payment services industry, fragmentation is still widespread. Some Member States have also decided to take on this daunting ASPSP task at a national level, with the national central bank taking a leading role, which exacerbates this fragmentation. Various API standards have emerged which have also contributed to the fragmentation, despite the fact that the two particular sets of standards have been pushed to the forefront. The API Evaluation Group sought to curb this fragmentation and published an API functionalities document on 10 December 2018 to serve as guidance.

Certain regions around the world have used Europe's PSD2 as their inspiration to move the banking world into the modern digital age with the concept of open banking, or as PSD2 refers to it "access to accounts" also known as "XS2A". Whilst such regions may have sought inspiration from Europe, perhaps Europe could see how other countries or regions in the world are handling the *implementation* of open banking and learn from them?

Asia-Pacific Region

As at time of writing (early 2019) Asia-Pacific countries such as Indonesia and Malaysia acknowledged the importance and potential of open banking, and have had government-backed discussions on the use of APIs for the provision of financial services. Other countries in the Asia-Pacific region, such as India and China, have also been proactive, with initiatives taking place outside the regulatory space. Australia and Hong Kong are at a rather advanced stage with their implementation plans on the use of open banking. Australia is certainly a good example of how open banking is being handled from a regulatory perspective, especially with customer data protection at the forefront of the project. Hong Kong comes a close second with its carefully planned phases of implementation.

Australia

In Australia, "open banking" is a regulatory initiative that is focused on the protection of consumer data and forms part of the Consumer Data Right. Banking is the first sector in which this Right will be applied. Initially, "open banking" in Australia will be limited to accessing account information and payment initiation will not be implemented at the outset. However, unlike PSD2, the selection of types of accounts that can be accessed is wider than in the EU, and will also include mortgage accounts. Nevertheless, Australian customers will not have the right to request deletion of their personal information under the Privacy Act, while in the EU it must be allowed in order to comply with the General Data Protection Regulation (GDPR).

The introduction of open banking in Australia is divided into different phases, whereby different types of accounts and related information must be made available during each phase, starting on 1 July 2019 with four major Australian banks and the remaining Australian deposit-taking institutions to comply by 1 July 2021, unless the Australian Competition and Consumer Commission (ACCC) determines otherwise. This is in contrast with the EU, where PSD2 is applicable to all banks in the EU that offer payment accounts, regardless of their size.

Under Australian regulations, third parties that participate in open banking will also be obliged to share their customer data, which is different from the PSD2 rules which state that only ASPSPs are obliged to share such data. Moreover, only accredited data recipients may receive open banking data, with the ACCC determining the criteria for, and method of, accreditation. This is similar to PSD2 rules whereby third-party providers (TPPs) must be registered with a national competent authority.

Hong Kong

On 18 July 2018 the Hong Kong Monetary Authority (HKMA) published the *Open Application Programming Interface (API) Framework* for the Hong Kong banking sector, which provides that open banking will be implemented in four phases starting with the provision of account information. Payment initiation will be offered on an API at a later stage. Initially it will be compulsory for the large banks to participate in the implementation, while other banks will be able to join in the future. The HKMA launched an open API on its official website on 23 July 2018.

The Open API Framework lays out detailed expectations on how banks should onboard and maintain relationships with third-party service providers (TSPs) in a manner that ensures consumer protection. With the release of the Framework, the HKMA expects the large banks to deploy the various phases within determined timelines, starting from late 2018, to ensure smooth implementation.

In Hong Kong, banks will retain control of the customer relationship and data, and can *choose* which TSPs to collaborate with. This is in contrast to PSD2 and open banking in Australia, which generally obliges banks to share customer data (upon the customer's request) with accredited parties. As at early 2019, there are no rules yet in Hong Kong as to TSP regulation and registration.

Conclusion: What Can Europe Learn?

While PSD2 sought to provide ASPSPs with time to prepare their systems for the acceptance of TPPs, in practice the deadline provided has been rather overwhelming for ASPSPs, especially those with fewer resources. The Commission could have provided different phases for different types of ASPSPs, depending on their size. In Hong Kong the implementation of open banking was made compulsory for the large banks, with other banks being allowed to join in the future. Similarly, in Australia, the implementation of open banking will initially take place with the four major banks.

Furthermore, using Australia as an example, the implementation of open banking in Europe could have started first for account information services, with the intention to evaluate its success or otherwise in order to prepare for the use of APIs for payment initiation services at a later stage. Hong Kong also planned the open banking implementation phases with account information first and payment initiation to be offered on an API at a later stage of the implementation.

Europe Can Learn From Others

By 14 March 2019, ASPSPs in Europe must have their APIs ready for testing by TPPs and the aforementioned RTS will become fully applicable from 14 September 2019. Therefore, it seems that full implementation of open banking for account information services and payment initiation services in Europe should be ready by the end of 2019. It remains to be seen whether such ambitious deadlines are met by various ASPSPs, as well as the national competent authorities and TPPs that will be evaluating and testing the APIs presented by the ASPSPs. Commencing the implementation of XS2A principles with account information services only would have helped to ease the burden of ASPSPs and could possibly have helped to avoid staggered implementation in various Member States.

Taking Back the Power: Regulations in the EU are Changing the Face of Banking

By Frans Labuschagne
Country Manager UK & Ireland, Entersekt

Businesses, whether legitimate or illegitimate, have long been gathering detailed information about consumers so that they can use it for advertising or fraud, while consumers had no choice but to sit back and watch it happen with a sense of helplessness. Until recently, this was acknowledged as the status quo, but things are changing as we enter a new era. With the advent of new regulations in the European Union (EU), consumers can take back their power. Regulations such as the General Data Protection Regulation (GDPR) and the second Payment Services Directive (PSD2) mean that consumers have more choice over when and how companies collect their data, as well as how they pay for goods and services online.

What Do the Regulations Mean for Consumers?

In summary, GDPR gives European consumers more control over their personal data and the information organizations can collect on them, while also setting out regulations to better protect this information. Specifically, GDPR stipulates that "opt out" measures are not good enough if an organization wants to gather and share information about its consumers. Instead, consumers must now "opt in" if they agree to share their information or receive communications, and they can also expressly state whether they consent to their data being shared with third parties.

PSD2 is not a new concept; the regulatory technical standard (RTS) addressing strong customer authentication (SCA)

mandates that banks have a test-bed environment available by 14 March 2019 and for the go-live to be fully compliant by 14 September 2019. It was adopted by European parliaments in 2015 with the aim of contributing to a more integrated and efficient payments market, levelling the playing field for payment service providers, driving competition (which lowers the cost of payments) and protecting consumers by making payments more secure.

How Does This Change Banking?

This directive for SCA will fundamentally change how consumers access their financial data as well as how, and with whom, they transact. Additionally, to promote competition in financial services and improve ease of use for consumers, PSD2 means that banks are no longer the only institutions in control of consumer financial data and initiation of payments.

PSD2 is paving the way for open banking – using application programming interfaces (APIs) and open source technology to allow third parties, such as data aggregators, to access the data traditionally held by banks, and build applications and services around this data. This means, for example, that a consumer's accounts at multiple providers (e.g. insurance companies, payment services, credit card issuers and mortgage providers) can be seen all at once. All account information, financial products and transactions can be seen on a single dashboard, analysed into an overview of the consumer and, with the consumer's permission, shared with third parties so they can tailor services around the consumer's specific profile.

This opening of banking offers consumers more freedom, not only when it comes to accessing and sharing financial data, but also when transacting. Consumers can now use Facebook or Google to pay their bills, make peer-to-peer transfers and analyse their spending while still having their money safely in their bank accounts.

What About Security?

Greater freedom typically equates to less security, more exposure and additional risk. In fact, that's why the European Banking Authority (EBA) mandated increased security, partly in the form of SCA. This entails using a combination of security measures, which is proving to be the only way to stand up to the increasing complexity of fraud today.

One way of providing an authentication measure that is simultaneously secure and less disruptive to the consumer is by using the power and ubiquity of the mobile phone. Rather than requiring consumers to rely on one-time passwords or cumbersome security tokens, mobile devices – if identified definitively by a digital certificate – can be used as one factor of authentication. For example, imagine a scenario in which a consumer initiates a purchase online and, to verify that purchase, an authentication window pops up on their mobile phone. All the consumer has to do is tap "accept" or "reject" on the device. It's a quick and seamless interaction that leaves the consumer feeling empowered and reassured, because research has shown that consumers do want to take control of the security of their personal information.

To augment security, PSD2 requires a second factor of authentication, which could be, for example, a PIN, the user's GPS location or a biometric input. For added security, banks and other financial service providers should implement authentication solutions that provide a separate, bidirectional channel between their services and their users' mobile devices. Encrypted, push-based authentication requests and responses can then be exchanged without fear of interception and modification. This secure channel provides a second factor of authentication without the user even having to switch apps. As well as authenticating digital logins and financial transactions, this will enable the authentication of card-not-present payments using the same interface, thus providing a consistent customer experience across multiple digital channels.

Changing Consumer Expectations

These regulations and open banking mean a huge increase in competition in the financial world, and banks are going to have to put up a fight to keep their customers loyal. New products and new ways of managing money will not be enough; banks will have to put their consumers first, because consumers can take their business elsewhere; and it is becoming increasingly easy for them to do so. Banks now need to provide, and exceed, the level of digital experience that consumers expect as standard, from being able to access all their accounts in a single app, to the information and alerts they need when they need them, to providing a level of service that cannot be found elsewhere.

This change in customer expectation, and the increased digitalization of everything, may be why we are seeing more and more banks experimenting with their APIs, collaborating with FinTechs and setting up innovation labs.

The Opportunity for Banks

As the adoption of SCA takes hold and new forms of authentication are delivered, historic banking processes need to be updated. Part of the reason for the change, from direct access solutions to SCA services, was to improve customer security. However, even with these standards, financial institutions still also focus on their individual security needs. This approach results in banks taking different approaches to the challenge of digital identification.

However, the delivery of a world-class SCA framework that allows collaboration through a common identity solution is gaining traction. Taking an approach that puts the customer and their security at the centre, with cross-institutional acceptance of the resulting digital tokenization in SCA delivery, would mean that citizens can secure their future, whilst at the same time taking advantage of the benefits of open banking, PSD2 and SCA.

If implemented with security and user experience in mind, the changes introduced in accordance with the new regulations – especially with cross-institutional acceptance of the resulting digital tokenization in SCA delivery – could present an opportunity for banks to instil customer trust, leading to an increase in the number and value of transactions, while at the same time effectively eliminating fraud. Banks that embrace these new regulations with a smart, innovative and customer-centric approach will reap all the rewards and secure their place in a changing financial landscape, from better customer satisfaction to lower fraud levels: security and privacy can be a win on all fronts – exactly the benefits that open banking, PSD2 and SCA were intended to provide.

Achieving Control Effectiveness and Sustainable Compliance Using Nine Factors

By Ciske van Oosten
Global Manager – Intelligence, Verizon

The lack of sustainable control environments is a top contributor to ineffective controls and data breaches. Sustainable security and compliance are achieved by demonstrating a consistent capability to maintain ongoing operation of all required security controls. This capability prevents or minimizes future deviation from required performance standards. Organizations achieve sustainability by design (i.e., by building sustainability into the functional, operational specifications of the compliance program and reinforcing it through frequent education, training and awareness). The 9 Factors of Control Effectiveness and Sustainability, described below, structure compliance programs effectively for data protection and establish key success factors in corporate security management.

Factor 1: Control Environment

Effective control environments require knowledgeable people who understand responsibilities and limitations and are competent and committed to organizational policies, standards and procedures – doing what's right in the right way. Management must create a security-conscious culture. Organizational culture determines the degree of the control environment's health – defined and enforced through values, priorities, management styles, standards, processes and organizational framework. A control environment with a defined internal control framework contributes substantially toward effective risk mitigation.

Any IT environment is susceptible to control deficiencies, leading to chain reactions that result in failures and vulnerabilities. While most security control failures are detectable and avoidable, poor management of control environments can leave your organization prone. Defining and documenting control environments are important steps toward sustainable compliance.

Factor 2: Control Design

Implementing "out of the box" security controls usually isn't sustainable unless combined with tailor-made documentation and specifications for operating in specific environments. Environmental circumstances and conditions influence security controls, which impact control performance. Multi-layered control systems create dependencies where one layer compensates for weakness in another. Systematic control design is imperative for predictable control performance, effectiveness and sustainability.

Neglecting to design and test security controls before deployment is a common mistake. Some organizations assume an environment is secure if design or operational issues don't surface. Deliberate control design helps to uncover control effectiveness limitations to predictably evaluate and compare results against documented control specifications and promotes consistent, reliable operations. Without this awareness, control systems can operate with hidden flaws that surface only when a control fails – with noticeable consequences.

Therefore, every key security control needs its own documented control design specification. This involves systematically specifying the purpose, function, scope, limitations and control dependencies, including control descriptions in their effective state and scenarios that could impact control effectiveness.

Factor 3: Control Risk

Controls can degrade without ongoing maintenance and lose effectiveness over time. This control risk is usually due to ineffective design and management of control environments.

Design deficiencies (Factor 2) and operational failures contribute directly toward unsustainable control environments. Organizations must be proficient at proactively detecting, responding to and correcting internal control failures. That requires fully integrated control risk management covering key areas of weakness: human error, IT failures, process failures and external events.

A defined control risk mitigation plan must be part of the organization's broader operational risk management strategy to avoid handicapping organizational abilities to protect sensitive data.

Factor 4: Control Robustness

Control environments operate in dynamic business and ever-changing threat environments and require multiple lines of defense. "Robust" environments continue to operate according to specifications and maintain steady performance despite disruptions, unwanted changes or attacks. Absorbing significant amounts of "damage" before failure results in continuous control operation and greater control environment stability.

Maintaining robust controls goes beyond keeping IT processes and components current. Such controls benefit from sound control environments (Factor 1), strong design, operation and maintenance of security controls (Factor 2) and consistent management of control risk (Factor 3).

Factor 5: Control Resilience

Control failures occur even in highly robust control environments – making proactive discovery and quick recovery essential. Control resilience combines areas of data protection, business continuity and organizational recovery to maintain states of informed preparedness to anticipate, withstand, recover and evolve from each control failure. Levels of control resilience are directly proportional to organizational ability to design and operate security controls capable of rapid recovery from disruptive events. This capability is paramount for maintaining effective and sustainable control environments.

Factor 6: Control Lifecycle Management

Monitoring and active management of security controls throughout each lifecycle stage is necessary from inception to retirement. Security control lifecycle management identifies and improves control design and support requirements. These lifecycle stages influence underlying support processes, operational efficiency and control effectiveness:

- Conception

- Design and build

- Testing

- Introduction and deployment

- Operation and monitoring

- Growth and evolution

- Maintenance and improvement

- Maturity

- Decline and retirement.

Actively maintaining Security Control Lifecycle Management (SCLM) for all controls offers immediate and long-term benefits for effective and sustainable data protection and compliance efforts. Integrating SCLM into compliance programs provides valuable measurements to record control effectiveness and management guidance as controls age and environments evolve.

Factor 7: Performance Management

Sustaining control environments is key to effective data protection. Controls must operate over extended periods without significant deviation from design and operational specifications. Internally developed performance standards measure control performance and allow for early identification and correction of performance deviations.

Data protection and compliance program performance management are essential management control processes to improve the performance and capabilities of system components (people, processes, technology) within control environments. These actions improve data protection performance and achieve goals within established timetables:

• Clarifying goals and objectives

• Setting standards

• Managing deviations

• Measuring and comparing outcomes.

Data protection, security and compliance objectives are too often overlooked in performance management processes – or siloed. Responsibilities for security or compliance goals should be integrated companywide as standard protocols. Performance management must be aligned with strategic goals, and corrective action for deviations from standards must occur with each of the 9 Factors.

In short, what gets measured gets done.

Factor 8: Maturity Measurement

With the mounting number of high-profile data breaches, demonstrating greater control effectiveness and data protection is increasingly important. Many organizations still have a wash–rinse–repeat approach that is focused on annual compliance validation for data protection instead of long-term development and maturity based on measurements and metrics.

Maturity models are benchmarks with structured levels that describe how well organizational behaviours, practices and processes can produce desired outcomes. They provide necessary directives for higher proficiency. Ongoing control environment improvement depends on defined maturity target levels to track degrees of formality and optimization of processes and capabilities.

Measuring control environment performance (Factor 7) and applying metrics creates underpinnings for reliable data protection and compliance capabilities growth.

Factor 9: Self-Assessment

The 9 Factors create new perspectives and enhanced guidelines to pinpoint PCI DSS (Payment Card Industry Data Security Standard) compliance risk. Developing in-house awareness and self-assessment competency promotes proactive detection of potential issues, rather than waiting for annual validation – or a hacker – to highlight problems. This aids in revising controls annually, while heightening defenses and streamlining annual validation of compliance audits. Regular internal self-assessment also improves internal and external communication with business units and stakeholders. It boosts confidence in proficiency and the five Cs – capacity, capability, competence, commitment and communication. Evaluating organizational performance against these criteria cultivates a culture where sustainable control environments are successfully developed and expanded.

Money Laundering Laws, Technology and Keeping Up With Criminals

By Nadja van der Veer
Co-Founder, Payments Lawyer, PaymentCounsel

By its very nature, the constantly evolving world of e-commerce, technology and globalization creates new opportunities for financial crime. Although governments and authorities are taking action, criminals continue to find ways around these measures.

Is Legislation Keeping Up With the New Age of Cybercrime?

The central guidance is the European Anti-Money Laundering (AML) Directive. There is now a fifth version designed to reflect the nature and speed of technological growth, but it will certainly not be the last.

We should not forget the practical impact of any legislative changes. When it comes to making an online payment, it is critical that this is smooth, swift and secure and that safeguards endorse, but do not stifle, lawful commerce. Unnecessarily strict requirements can have a detrimental impact on the e-commerce sector. Recent regulative AML and counter-terrorism financing (CTF) changes increase complexity and increase the cost of compliance.

Whilst the 4th AML Directive was being prepared, there were already talks about an update as a reaction to the 2016 Paris and Brussels attacks and the revelation of the Panama Papers; hence the arrival of the 5th AML Directive. It seems like the legislators did not anticipate the true impact and operational effect of these newly introduced measures. Payment companies continue to struggle to comply.

As part of the process to create comprehensive regulation in this area, we see the creation of lists of high-risk third countries/ non-cooperative supposed tax jurisdictions, objective indicators and other assumptions relating to enhanced measures or reporting. These are asked for without suspicion of money laundering. This is ineffective and unnecessary as the circumstances surrounding transactions should be the most relevant factors when assessing risk.

In reality, organizations are faced with a raft of legislation, guidelines and other positions published by bodies such as the Financial Action Task Force (FATF), European Supervisory Authorities (ESAs) and European Banking Authority (EBA). For example, the ESAs' (binding) risk factor guidelines set out factors for assessing risk and how to undertake customer due diligence (CDD). An array of factors must be considered, and a lot of detail gathered in relation to risk assessments and customer relationships. The time it would take to answer the required questions on a per customer basis, regardless of a high or low-risk assessment, is worrying. These extended obligations could potentially undermine the ability to take a risk-based approach.

While the legislator's position is understandable, there are other ways to mitigate money laundering risks.

Into the Hands of the Criminals

Astute criminals are constantly finding new vulnerabilities to exploit. The use of analytics and artificial intelligence (AI) to place dirty money strategically and then hide the trails is becoming the norm. More controls in one field, however, just result in wrongdoers finding alternatives. With so many companies involved in the payment process, tracking money laundering is almost impossible. What's more, cryptocurrency exchange platforms, third-party providers emerging under PSD2 and new payment services have all added to the cauldron. Using merchant accounts for third-party transactions (e.g. transaction laundering) is a significant risk.

What Should Happen Now?

Increased collaboration between industry and governments is needed. We are, however, still scratching the surface in terms of what's possible.

The focus for relevant technology should be around making the AML framework more robust. Fortunately, AI, distributed ledger technologies, biometrics and machine learning are rising. A variety of commercial RegTech solutions are also emerging, and these can capture untapped potential in the AML framework, helping organizations to leverage their data to greater benefit.

However, one worry here is that financial institutions are still performing their own know your customer (KYC) and monitoring using their own tools and data. The existing centralized Ultimate Beneficial Ownership registers do not go far enough. They are restricted in their effectiveness due to privacy and data protection concerns. A much-needed breakthrough would be a central government-backed KYC utility platform. This long-overdue initiative is now being set up in the Nordics and in France, but on a smaller scale.

Mindset Change

The collaboration that is desperately needed is not only about technology. All parties involved in online payments are, by their nature, involved in fighting money laundering. A mindset change, towards adequately deterring criminals through responsibility and international collaboration, is paramount.

This cooperation should not only involve legislators, governments, prosecutors and supervisory bodies, but also private organizations. Whilst cooperation between authorities is formalized, collaboration between financial institutions remains a missing link. Exchanging information between banks and non-banks can be indispensable.[1] Happily, some efforts (such as the UK's Joint Money Laundering Intelligence Taskforce) are already up and running and initiatives such as these will continue to grow and close down criminal activity.

Aside from operational cooperation, public bodies should also join forces with private entities to share intelligence to help identify new threats and assess what needs to be done to close off such channels.

Rethinking Compliance

New regulatory burdens and increased financial penalties have created a tick-box approach to KYC. Rather than contributing to addressing the root cause, this approach seems to do nothing more than satisfy the regulator.

A truly effective AML programme contains much more than the compliance function; it is driven by culture, people, structure and decision-making models. The position of Compliance Officer, for example, must be high in the chain, ensuring compliance decisions are made at strategic level. Compliance also requires a review of other areas such as internal or external development, data and security, and privacy/third-party risk. With some organizations embracing this, we're starting to see a new breed of compliance specialists evolve.

Conclusion

To allow the payments landscape to extend appropriately, cultural as well as legislative changes must be made, but the latter must be at the right time and with the right approach.

---

[1] An initiative launched earlier this year by Pay.UK in collaboration with Vocalink aims to bring together data from multiple banks.

Regulators must ask themselves about the actual changes that can be expected to be seen (or not seen) following the introduction of new legislation. Emerging trends in financial crime require a different regulatory mindset, one that might not require actual legislation. Regulators should not sit still, but instead innovate. They should look at enhancing reporting technology, testing RegTech solutions and empowering collaboration through centralized platforms. Compliance cannot be redesigned without incorporating the very best empowerment technology and changes in culture.

A combination of the above elements would significantly contribute to the development, effectiveness and structural integrity of the AML framework.

Dynamic Regulation Readiness – Implementing the 5th Anti-Money Laundering Directive

By Gary Pine
Chief Product Officer, W2 Global Data

Determining the best course of action when considering divisive new financial trends such as the rise of digital currencies falls to the various market regulators. While some expect regulators to be leading the agenda of change, others suggest the role of the regulators is to keep an active watching brief and intervene only when necessary.

Regardless of which side of the fence you sit, the consensus is that effective regulation needs to cater for a wide range of risk profiles, accommodating a wide range of modern business structures and operating models.

Focusing on continuous enhancement of anti-money laundering (AML) controls, supported by improved AML compliance procedures and more advanced monitoring approaches, the next significant regulatory reform is already upon us.

The 5th Anti-Money Laundering Directive

On 9 July 2018, the amendment of the European Union (EU) Anti-Money Laundering Directive (AMLD) came into force. The EU Commission proposed the revised AMLD in July 2016 as part of its Action Plan against terrorism announced in February 2016, after the terrorist attacks in Paris and Brussels, and as a reaction to the Panama Papers published in April 2016. The latter involved tax-related data leaks that revealed the widespread use of offshore bank accounts and other corporate vehicles in order to hide potentially illegal proceeds and transfer of funds.

The 5th AMLD obligates certain entities to fulfil customer due diligence (CDD) requirements when they conduct business transactions and have in place further policies and procedures to detect, prevent and report money laundering and terrorist financing. In a perfect world, such regulation would have advanced at the speed of such market developments. However, as the pace of change continues to quicken across the payments industry, it is becoming more difficult for regulations, or the regulators themselves, to keep up. In the absence of regulatory clarity, impatient innovators will push forward regardless.

Leveraging the Ultimate Beneficial Owner Register

One important change within the 5th AMLD is that the Ultimate Beneficial Owner (UBO) register – which Member States were already required to set up and maintain pursuant to the 4th AMLD – will now become a public register. The obliged entities are now required to report any discrepancies they find between the information held on those registries and what they identified during their own CDD or KYC processes. It is anticipated that public access will further improve the maintenance of the accuracy of the information contained in the registries – information which is typically pulled from a range of third-party external sources.

Given that many of the EU states have been slow to implement the requirements in accordance with the previous 4th AML/CFT Directive (AMLD4: Directive 2015/849), the updated set of obligations presents a new challenge for many of them.

Tooling Up for Future Regulation

It is clear that where innovation leads, regulation has to follow. A more dynamic "regulation readiness" approach is called for;

one that is contingent upon application programming interfaces (APIs) being used to automate and speed up decision-making as well as combining multiple services like identity validation and credit ranking alongside internal insights into end customer behaviours. For example, this could be a single, solution-oriented API that better positions an institution to examine and act on the important interactions and workflows critical to a 5th AMLD-compliant onboarding and monitoring process. This is not just for the near-term introduction of the 5th AMLD. Tapping into a variety of valuable data sources in real time is a key driver for the use of cognitive technologies within the ever-changing regulatory landscape.

The aim should be to reduce client onboarding and approval times from days to minutes.

Cognitive Technologies in Action

As the demands of AML obligations have increased, payment businesses are required to screen customers daily. This naturally produces many "false positives", or alarms that flag an issue that must be investigated but often proves to be unimportant.

Machine learning can facilitate sanctions compliance efficiency, decreasing the false positive rate as the platform learns from historical behaviour and experience. Such cognitive technologies support the acceleration of digitization initiatives while reducing costs – and while affording the possibility of personalized services in the pursuit of a much-improved customer experience.

Such cognitively driven analytics offer new insights into information that may have previously gone untapped by costly human investigators. Combined with new data sources, the latest advances in cognitive technologies continue to create innovation opportunities amidst the ongoing data revolution.

Available through "Software as a Service" (SaaS)-based offerings, RegTech businesses that take on such high-risk innovations as a

strategy – even if they fall outside the scope of existing regulatory frameworks – get to reap the rewards.

The Application of Data Science

Having gained popularity from social networking models, graph databases are now also being applied in many more areas – like fraud detection; the basic premise being that the sooner you can identify a suspicious behavioural pattern or a group of individuals who seem to be colluding, the faster you can block their activity.

This is particularly important as companies seek to identify second and third-level relationships that may not be readily apparent from data stored in traditional relational databases. If done properly, machine learning can clearly distinguish legitimate and fraudulent behaviours while adapting over time to new, yet unseen, fraud tactics.

Gathering greater insights from customer-derived data can also lead to the development of new single or "community-based" service offerings; pooling information among client institutions in the form of a utility. Access to a data source of would-be fraud events – that can be used as an early warning system to identify fraud at the point of application before substantial losses occur – would be invaluable.

Incumbents and Startups Face Different Challenges

Building on the terms of the 4th AMLD, the 5th AMLD is, in its simplest form, a refinement of previous terms – so compliance should not be too much of an obstacle for the entities that were already subject to the previous AML/counter-terrorism financing (CTF) requirements. For newly subjected entities, however, it will be a different story.

The enormous interest in virtual currencies has inadvertently created a few safe places for the money laundering of anonymously acquired funds and even hidden terrorist financing.

The 5th AMLD comes with a requirement for preventive responsibility by the cryptocurrency market.

The Principle of Proportionality

In the interests of effective and efficient regulation, the principle of proportionality should be applied at every step of the legislative and regulatory process; balancing the costs and benefits of regulation. If the regulation is disproportionate in relation to its objectives, the cost–benefit calculation is likely to be worsened. Consistent regulation should not, therefore, be based on a "one-size-fits-all" approach, but tailored to the characteristics of the institutions involved.

The 5th AMLD aims to reduce the capabilities to exploit identified loopholes by criminals and better CTF through increased transparency about who really owns a legal entity, broadening the criteria for assessing high-risk third countries and ensuring a common high level of safeguards for financial transactions from such countries. The 5th AMLD targets discrete but varied problems in an effective way, and if the payments industry can apply it in a collaborative and integrated manner, it will go a long way towards solving them.

eKYC: The Next Mountain for e-Businesses to Climb

By Philip Atherton
Chief Risk Officer, SafeCharge

The evolution of payments has brought increased opportunity to consumers and merchants alike. Businesses can reach a global customer base, and customers have increased flexibility in how, when and even where they want to pay. However, in order to ensure that business is conducted ethically and that both merchants and customers stay safe from online fraud attempts, regulations such as PSD2 have paved the way for strong customer authentication (SCA) and 3-D Secure V2.0.

Authentication checks to ensure online payments are secure are undoubtedly vital in today's digital age, yet remain a complicated process for e-commerce merchants. Furthermore, online regulated industries – such as gaming and Forex – require increased authentication measures, such as electronic know your customer (eKYC), to protect both customer and merchant. Below, I explore the challenges of online customer authentication and show how technology can be used to increase security while maintaining a smooth user experience (UX).

The Difficult Nature of KYC

The need for KYC requirements has long preceded the explosion of e-commerce and regulation. Rooted in financial services, the essence of these requirements is exactly what it says on the tin; it's the process of verifying the identity of a customer before or during the time they start doing business with an organization.

With the evolution of technology and the globalization of financial services, the legacy KYC policies used by existing regulated businesses must adapt to keep pace.

The Rise in Fraudulent Activities

eKYC's main objective is to ensure that merchants in regulated industries have sufficient information to properly identify and verify a customer's identity in order to ensure they are not the victim of fraudulent activity or any money laundering activities. The technological boom has made the verification process more complicated, as it has created more opportunities for criminals to exploit organizations' failures in their own onboarding processes. From applying for a loan and opening a bank account to playing blackjack on a computer or mobile device, businesses now need to verify their customers without ever meeting them, and faster than ever before. With more and more business now online, customers can conveniently carry out authentication processes online from the comfort of their own sofa. While this has certainly made it easier for customers and increased satisfaction, it has also increased the opportunity for fraudsters to take advantage of the situation.

Digital fraud attacks have become more sophisticated in nature and they are affecting a wide variety of sectors. From advertising to gaming, companies across the board have suffered significant monetary losses. A recent announcement from the leading fraud-prevention body CIFAS (Credit Industry Fraud Avoidance System, founded in 1988), has shown that there were 174,523 cases of identity fraud in 2017, with 95% of these cases involving the impersonation of an oblivious victim; 80% of fraudulent applications were made online.

The cost and prevalence of fraud for both businesses and consumers is simply too high to be ignored, and businesses need to ensure that they have the technology in place to safeguard them from fraudulent activities and keep their customers safe.

The Crossroads Where eKYC and UX Meet

With fraudulent activity on the rise, many businesses know they need to be more diligent in their verification process. However, as businesses continue to move online, customers are becoming digitally native and are growing accustomed to an "instant society", where they can access anything at the click of a button and get their desired results in a matter of seconds. This can create tension when trying to juggle a smooth and instant customer experience whilst remaining safe from fraud. There is often a trade-off; the more checks and verification stages implemented, the worse the UX. When playing a fast-paced game online, no customer wants to jump through ten hoops before they can even start to play.

On the flip side, an instant approval can sometimes be the result of a lax confirmation process that does not contain all the necessary checks needed to remain compliant with regulation. It's a difficult balancing act between safety and maintaining a frictionless experience for the customer, as a turbulent verification process at the end of a customer's transaction journey could lead to cart abandonment and decreasing customer loyalty.

Automation: The Way Forward

Building the right verification structure that takes technological advancements, increased digital fraud and UX into consideration is key. The challenge for businesses is to deliver smart authentication solutions that fit into the customer's journey without affecting the seamless checkout experience.

Introducing automation into identity verification could make the balancing act a lot easier for all merchants, including those in regulated industries. By unifying multiple validation checks, automated verification allows businesses to create a smooth onboarding experience. Rather than adding friction by forcing users to prove their identity at each stage, automation allows businesses to run various checks at the same time, creating a successful experience for the customer without compromising compliance requirements. In doing so, users maintain a positive UX and are more likely to use the same business platform again. This helps businesses maximize their sales conversion, reduce drop-off and abandonment rates, and strengthen customer loyalty.

Through automation, businesses also eliminate the lengthy, painstaking process of manually verifying each customer's documents for KYC checks. Not only does this minimize the risk of error – which in itself amplifies customer frustrations and increases abandonment rates – but it also helps businesses cut their costs significantly. By automating the verification process, businesses can reallocate their capital to other revenue-generating functions of the business, empowering them to create new growth opportunities.

Traditional Approaches are Not Enough

In order to ensure that both businesses and customers are able to take advantage of the benefits of an online global marketplace, security and fraud prevention measures must be in place and updated regularly. Traditional means of validation are no longer fit for today's digital world. Automation solutions are required that can comply with eKYC regulations in different jurisdictions whilst maintaining a smooth experience for customers; bridging the gap between these factors and leaving businesses with the confidence to onboard anyone, anywhere in the world.

AML Systems After Madoff: Ponzi-Identification Using "Complexity"

By J.B. Beckett
Consultant, New Fund Order

Could the use of complexity stop the next Madoff fraud? How can a Ponzi scheme be detected in a universe of money transfer transactions where attacks may be undetected for prolonged periods of time?

Eradicating the causality of Ponzi schemes is a Rubicon which regulators have failed to cross. Such schemes are perpetuated through the unassuming bank account. Can anomaly identification help prevent Ponzi schemes in future?

What is a Ponzi Scheme?

Ponzi schemes (named after the fraudster, Charles Ponzi) are investment schemes that attract cash deposits on the prospect of future returns but typically pay out existing clients using the deposits from new investors. Eventually these schemes run out of cash but can exist for many decades so long as clients are content and redemptions covered. Why did Madoff happen? I could cite you Orwell, Nietzsche or even Confucius; or any other commentator of the human condition, but it is more useful to consider what actually happened.

About Madoff

For those who don't recall, Bernie Madoff ran the largest known Ponzi scheme in history; US$65 billion was defrauded from the US$177 billion deposited. The fact that the collapse of the Ponzi followed the credit crisis in 2008 only made the US nation's reaction all the more dramatic. In 2009, something in the American psyche broke.

On 12 March 2009, Bernie Madoff pleaded guilty to 11 federal crimes of operating the largest private Ponzi scheme in history. Accusations and investigations were brought against Madoff over the years, both externally and internally. In 2000, Harry Markopoulos alerted the Securities and Exchange Commission. After failing to replicate Madoff's returns, Markopoulos concluded they were mathematically impossible. Madoff was either front-running his order flow, or his wealth management business was one massive Ponzi scheme. In his 17-page memo entitled "The World's Largest Hedge Fund is a Fraud", he specified 30 numbered red flags across 14 years of Madoff's trades. He approached *The Wall Street Journal* in 2005, but its editors failed to pursue.

The Sins of the Deposit

Instead of investing deposits, for two decades Madoff simply deposited clients' funds into his business account at Chase Manhattan Bank (part of JPM), and paid out of that account when they requested withdrawals. To pay off those clients, Madoff needed new investors.

During the 1990s, according to prosecutors, JPM Bank employees raised concerns. One arm of JPM even pulled out of a Madoff investment in 1998 after "too many red flags" were raised. By autumn 2008, JPM had redeemed a US$200 million investment from Madoff, without notifying clients or authorities. In January 2007 and July 2008, transfers from Madoff's accounts triggered JPM's anti-money laundering (AML) software, but JPM failed to file a suspicious activity report (SAR). In October 2008, its UK subsidiary filed a SAR with the Serious Organized Crime Agency.

As the credit crisis intensified, investors tried to redeem US$7 billion from Madoff. By November 2008, the account balance had dropped to low levels. US$300 million in new money came in, but US$320 million flowed out; leaving the account marginal to meet redemptions in November.

JPM Bank, which at one point had well over US$5 billion, fell to US$234 million. Despite a rush of new investors, it still wasn't enough to offset withdrawals. Banks had stopped lending; Madoff knew he could not borrow enough to cover the outstanding redemption requests. He instructed the remaining account to be paid out to relatives and selected clients.

JPM should have identified that money deposited was not being transferred to an investment account. JPM should also have flagged net flows sooner. The error lay in JPM's AML systems and process. Poor AML was the root cause of the Madoff Ponzi scandal.

Starting Assumptions for an AML System

The starting assumptions for a good AML system are:

- Prevent the *placement* of assets from criminal, terrorist or sanctioned sources.
- Prevent the *layering* of assets, from prohibited sources, into deposit and investment.
- Prevent the *integration* of prohibited assets being paid back.

Failings of JPM's AML

The failings of JPM's AML were therefore:

- Failing to identify the anomaly and malignant purpose of the account.
- Not identifying that deposits made were not moved into an investment account.

- Failing to identify patterns between deposits and withdrawals.
- Failing to quickly escalate a SAR to the authorities.

The Aftermath

In 2014, *Forbes* magazine reported: "Madoff kept the bank account at the centre of his fraud". JPM entered into a "deferred prosecution agreement" with prosecutors to resolve two felony charges under the Bank Secrecy Act. The bank admitted to not filing a SAR after red flags were raised, and having inadequate AML compliance procedures.

Where PayTech Can Help: Anomaly Anti-Money Laundering Software (AAMLS)

Most AML systems were designed to stop the proceeds of crime and terrorism being laundered. But they still struggle to identify anomalies (fraud) perpetuated by existing customers moving between domestic and foreign accounts. A robust AAMLS solution could include:

- Geotagging of money paid in, paid out and the source and beneficiary of funds.
- Automated suspicious activity reporting to remove human negligence.
- Codifying every deposit and settlement for intent and behaviour.
- Measure sequencing the risk of outflows to inflows to detect "burn rate".
- Rules-based modelling on a set of assumptions and characteristics.
- Machine learning to identify characteristics of arising fraud.
- Anomaly identification based on complexity approaches.

Applying Complexity Rather than Modelling or Machine Learning

In his *principle of incompatibility*, L. Zadeh assumes that finding a small anomaly in a highly complex system is improbable because of "insufficient precision". This leads to small anomalies slowly causing major issues. AML systems have become more sophisticated through modelling and machine learning, yet remain fragile to this principle. Dr Jacek Marczyk, who invented model-free quantitative complexity management (QCM), notes:

Complexity doesn't need to be modelled – it can be measured based on raw data. Models are based on assumptions, which are prone to error. Building (complex) models of something that is already complex is a highly subjective and risky exercise. Meanwhile a machine learning system must see a given anomaly a sufficient number of times in order to learn to recognize it. In most cases, however, one cannot afford the luxury of multiple failures in order to learn to recognize an anomaly!

So, the starting assumptions for an AAMLS are:

- A model-free approach needs only raw data over a period of time.
- Anomaly detection requires two things: (1) to define the anomaly and (2) to capture when anomalies change.
- Deposits in, and withdrawals out, form a "universe" over time.
- The structure of the "universe" is mapped such that high complexity implies fragility.

- Resilience is a function of the deficit/surplus of net flows.
- Highly complex systems behave in a myriad of modes – and can switch from one mode to another without warning.
- Deposit and withdrawal identity/behaviour in isolation may appear normal.

A Ponzi will present itself as upward complexity with a gradient proportional to the scheme's expansion. Typically, we are looking for a loss of structure due to "decorrelation" between entries on the account ledger, and a subsequent change in the topology of its complexity map. With typical AML systems, the anomalies lack sufficient magnitude to rise above the "noise floor" to be flagged. In QCM, numerous small transactions will not hide a Ponzi because it is scale-independent; the magnitude of the transactions doesn't affect the complexity.

Conclusion

Today's AML systems remain misguided and ill-equipped to stop the next Madoff. Reliance on modelling and machine learning incurs further fragility. When a Ponzi scheme enters the bank's "universe" it will add structure, hence complexity. By using complexity, we can change the focus of AML systems from simple client identification to anomaly identification, optimizing payments analysis, automating the SAR process and removing human error. As a result, we can spot Ponzi schemes before they damage the integrity of our financial systems.

Blockchain Regulation Around the World

4

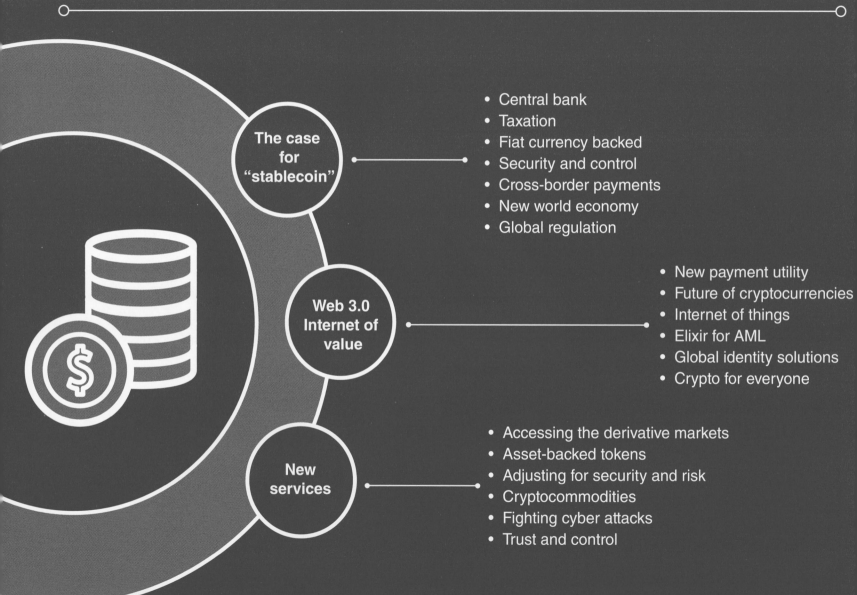

BLOCKCHAIN REGULATION AROUND THE WORLD

The case for "stablecoin"
- Central bank
- Taxation
- Fiat currency backed
- Security and control
- Cross-border payments
- New world economy
- Global regulation

Web 3.0 Internet of value
- New payment utility
- Future of cryptocurrencies
- Internet of things
- Elixir for AML
- Global identity solutions
- Crypto for everyone

New services
- Accessing the derivative markets
- Asset-backed tokens
- Adjusting for security and risk
- Cryptocommodities
- Fighting cyber attacks
- Trust and control

Executive Summary

In this part we explore the new world of blockchain and cryptocurrencies. This area has had plenty of hype over the few years since its creation by Satoshi Nakamoto in 2009. We start with a helpful introduction of how it works and how regulation is attempting to be applied. We move on to look at the way in which it is regulated around the world and this is quickly followed by a look at central banks and how they are adapting to the potential of having their currencies on the blockchain. The chapter from the Ukrainian National Bank has some radical views on the future of the economy and taxation based on a blockchain environment.

Moving on, we take a very pragmatic view of the regulatory landscape and where it is headed. Next we look at Web 3.0 and the growth of value back exchanges on the blockchain, but end by asking whether the solution actually defeats the original purpose of cryptocurrencies. We then delve into the possibility that distributed ledger technology (DLT)-based currencies could solve money laundering and identity issues in the future, and that crypto could become mainstream within five years.

Finally, we take a look at some other areas where blockchain solutions can work in the payments industry. We consider how smart contracts can be deployed to simplify and build trust into other areas like derivatives and commodities trading. And how stablecoins can provide a means of settlement in the crypto community and how cyber-attacks can be reduced through DLT solutions.

It's a truly exciting look into how tech can transform an industry.

Understanding Cryptocurrencies, Blockchain Technology and Regulations

By Veronica McGregor
Chief Legal Officer, Shapeshift

Recently, Grand View Research reported that by 2024, the global blockchain technology market size is expected to reach US$7.59 billion. The use cases for blockchain technology are plenty, ranging from smart contracts to RegTech, real and personal property transfer, securities exchanges, voting and more. This is not only indicative of the significant and growing interest in blockchain technology, but illustrates that no matter what the context, blockchain technology will almost certainly impact your business and life. And soon.

Notwithstanding the expanding universe of possibilities, blockchain technology was born as a payments technology and many of the most compelling use cases involve moving units of value, often referred to as "digital assets". It should come as no surprise that the payments industry, already one of the most dynamic sectors in financial services, continues to evolve, propelled by blockchain-related innovations from established players and FinTech firms alike.

Chief among the developments in payments are the increasingly diverse options in cryptocurrencies. While still shrouded in mystery and suspicion by many who have yet to fully comprehend it, the development of cryptocurrencies is happening at a rapid pace.

Below are the basics of blockchain technology and cryptocurrencies, followed by a brief discussion of the state of global regulations surrounding each.

On Blockchain Technology

"Blockchain" is a buzzword these days. But what's behind this powerful technology, and what unique properties does it have?

Introduction to Blockchain

First introduced for Bitcoin, the blockchain was a revolutionary concept when it was conceptualized by Satoshi Nakamoto in 2008. At its core, it's a distributed ledger or a database that requires consensus between all of the involved parties.[1]

This approach worked for the Bitcoin network and has since been adopted by many other digital assets. Distributed ledgers are professed by many to be the best decentralized method for making secure, trusted transactions for a number of reasons. The foundational concepts of blockchain technology are:

- **Decentralization.** Unlike transactions that are made with banks, blockchain transactions aren't centralized to banks and federal governments. Removing this level of authority puts financial freedom in the hands of everyone.

- **No third parties.** Third parties have often been the source of trust in common fiat transactions. Blockchain technology replaces these third parties with a community-shared database. In other words, you trust your peers rather than a faceless entity.

- **Transparency.** All blockchain transactions are publicly viewable. When it comes to digital assets, you can enter a transaction ID in a block explorer and see a recorded transaction. Each transaction ID is completely unique.

- **Resistance to censorship.** Governments and corporations can often censor transactions if they wish, but blockchain technology is resistant to this. The blockchain model is meant to allow non-discriminatory transactions based on an agreed set of rules. Everyone utilizing the network is bound by the same set of rules.

---

[1] *Note:* You will often hear the word "crypto" – a term that originates from the word "cryptography". In this context, it means using cryptography, maths and computer science to make sure that currency can't be faked, and each transaction record is real and immutable.

- **Immutability.** The blockchain is fully immutable, which means that transactions cannot change. Transactions are irreversible, meaning that even in the unlikely event that a network was successfully attacked, existing transactions could never be undone.

- **Security.** Because all blocks within the blockchain are connected to one another, tampering with a single block requires tampering with all of its connected blocks. Not only is this difficult, but there are other protections that the blockchain offers. Personal digital signatures – known as private keys – are another measure of security to ensure that digital assets are not misappropriated. In order to successfully attack a blockchain, at least 51% of the network would have to be changed at the same time. Since this is nearly impossible, the blockchain is much more secure than previous payment systems.

The Building Blocks

There are three fundamental components to the blockchain. The technology depends on:

- **The distributed ledger.** This is a database fuelled by a community of nodes. Each node that participates in the information processing required by the database will process each transaction. This ensures that no central authority is needed to confirm blockchain transactions.

- **The consensus mechanism.** When enough of the individuals utilizing the distributed ledger meet consensus – or agree on a transaction – the transaction is confirmed and considered successful. This is possible via special, blockchain-specific algorithms.

- **Public-key cryptography.** Public keys can be shown to anyone, which is why they are referred to as "public". Private keys, in contrast, should only be known by the user. This is the part of your key pair that ensures only you have control of your digital assets. Public-key cryptography is used on the blockchain to encrypt data and create digital signatures. In both cases, the user must have the private key to access the necessary information for blockchain interaction. Someone with the correct key pair can create a confirmed digital signature or decrypt any encrypted data. This is why your private key must remain secret.

These components are what ensure that the blockchain is correct and dependable. Because of its building blocks, blockchains are designed to be one of the most accurate database types ever created.

Creative Uses for Blockchain Technology

While it is most commonly associated with cryptocurrencies, blockchain technology has a number of different applications. It functions both as a platform and as a record-keeping system, making it a concept of interest to many. Blockchain technology has a number of unique use cases, some of which include:

- **Markets.** Digital tokens are often compared to physical assets or stocks. Blockchain technology ensures that ownership is absolute.

- **Finance.** Blockchain technology tracks transactions and balances, making it perfect for financial services companies.

- **Identity protection.** While the blockchain guarantees that ownership is absolute based on private-key ownership, there is no background check. You do not need to provide your name, any government-issued numbers or your home address.

- **Crowdfunding.** Some cryptocurrency companies, such as Acorn, think that crowdfunding and blockchain technology should go hand-in-hand.

- **Healthcare.** Many believe that blockchain technology could change the healthcare industry. From patient records to disease tracking, blockchain companies are using the technology to improve the future of the world's overall health.

- **Tourism.** The tourist industry hopes to utilize blockchain technology too. Ridesharing has had a surge in popularity, and companies involved in the blockchain space hope to get in on the action.
- **Retail.** For retailers, the middle man can cause headaches. That is why companies like OpenBazaar have decided to launch blockchain-based markets.

Now that you understand the basics, the rest will start to make sense too.

A Primer on Cryptocurrency

To put it simply, cryptocurrencies are digital assets. Most digital assets are decentralized, which means they are not controlled by a single governing body, and this is one of the features that distinguishes them from traditional fiat currency.

Since cryptocurrency is decentralized, it is important that some rules exist to ensure that transactions involving digital assets are legitimate.

The blockchain, as described above, is essentially a list of validated blocks, each linking to its predecessor all the way to the genesis block – storing all transaction data, chronologically tracking the public digital asset transactions that take place all over the world.

While this may sound simple, this level of data storage takes an incredible amount of work. That is why computers called miners are constantly processing advanced computations to confirm transactions. When someone chooses to use their personal hardware to mine, they are issued a small amount of crypto called a block reward. This is called "mining".

Bitcoin

Although Bitcoin was the first and remains the most well known, there are more digital assets than ever online today. With new "coins" and new people entering the market, it can be hard to keep track of all the tokens that the crypto ecosystem has to offer.

Bitcoin is the original digital asset, created by Satoshi Nakamoto. But at its core, Bitcoin is a collection of concepts and technologies that form the basis of a digital money ecosystem.

Satoshi Nakamoto introduced the Bitcoin network as a concept in 2008, hoping to decentralize online payment processing. It enabled people to transact without a third party. While some have claimed to be the person behind the Bitcoin network concept, the true identity of Satoshi Nakamoto is still unconfirmed.

The Bitcoin network can be hard to understand, as it is a complicated subject. You can learn more on the Bitcoin website.

Regulations

Because cryptocurrencies are still relatively nascent, and the global regulatory environment is always slow to adapt to new technology, there is quite a steep learning curve for lawmakers to understand blockchain and cryptocurrency. Blockchain is unlikely to be regulated as technology, but will be regulated in the use cases. For example, banks choosing to use blockchain in their operations will likely need to meet certain standards to satisfy banking regulators. Likewise, those utilizing blockchain for securities registration and transfer will face similar scrutiny by securities regulators.

Regulation of Cryptocurrency

Although clear regulation has been scarce, with some countries imposing outright bans on virtual currencies, some jurisdictions have successfully issued guidance or even regulation on various aspects of the cryptocurrency ecosystem. Still other countries have simply issued warnings about the risks associated with buying digital currencies.

For those doing more than simply issuing warnings, the potential for money laundering has been chief among the concerns of global regulators. Some countries have developed new regulatory regimes to specifically address the industry, while others have instead attempted to fit the new technology into existing regulation. In the USA, federal regulation of other types of financial services was simply expanded to cover convertible virtual currencies, but there are also a few specific state laws covering virtual currencies. Other countries, such as Japan, have enacted crypto-specific laws in recent years.

Regulation of virtual currencies is tricky because the transactions within the payment systems, such as Bitcoin, are anonymous. The USA has chosen to regulate the exchanges on which currencies are bought and sold as a means to control for money laundering and fraud risk.

Legal Treatment of Cryptocurrency

One of the first legal issues to arise was how to characterize cryptocurrencies. In the USA, the Internal Revenue Service issued guidance stating that crypto was to be treated, for tax purposes, as property (rather than currency). Still another US regulatory agency, the Commodities and Futures Exchange Commission, has stated that cryptocurrencies are to be treated as commodities. Other jurisdictions, such as Germany, treat cryptocurrencies as financial instruments and require that they be taxed as "capital". With so many varying laws and regulations, it can be difficult for those in the industry to develop an effective and reasonable compliance programme.

The advent of initial coin offerings (ICOs, or token sales) raised still more concerns for regulators, as many of the first entrants into this area resembled securities. In the USA, the Securities and Exchange Commission has issued guidance on the subject and has also issued enforcement actions against some of the more egregious examples.

As regulators around the globe struggle with how to protect consumers, the financial system and control of money laundering, innovators in the space continue to develop more models and use cases – often in the absence of clear legal guidance. Such is life in FinTech.

Blockchain, Cryptocurrencies and How They Fit Within Current Payments Regulation

By James Burnie
Senior Associate, Eversheds-Sutherland (International) LLP

Andrew Henderson
Partner - Financial Services, Eversheds-Sutherland (International) LLP

and Andrew Burnie
PhD Student, Alan Turing Institute and University College London

What is a Payment Service?

At its core, payment services constitutes enabling the movement of value, traditionally in the form of fiat currency, from a client to a third party. This "movement" does not constitute a physical movement of money, rather what is happening is that one ledger, that is held between the client and the payment service provider, is altered to reflect the fact that the client has a right to less money, and the ledger of the third party is altered to reflect the fact that it has a right to more money.

The role of a payment services provider, therefore, is to enable the alteration of different ledgers to reflect changes in amounts owed.[1]

Figure 1: **The movement of value**

---

[1] Please note that in this chapter, references to "payment service provider" will be to the entity performing this function in the broadest sense.

As the number of users of the payment service increases, so does the number of ledgers. Given the nature of this system, there is a natural role for blockchain, which is "*essentially records, or ledgers, of electronic transactions, very similar to accounting ledgers*".[2]

The Three Key Blockchain Payment Models Explained

The potential role of blockchain in facilitating the movement of value has been recognized since its inception with Bitcoin. There are currently broadly three different models by which this is achieved.

Model 1: The Use of Cryptocurrency to Make Payments Directly (e.g. the Bitcoin Model)

Originally, Bitcoin was intended to "*allow online payments to be sent directly from one party to another without going through a financial institution*".[3] However, as some participants may not be sufficiently technology savvy to operate their own wallet, or do not want the hassle of doing so, they may delegate the operation of their wallet to a payment service provider.

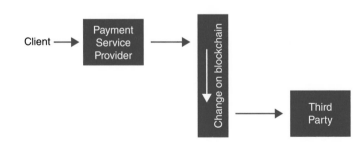

Figure 2: **Model 1**

---

[2] ESMA Report, "The Distributed Ledger Technology Applied to Securities Markets", p. 4.

[3] Satoshi Nakamoto, "Bitcoin: A Peer-to-Peer Electronic Cash System", p. 1.

Model 2: Fiat Models Using Blockchain to Facilitate Payments (e.g. RippleNet[4])

Another use of blockchain may be to facilitate movements of fiat currency, whilst minimizing the use of a cryptocurrency. The purpose of these models is to improve on the existing infrastructure for moving fiat value, whilst avoiding the volatility and risk of using a cryptocurrency.

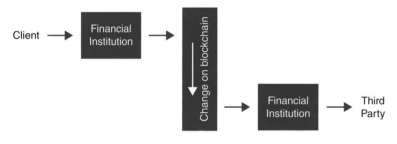

Figure 3: Model 2

Model 3: Stablecoin Models Whereby Payments are Made in Cryptocurrencies Pegged to/Exchanged for an Underlying Fiat Currency or Other Liquid Asset (e.g. Tether[5] and Dai[6])

Stablecoins are a subset of cryptocurrencies designed to minimize the risk of volatility. There are various ways in which greater stability for a token can be achieved; however, it is common for stability to be provided through some form of linkage to an underlying asset (e.g. a fiat currency), which can be liquidated in the event of a fall in the cryptocurrency.

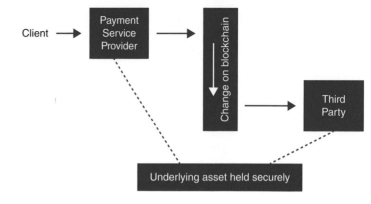

Figure 4: Model 3

Navigating the Current Regulatory Framework

Before blockchain, there were various pre-existing regulatory frameworks governing the provision of a payment service by controlling the movement of fiat currency. The existing systems often apply on a definitional, rather than a functional, approach (i.e. they apply on the basis of whether a model falls within the definition of the scope of the relevant legislation). As such, they broadly apply to the different blockchain models set out above as follows.

Model 1

As there is no fiat currency involvement, this model has often fallen outside the regulatory system.[7] However, given that the functionality of these tokens can be analogous to traditional payment services, there have been moves to incorporate them

---

[4] https://ripple.com.

[5] https://tether.to.

[6] https://makerdao.com/en/?no-cache=1.

---

[7] For example in Europe, payment services have traditionally been applied to banknotes, coins or scriptural money, see Article 4 of Directive 2015/2366 ("PSD2").

into the existing framework.[8] This type of token is increasingly being recognized as a distinct subgroup of crypto-assets.[9]

Model 2

Here there is a movement of fiat money, and on this basis existing payment service regimes will apply. The core issue here is that these regimes are based on pre-existing payment models, using a multi-ledger system, and so requirements, for example designed to ensure reconciliation of the different ledgers, may not be suitable for a system premised on a single ledger system.

Model 3

The regulatory treatment of this model is contingent on the stabilization mechanism used. At a high level, there are two options. The first is whether there is a direct correlation between each token and fiat currency on a 1:1 basis. This would be the case if, for example, a client pays USD into a bank account, and in return receives tokens which, at a later date, can be converted back into USD, at the same rate,[10] meaning that functionally, it acts as a "voucher"[11] for the fiat currency.

---

[8] For example in Singapore, the Payment Services Bill expanded the existing legislation to include virtual currency services and the 5th Anti-Money Laundering Directive (MLDS) especially applies AML to cryptocurrencies.

[9] Although the label used by regulators for this group may vary (e.g. being unregulated tokens (previously referred to as "exchange tokens") – UK Financial Conduct Authority Guidance on Cryptoassets or "payment tokens" – European Banking Authority Report with advice for the European Commission on crypto-assets, https://eba.europa.eu/documents/10180/2545547/EBA+Report+on+crypto+assets.pdf).

[10] For example, see USDC: https://support.usdc.circle.com/hc/en-us/articles/360016278791-What-does-it-mean-to-tokenize-USD-What-does-it-mean-to-redeem-USDC-.

[11] For further analysis of voucher-type tokens, see "Developing a Cryptocurrency Assessment Framework", 10.5915/LEDGER.2018.21 (https://ledgerjournal.org/ojs/index.php/ledger/article/view/121).

This stabilization mechanism often leads to the token falling within the European Directive on Electronic Money (Directive 2009/110/EC, "EMD 2") – e-money being defined (in Europe) as "*electronically…stored monetary value as represented by a claim on the issuer which is issued on receipt of funds for the purpose of making payment transactions…and which is accepted by a natural or legal person other than the electronic money issuer.*"[12]

Alternatively, a stabilization mechanism may be provided by either acting as vouchers for non-fiat assets, or linked to fiat on a basis which is not 1:1. Where this is the case, the token may fall outside local definitions of electronic money and, as such, outside regulation.

Setting Up for the Future

As blockchain becomes widely explored and gradually applied, regulators globally[13] are becoming sensitive to the need to avoid arbitrage between blockchain-based systems and other systems. In particular, they are focusing on ensuring both that there are proper anti-money laundering and know your customer procedures in place, and the security of funds, as these issues pose the greatest risk for consumers and markets, respectively. Commercially this means that, when setting up payments systems, firms should focus on implementing robust systems and controls on these aspects to future-proof the business for future regulatory change.

---

[12] See Article 2 of "EMD 2".

[13] Often this is done by explicitly referring to crypto-assets as being captured within the regulatory framework, as has been the case in Abu Dhabi, Gibraltar, Malta and Singapore. Other regulations are moving towards extending the regulatory framework to include crypto-assets (e.g. the European Securities and Markets Association is calling for a pan-European approach to cryptocurrency).

Blockchain and Beyond

By Samiran Ghosh
Independent Consultant / Startup Advisor

The legal status of cryptocurrencies, and the regulatory framework around them, vary across the world. Since blockchain is the underlying technology, the regulatory status of cryptocurrencies in a country also has a direct bearing on the progress of the technology there. With the current rise of blockchain technology, some governments around the world have already issued the first blockchain-related laws.

It is interesting to note that what we take as a matter of course today were objects of fear and ridicule not so long ago. As per the *Smithsonian Magazine*, at the turn of the 20th century, motor vehicles were handmade, expensive toys of the rich, and widely regarded as rare and dangerous. Similarly, according to the BBC, when Faraday first generated electric power in 1831, there was widespread fear of electric shocks and, according to *The Economist*, in the 19th century people worried that telegraph wires were affecting the weather or were a form of black magic. Trains were thought to cause nervous disorders. Today, a ban on the above innovations would be unthinkable to many. History has taught us that the regulation of new and disruptive technologies is more appropriate than their prohibition. This applies to crypto-assets as well.

While the global community wants consensus on cryptocurrency regulation, national governments are making their own manoeuvres and it is important to understand the intentions behind them. For instance, small countries like Gibraltar, Bermuda and Liechtenstein are attempting to attract new capital and become crypto-friendly as a result, whilst the Republic of the Marshall Islands and Venezuela issued their own tokens to oppose external financial influence and the growth of Bitcoin.

The word "regulation" was enough to send a shudder down the spine of the crypto community. One of the primary drivers behind the success of blockchain is an anti-establishment set of beliefs.

Conceding to regulatory bodies in what resembles an attempt to fit into the existing financial framework seems to counter the beliefs upon which the blockchain ecosystem was built. Yet it has become abundantly clear in the past year that in order for cryptocurrencies to succeed, there will need to be some degree of assimilation with the traditional way of doing things. Sure, blockchain as a technology has given rise to true peer-to-peer borderless transfer of value, and innovative ways to raise capital or invest in promising projects, but we have also seen the other side of the coin: cryptocurrency being used as the primary exchange of value for illicit activities, and people taking advantage of the uneducated investor through scam initial coin offerings. As nefarious and anti-crypto as regulation once seemed, some in the crypto community are slowly warming to, or even welcoming, the impending increase in the regulation of the blockchain ecosystem.

Getting Onboard the Regulation Bandwagon

On 20 March 2018, the G20 countries gathered in Buenos Aires to discuss the possible regulation of cryptocurrency. Argentina, Australia, Turkey, South Africa and the UK proclaimed that they had decided not to regulate cryptocurrencies. While blockchain is still in its infancy, governments around the world recognize the value of distributed ledger technology. The European Commission recently launched the EU Blockchain Observatory and Forum, however, investing over €80 million in blockchain projects that support the use of blockchain in technical and societal areas, with €300 million more to be allocated to blockchain implementation by 2020. Blockchain regulation will continue to evolve and gain acceptance in the years ahead.

Addressing Our Fears

So, what are we all afraid of? What does "regulation" even mean in the context of cryptocurrency? Will technology follow regulation, or will it be the other way around?

Some might say that regulation means acceptance of technology as part of mainstream business – ready to scale and be adopted by all. When "regulation" is mentioned in the context of cryptocurrency, it is usually with reference to two main concepts: know your customer and anti-money laundering regulations, and the regulations surrounding the issuance and trading of securities. Regulations are created for a reason. In the case of securities, the intent of regulations is to protect investors and make sure that funds are being used for their intended (and legal) purposes.

Each country has its own views and many also have laws around cryptocurrencies. Typically, whilst blockchain is welcome, virtual currencies are not. Since it cannot be undiscovered, a framework needs to be put in place that manages this ecosystem.

There is definitely a case to be made for cryptocurrency:

- *It can reduce the incidence of fraud:* being digital in character, cryptocurrencies cannot be counterfeited or reversed arbitrarily by the sender.

- *It can reduce identity theft:* (current) credit cards operate on a "pull" basis, where the merchant initiates the payment and pulls the designated amount from the cardholder's account. When you give your credit card to a merchant, you give him or her access to your full credit line, even if the transaction is for a small amount. Cryptocurrency use a "push" mechanism, which allows the cryptocurrency holder to send exactly what he or she wants to the merchant or recipient with no further information.

- *It can provide everyone with access to commerce:* there are approximately 2.2 billion individuals with access to the Internet or mobile phones who don't currently have access to traditional banking and monetary systems. These individuals are prime candidates for the cryptocurrency market. Since cryptocurrency is not bound by the conventional banking system, it has the potential to truly be an international medium of exchange and a viable alternative to existing mechanisms.

Conclusion

A cryptocurrency's purpose is to enable someone to become their own bank, to take control of their own financial destiny. It allows us to no longer depend on any institution to store value and send it from one place to another on the planet. It seems simple, yet the implications are mind-boggling.

Where the Internet brought freedom of information to the world, Bitcoin and its distributed ledger system, the blockchain, aim to bring freedom of financial activities (e.g. movement of value peer to peer) to the world.

Will Central Banks Adopt the New World Economy of Cryptocurrencies?

By Aarón Olmos
Economist and Professor of Cryptocurrencies

Since the creation of the Central Bank of Sweden (Sveriges Riksbank) in 1688, the need to control monetary flows became evident. Central banks control one of the most important elements in the political and economic game of the states, money. The urgency of creating a means of exchange, divisible, fractionable, reserve of value and unit of account goes back more than 5,000 years in history, but it is with the central bank that money becomes a key piece of the economic dynamics of the nations, as a reflection of the levels of national production, an indicator of the cost of living, a reference for price systems and a focal point for several schools of economic thought.

A Vision of Money

In 1976 Professor Frederick von Hayek, member of the Austrian School and winner of the Nobel Prize for Economics, published his book *The Denationalization of Money*.[1] This book highlighted the need for a free monetary system and economy of central banks, considering them the cause of the greatest distortions in the economic dynamics of countries with fiscal deficits; here monetary policy, far from correcting the present structural problems, aggravates them. In this sense, Hayek even refers to the need for free choice, on the part of people and companies, for the type of money that represents them. He went on to show a vision of a type of money denationalized and independent of the economic policy

of some country or state – not dissimilar to the definition from Satoshi Nakamoto in his original paper that formed the basis for the development of Bitcoin.[2]

This idea gained more interest after the unilateral abandonment of the gold standard by the government of Richard Nixon in 1971, leaving open the possibility – on the part of the Federal Reserve – to continue issuing money without real support in a historical fractional reserve scheme that further expanded the amounts of US dollars in the markets, supported only by its internal productive capacity. In this sense, people and companies were connected to a money of mandatory acceptance (fiduciary money), which is in a relationship of dependence with the economic policies that governments establish in the search for medium and long-term equilibria in their markets, leaving the value of labour, savings and investments affected for good or bad by the result of the monetary policies of central banks. This was the start of fiat currencies and the end of gold-based economics.

Creating Options

It is for this reason that the regulation of the price of money (interest rate), through monetary policy tools, was made increasingly necessary by the central bank to establish control over an increasingly unstable market where, as a result of its own intervention, the intrinsic value of the coin is progressively lost and, with it, the result of the work of the people and the returns on the investments. This is where the idea of Professor Frederick von Hayek no longer looks so outlandish. What if, providing conditions for the creation of a denationalized type of money existed, it became a real option for fiduciary money for people and companies globally? The answer to this question came from the greatest technological serendipity of the 20th century, and the idea of privacy, anonymity and immutability in the transfer of data.

---

[1] F. von Hayek, *The Denationalization of Money* (London: Institute of Economic Affairs, 1976).

[2] Satoshi Nakamoto, "Bitcoin: A Peer-to-Peer Electronic Cash System".

In 1991, Vinton Cerf and Tim Berners Lee created the largest dematerialized value-transfer market that anyone has ever imagined – the Internet. This new virtual space began to change social and production relations almost immediately, with commerce being one of its first activities – in the hands of eBay and Amazon – in an area unexplored by traditional economic policies, as well as by governments. In an interview given to John Berthoud, President of the National Taxpayers Union in 1999, Professor Milton Friedman, a member of the Chicago School and winner of the 1976 Nobel Prize for Economics, questioned what the tax treatment of technology companies like Microsoft should be in a market of growing electronic commerce, where it was even possible to create a digital form of denationalized money which would pose a great difficulty for the Internal Revenue Service (IRS) when collecting taxes in an eminent virtual market.

This new market lives in a digital economy, as defined by Don Tapscott in his 1995 book,[3] where the Internet, electronic commerce, social networks, digital transformation and blockchain protocols for the development of the Bitcoin network have a great impact on all economic, political and social systems, changing everything we do. We are in the midst of a digital revolution, or 4th Industrial Revolution, as explained by Klaus Schwab in his 2016 book.[4] This implies an epochal change where "data" is the new value, enabling spaces for the development and adoption of alternative means of payment, in non-vertical organizations and open to production methods with intensive use of technology, changing the concept of money and things in the minds of people and companies globally.

A New Money

This is how money 2.0, or people's money (cryptocurrencies) was born. A means of change and virtual system, decentralized, distributed, denationalized and accepted worldwide by the endorsement given by the blockchain protocols, being transparent and easy to use, verifiable, open, inclusive and in constant evolution. This alternative means of payment privileges privacy, anonymity and immutability in the transfer of data, leaving outside the operation reliable third parties and governments, in a structure where the consensus of their peers and the shortage programmed by design of their cryptocurrencies, give use value linked to a project that creates the market where its price will fluctuate, depending on supply and demand caused by human needs.

This new way of creating, transferring and treasuring value does not establish a relationship with the traditional monetary path, where central banks concentrate power and regulate the money market. In this sense Andreas Antonopoulos, in his book *Internet of Money*, vol. I,[5] states that the means of payment based on blockchain will create new scenarios for governments and central banks, which will automatically close because they will lose control of a valuable historical asset, money. Given this reality, the central bank is the authority that can make the choice between its regulation and its adoption. This new economic system will have a proven distorting effect on the traditional monetary systems, in terms of Hayek. For this reason, the central banks, by refusing to adopt, will regulate in favour of more control and centralization of money and monetary power, rejecting any tool that changes their status quo.

From Stranger to Friend

Bitcoin and cryptocurrencies were once simply data created in an ecosystem controlled by an algorithm, reliant on nodes of computers worldwide to validate exchange operations between perfect strangers whose anonymity and privacy are extremely

[3] D. Tapscott, *The Digital Economy: Promise and Peril in the Age of Networked Intelligence* (New York, McGraw-Hill, 1995).

[4] K. Schwab, *The Fourth Industrial Revolution* (Harmondsworth: Penguin, 2016).

[5] A. Antonopoulos, *Internet of Money*, vol. I (New York: Merkle Bloom LLC, 2018).

valuable. They are now powerful dematerialized value-transfer vehicles, which, by global consensus, can replace traditional fiduciary money by changing the rules of the game.

Bitcoin has become the standard for the development of innovative solutions, which reduce bureaucracy, increase security and promote global inclusion in a new cryptographic money system whose demand is on the rise.

For this reason, in the digital Darwinism posed by the new economy, central banks need to adapt or die. That is their challenge, but will they accept it?

The Case for a National Cryptocurrency

By Dmitro Nikolaievskyi
Lawyer, Ukrainian National Bar Association

The preservation of a sensible balance between the needs of nation state sovereignties on the one hand, and the blurring of borders for such exchange on the other hand, lies in the implementation of national cryptocurrencies, created by the state, which are not new money, but a new, more effective form of old money. In its most simplified form, we could refer to national cryptocurrencies as tokenized national currencies.

When we talk about national cryptocurrency, its technological implementation is based on the use of cryptographic algorithms, which will provide for stable and safe functioning of the whole of its chain as an independent payment system. This mechanism offers protection from inflation risk, as it will not allow a state currency unit to circulate both in normal and in tokenized form at the same time. For its implementation, the introduction of a national cryptocurrency unit will automatically require the elimination of an equivalent unit of the normal currency.

A national cryptocurrency could be introduced and distributed through a newly created special state authority – a national cryptocurrency exchange. The first and foremost function of this state authority will be to provide regulative, methodological and technical support for the national cryptocurrency system to function. It would also be logical to assume the requirement for a platform for trading crypto-assets between any market subject to national cryptocurrency exchange, thus providing them with both high speed and increased safety of exchange operations, provided by the protection of deposits of exchange participants stored under state warranties.

Tokenized currency units would have new properties, which are not inherent in previous classical non-cash money.

Basic properties would include the possibility of a national cryptocurrency being able to perform functions of a national payment unit functioning outside the banking system, as well as the potential to participate in processes of conclusion and automatization of performance of smart contracts. Their actual potential could be incomparably higher.

Upward Direction of Travel

Various countries are in the process of introducing e-government projects and systems, but the general trend is to widen both their functions and spheres of application. The introduction by countries of their own national cryptocurrencies will allow them to raise the functionality of such systems to a new level. There are already design projects for reliable and high-speed state resources, utilizing blockchain technology.

The interoperability of these state registers, supplemented with a high-tech tool like a national cryptocurrency, would allow the creation of e-government systems for a new generation, allowing minimal practical human intervention in solving routine issues of state administration whilst at the same time increasing the speed, reliability and sustainability and administration of such systems.

Taxing Your Share

But the potential of the new form of money discussed is not limited to this. It could serve as the basis for introducing a brand new concept of taxation, the basic principle of which would shift from "income" taxation to "turnover" taxation. This could lead to the transformation of tax authorities, allowing states to collect taxes from their tax residents in real-time mode at the moment of carrying out taxable activity in real time and with practically no cost.

One further peculiarity of a national cryptocurrency is the fact that countries would be able use it to tax other cryptocurrencies used in their country. This would finally make it possible for all the participants of a cryptocurrency market to work within the legal framework.

The charges on transactions between standard cryptocurrencies such as Bitcoin and state-owned cryptocurrencies would be (in effect) state taxes, which could automatically be deducted by the system when performing transactions. This tax will be more like turnover tax with cost-free administration. This would give the state, which earlier had no clear picture of how a new tokenized economics could be integrated with classical economics, an effective tool for its implementation.

National cryptocurrencies have their own development potential. Having successfully implemented a new economic model, countries will start issuing tax tokens. This will allow a more flexible approach to tax policy. e-Government systems, improved by integration with national cryptocurrencies, will develop into the systems of automatic law enforcement, allowing the exchange of goods, services, intellectual property or labour resources freely and across borders without the necessity of studying the legal framework of this or that jurisdiction and without the need for taxpayers to calculate and pay any type of tax payments on their own. All this will not just be possible, but is essential for the intellectual technological evolution of mankind.

Act Now

This is why it is of essential importance for national states to start implementing brand new technological tools as soon as possible, allowing them to optimally regulate the rapidly growing digital reality with a view to its specific features, to create conditions for its objective development on the basis of a new public consensus.

Regulation and the Future of Blockchain: Which Approach Will Succeed?

By Judie Rinearson
Partner, K&L Gates

One memorable moment at Money2020 USA in 2018 was when Sopnendu Mohanty, the influential Chief Fintech Officer of the Monetary Authority of Singapore, was asked to give one-word replies during his interview:

> *Moderator:* Cryptocurrencies?
>
> *Mohanty:* Over-rated.
>
> *Moderator:* Blockchain?
>
> *Mohanty:* Under-rated.

Mohanty's comment on blockchain flies in the face of those who have argued that the blockchain has become over-hyped and cannot live up to the buzz that surrounds it. Yes, there is no question that the blockchain has been hyped, but this is still early days and the good news is that the significant opportunities presented by the blockchain or, more appropriately, distributed ledger technology (DLT), are now being realized around the world.

As a lawyer, one concern I have is the impact of premature regulation. We know that it's not really the DLT itself that is regulated, but the applications that work on the technology. The most famous application using DLT is Bitcoin and other cryptocurrencies. From my review of global regulatory trends, there are four distinctly different regulatory approaches:

- *Early and distrustful regulation.* As seen in the USA, where regulators early on passed a range of anti-money laundering (AML), licensing and consumer protection laws. US law enforcement has also pursued punitive enforcement actions against DLT startups.

- *Initially open but with later regulation.* More typical of the UK, where regulators have issued some warnings, but overall the Financial Conduct Authority (FCA)'s sandbox has welcomed DLT products. Now, the UK is publicly moving towards more specific regulations.

- *Welcoming regulation.* Jurisdictions that openly welcome new cryptocurrency businesses, with some appropriate regulation, but with favourable tax treatment. Gibraltar and Malta are both jurisdictions that welcome cryptocurrency companies, while establishing a clear, tax-friendly, but not too burdensome regulatory framework.

- *Absent or prohibitive regulation.* There are multiple jurisdictions that have simply been silent in the face of growing investor enthusiasm for DLT products and services. These jurisdictions are taking a "wait-and-see" approach, allowing others to pursue regulation first. Others simply ban such products without considering the consequences.

Ten years from today, which of these approaches will prove to be the most influential and successful? Let's take a closer look.

The USA's Distrustful Approach

The US Treasury Department's Financial Crimes Enforcement Network (FinCEN) issued the first US regulation of cryptocurrencies on 13 March 2013. It caused a global ripple of surprise and anxiety across what was virtually an unregulated industry. It also veered the USA towards a regulatory approach of licensing, regulating and restricting "virtual" or cryptocurrencies. While other countries have issued guidance and established sandboxes, the USA leads in terms of laws and enforcement actions related to cryptocurrencies and initial coin offerings (ICOs):

- FinCEN – administrators and exchangers of virtual currency must register as a money services business, implement an effective

AML compliance programme, and comply with certain customer data collection and retention requirements.

- At the time of writing, 13 US states have issued guidance or regulations requiring certain cryptocurrency businesses to be licensed or regulated; in contrast, 16 states have decided, for now, not to regulate cryptocurrencies.

- Similarly, at the time of writing, the US Securities and Exchange Commission (SEC) has brought 29 enforcement actions against companies engaged in ICOs and other token sales/exchanges deemed to be unlawful sales of unregistered securities. See https://www.sec.gov/spotlight/cybersecurity-enforcement-actions.

As a result of the US regulatory approach, many companies have opted to leave the USA, or to cut back their operations or product features in the USA. Product launches are delayed. Headquarters and employees are transferred to other locations. Only the largest companies have the resources to obtain the necessary licensing.

Have these laws and enforcement actions made US consumers any safer? Many argue that this is not at all clear. With the extent of global communications and technology, US consumers and investors looking to invest can go outside the USA to make the same purchases, although due to legitimate fears of extra-territorial US enforcement (in order to make a purchase from a non-US token issuer or cryptocurrency exchange), many US consumers must establish bank accounts outside the USA, use a virtual private network to hide their location or even lie about their nationality.

On the other hand, there is no doubt that the US regulatory landscape discourages criminal elements from launching shady products in the USA. And it encourages many companies to seek licensing, establish effective AML policies, and provide clear and conspicuous disclosures to consumers.

Watchful and Slowly Moving Towards Regulation

Originally, the UK did not specifically regulate cryptocurrencies, finding that the market did not pose a material risk to monetary or financial stability in the UK. As a result, the blockchain and cryptocurrency market flourished in the UK for many years.

On 19 September 2018, however, a UK Treasury Committee published a report on crypto-assets which concluded that regulation was needed for the "Wild West" crypto-asset market. The UK government and the FCA issued a response in December 2018, noting that they shared "*the Committee's concerns on crypto-assets, including the lack of regulation, minimal consumer protection, and anonymity aiding money laundering*". The government and FCA now plan to hold a series of consultations about how to mitigate these risks. Many anticipate a significant increase in regulation.

Welcoming Regulation

There are jurisdictions that have not only lightly regulated cryptocurrency, but as the market developed, implemented progressive laws that welcomed cryptocurrency companies.

For example, Gibraltar established a well-defined regulatory framework for cryptocurrency exchanges, and also instituted business-friendly taxation terms such as a 10% corporate income tax rate.

Similarly, Malta recognizes cryptocurrencies as a medium of exchange and does not charge value-added tax on transactions exchanging fiat currency for crypto.

Absent Regulation or Prohibition

There is still a long list of countries that have been either silent on cryptocurrency regulation (such as Chile or Portugal) or have simply banned them. Most notably, China's central bank banned financial institutions from handling Bitcoin transactions in 2013, and later banned domestic cryptocurrency exchanges and ICOs in 2017. Other countries that take an outright ban approach include Egypt, Bolivia, Iraq and Pakistan.

Neither of these approaches does their citizens or local businesses any good. Both are short-sighted, but with the pressure of changing and disruptive technologies, perhaps they are the only approaches they could muster.

Conclusion

As the 2018 Report from the US Library of Congress on Regulation of Cryptocurrency around the World[1] indicates, despite disparate tax treatments, there is a fairly narrow range of approaches taken by countries on how to regulate cryptocurrencies. Certainly, regulation of new and emerging payment products is not an easy task. Regulators need to balance the needs of a growing industry with the protection of citizens and investors.

From my perspective, countries that impose quick and early regulation risk stunting economic growth and ceding emerging payment leadership to other locations. Similarly, those who turn a blind eye, or simply ban such products, also impede innovation and ultimately hurt both their consumers and businesses. It is those countries that start the process slowly and cautiously, by setting up task forces, studying the development of laws in other jurisdictions, and consulting with banks and industry, that are more likely to achieve the delicate and rare balance of "good regulation".

---

[1] See https://www.loc.gov/law/help/cryptocurrency/cryptocurrency-world-survey.pdf.

Web 3.0 – The Internet of Value

By Eleftherios Jerry Floros
Entrepreneur and Investor, MoneyDrome Edge Ltd

Blockchain infrastructures and personal data marketplaces are the hallmarks of Web 3.0 and will have the same impact as the Internet did on the interconnectedness of the world. The crucial difference will be that the ever-evolving blockchain protocol will create the "Internet of value", allowing for real-time peer-to-peer transfers of value across the world. We move from the current Web 2.0 paradigm of Google and Facebook, thereby removing the need for intermediates – disintermediation in blockchain parlance – so it will create a network without a reliance on trust, where participants can engage in commerce and business knowing that every transaction is transparent, time-stamped and tamper-proof, validated by a vast global network of distributed ledger technology that is updated concurrently and immutably.

Getting Smart

The use of "smart contracts" will enable many business practices to be simplified. That is, by the use of contractual obligations that can be coded into the protocol so that a transaction is insured, by virtue of a public traceable record that can be verified at any time, but cannot be reversed or corrupted in any way. More importantly, the exchange of value – meaning payment – will be instantaneous and irreversible, fostering a new global trade for goods or services. Technology will benefit society, as opposed to today's economic system that primarily benefits the corporate world.

There is, however, a challenge in that today's blockchain is slow and cumbersome. The blockchain protocol uses a "public key" and a "private key" to validate a transaction, which makes it difficult for the general public to use blockchain at all. These challenges have been overcome by brilliant visionaries such as Vitalik Buterin, who developed a new blockchain called "Ethereum", a protocol that uses "smart contracts" that validate transactions and ensure that all parties get their fair share.

One example of where smart contracts are starting to be used as a "means of exchange" is the music industry. Traditionally in the music industry, the record label of a band decided who got paid and when. This created many problems for the bands signed with a record label, because the latter would receive payment for every record sold immediately, whereas the band itself would have to wait months – or even years – to get paid. Using smart contracts, all parties get paid instantaneously for every music item sold, thus creating a fairer system that benefits all the parties involved as well as the entire music industry.

Developing the Next Generation

As promising as Ethereum may be, it will require many iterations before it becomes useful for the average person. At present, there is massive global competition to develop the next version of blockchain – one that is faster, better and can be used by anyone. Blockchain is governed by the protocol which ensures that every transaction is validated independently and cannot be reversed. As blockchain is open source, it can be improved continuously by coders around the world without any controlling authority.

New global commercial networks will be able to conduct business and exchange goods and services, bypassing the corporate titans of today. Global giants such as Amazon, Apple and Google will be forced to rethink their business models that put corporate profits and investors' return on investment at the forefront instead of the consumer that buys their products. Technology will open an entire new dimension for global trade and commerce as goods and services will be exchangeable without the involvement of an entire network of third parties or intermediaries. By removing all obstacles to global trade, new business models will emerge that do not exist today.

Robotics on Blockchains

At present, there is talk about the creation of "autonomous economic agents" (AEAs), which are value-creating entities on the blockchain that are devoid of human interaction and legally binding. To demystify the complexity of AEAs, these "entities" will be able to scour the global blockchain network for market inefficiencies – such as supply and demand – and profit by taking advantage of any price differences. In short, they are money-making machines that will transform wealth creation the world over.

Adopting Stability

All blockchain transactions are settled – by default – in cryptocurrency, which poses the next challenge. Using a decentralized and borderless digital currency, the value of which is determined solely by the market forces of supply and demand, makes it highly volatile and doing business difficult. During the transaction, the value of the exchange will be fixed and both parties to the transaction will receive their part of the exchange. However, following the transaction, that value may have either gone up or down significantly, and herein lies the challenge. If the value has gone up, the buyer/seller will be happy, but if not, one party to the transaction will be unhappy and may feel cheated.

The solution is the new "stablecoins" that would counter the effects of supply and demand that affect the value of crypto. However, this defeats the purpose of a cryptocurrency as, by being pegged to fiat currencies, it is by default part of the very society it is trying to change: another paradox of payments.

Blockchain – An Elixir for Anti-Money Laundering?

By Bhagvan Kommadi
CEO, Quantica Computacao

Introduction

Two Harvard Business School professors compared blockchain to Internet messaging and, while it may not be disruptive, it represents breakthrough strategic thinking from a technology perspective. It has the potential to completely rewrite industry business models, rewiring the workflows and changing the way we arrange, record and verify transactions. Blockchain systems can provide the basic infrastructure and tools for various areas within risk management and anti-money laundering (AML). The blockchain platform facilitates faster client onboarding and implementation of know your customer (KYC) compliance.

Cryptocurrencies

A cryptocurrency is a digital or virtual currency that utilizes cryptography to verify, make, approve and control its exchange transactions through the blockchain. It can be traded for different monetary forms, items and administrations. The whole system is utilized to screen and confirm both the production of local tokens through mining, and the exchange of tokens between clients. Mining is the procedure by which monetary exchanges are confirmed and added to accounts in general record and blockchain. Bitcoin is the first digital money which came to open notice in 2009; other digital forms of money include Ether, Ripple and Litecoin. As of late, economists, central bankers and monetary experts have communicated their reservations on the "fate" of this form of currency.

Blockchain

A blockchain is a distributed ledger which provides direct transactions between two entities – the originator and the beneficiary – and the verification of their credentials. The blockchain can issue a digital certificate for verification. "Miners" receive an award when a block is accepted. The proof-of-work process consists of checking a nonce value in the block to abide by the mining condition. A nonce is an integer which has the block ID, data and hash of the latest block. A chain of blocks can be created with every block having a link to the previous block's hash. A blockchain framework keeps track of parties which have control of, or access to, a company's records and keeps the data organized. It consists of rights, commitments and obligations identified with those records, and the representation of the transactional records. The framework provides information access and visibility to members and regulators.

A typical blockchain platform will have a smart contract engine, business tools, developer application programming interface, and capabilities to connect and message different blockchain protocols. A blockchain implementation which can connect to different blockchains is useful in wealth management. This implementation is valuable in trading, where you need to connect to different exchanges having multiple blockchain implementations. Blockchain can be used for making payments, trading, loan processing and auditing trails for regulators. Blockchain can consist of modules and components related to risk management and AML to help financial firms.

Regulations

In a regulations-based blockchain framework, members – whether national banks, corporates, private banks or some other related entities – will most likely offer data on all exchanges by adding to the all-encompassing appropriated record. Techniques used in the regulations framework tend to recognize and examine the transaction information in complete dimension. Regulators will screen the action of numerous dimensions and decide the danger of a particular exchange directly, in a substantially more logical and important way.

There will be no compelling reason to build and keep an enormously large framework when blockchain is implemented as a distributed ledger. The framework will be refreshed for regulatory experts of worldwide dimensions in an exceptionally opportune way. Every transaction exchanged is checked and approved by a concerned person taking an interest in the framework, without the requirement for unified oversight. The transactions can be recorded utilizing private encrypted keys by both the originator and the recipient. The substantial transactions exchanged among organizations and corporates will be carefully recorded in the blockchain regulatory framework.

Anti-Money Laundering

Tax evasion is the procedure whereby cash from illicit transactions is shown as originating from a lawful source. The most straightforward way to do this is to record these illicit gains as being deals made by a genuine business. Such exercises are exceptionally difficult to spot without leading an intensive review. The smart contracts which are part of the blockchain-based AML framework would almost certainly utilize inbuilt techniques to mechanize money laundering extortion identification. The framework would have the capacity to identify and warn of any suspicious transactions. At the point an exchange was made, it would be examined by the system and the government. The transactions involving digital currencies and other forms of currency authorized will also be examined.

Identity Management

"Advanced personality" is one of numerous difficulties with cryptocurrency, web commerce and digital money applications. Online identity administration requires an expanded dimension of security conventions to anticipate misrepresentation and stay consistent with The Bank Secrecy Act of 1970 (BSA), also known as the Currency and Foreign Transactions Reporting Act, is a US law. With cryptographic checks, delicate customer information could be discovered by a money-related foundation to distinguish the individual applying for credit, opening a record, or getting their personal data.

Advanced personality upgrades can enable money-related foundations to meet the consistently changing KYC and client due diligence (CDD) requirements, while at the same time diminishing the expenses related to actualizing a strong KYC programme. A blockchain-based KYC framework will utilize sensible ingenuity, as to the opening and support of each record, as to the opening and support of each record. It will be utilized to know the fundamentals of each client and have a concerned specialist for individual follow-up.

The CDD framework improves the exchange and action profiles for every client's foreseen movements. It consists of examining, evaluating and reviewing dangers related to the client or the record and recording discoveries. Blockchain utilizing smart contracts can radically decrease manual procedures in regard to CDD procedures, such as onboarding, reconnaissance and revealing KYC surveys, personality and record possession confirmation, sanctions screening and hazard appraisal.

AML and CDD issues are related to the high level of false positives for suspicious activities – currently between 90% and 95%. Another reason for the high number of false positives, as observed from Finance Industry Regulation Authority test discoveries, is the poor quality of information and inadequate value-based data. Subsequently, money-related organizations must spend huge assets and labour processing various alarms for authentic monetary exchanges. Another qualification of circulated record innovation for CDD procedures is the arrangement of specific points of interest in correlation with existing frameworks concerning security and versatility against a digital assault or framework breakdown. Compared to existing frameworks, advanced encryption strategies could offer an extra layer of assurance to pools of data stored on blockchain.

Biometric-based identification using blockchain offers multiple applications such as Secretary of State business enlistment records, monetary administrative oversight, checking high dollar exchanges, higher-risk clients, AML/KYC account onboarding and affirming that web accounts are attached to known people. Blockchain identity can help speculative firms limit their introduction to different AML/KYC administrative commitments. It can also be useful in deploying a successful onboarding process in high-risk illegal and tax-avoidance geographic areas.

Facilitating Online Crypto-Payments Now and in the Future

By Evgeniya Mykulyak
COO, B2Broker

The growing demand for online payments using cryptocurrencies has undoubtedly made its mark on the payment industry and, as a result, we have seen the emergence of more and more specialist payment service providers (PSPs) to cater for these needs. These advancements in the industry have made the requirement for a cryptocurrency payment gateway a necessity for many businesses. Further developments in this area are set to reshape the payments ecosystem and the future of money will be transformed.

The Emergence of Cryptocurrency Payment Platforms

Cryptocurrency emerged in 2009 with Bitcoin, the first decentralized currency. The aim was to create a secure and anonymous means of transferring value but, as further developments quickly unfolded, it soon paved the way for a whole new value transference. The last decade has seen technological developments in this sector progress at an unprecedented rate, and the huge popularity of cryptocurrencies has impacted on many areas, especially the payments sector.

Until recently, online business enterprises and merchants were limited to the more traditional methods of payment, such as credit/debit cards and various payment providers such as PayPal, Neteller, Skrill, etc., but now – with the increasing demand for crypto-payments – the payments industry has moved forward in leaps and bounds.

Growth in Demand for Online Payments

The growth in demand for online payments using cryptocurrencies has greatly impacted the payments industry and created a demand for new, specialist PSPs to address the growing need for faster and more cost-effective solutions compared with the service offered by traditional PSPs.

The financial benefits are simply too big for companies to ignore, and it is clear that this will continue as blockchain continues to establish itself in the future of payments. These kinds of solutions will be even more in demand.

There are several benefits of allowing customers to purchase with cryptocurrencies. They offer existing customers a new method of payment, offer access to new customers who wish to use cryptos to purchase goods or services, and reduce costs associated with more traditional payment methods like credit cards. Accepting crypto-payments also offers customers discretion when it comes to payments, which are, in turn, secure and stored on the blockchain ledger indefinitely.

Current Trends and Payment Regulation

Cryptocurrencies, as we know, have undergone turbulent times in the last year or so and the industry continues to bear the brunt of recent events. One such event was the Visa and Mastercard implementation of a ban on Forex, binary, crypto brokers and initial coin offering transactions in October 2018. New restrictions and increasing anti-money laundering concerns have resulted in crypto being a heavily regulated area with higher operating costs, thorough KYC checks and fund validation for all those involved.

These factors, and regulation in particular, have created continued uncertainty within the industry. In the crypto space, each country has different regulations and it is quite different from the regulation of the traditional banking institutions that we are accustomed to.

But it is still early days and the industry is still finding its feet, so it is not very different from other industries which are experiencing similar growing pains. The crypto industry still has to mature, but I am certain that we will continue to see many positive developments in this area. There are many big players already in the market who would not have invested in this industry on a whim.

One prominent industry leader recently declared: "We're two years away from everyone using Bitcoin…people will have almost no use for cash in just five years and only criminals will want to use it as Bitcoin and cryptocurrency transactions can be tracked."

Certainly, we will see more changes and the necessity for more stability and security where payments are concerned, but the potential for growth in this industry is huge. Recent events have contributed to reshaping the payments ecosystem and will continue to do so. I believe the future of money will be transformed. This is just the beginning.

A New Law for Derivatives Markets and the Use of Smart Contracts

By Omar Bairan
General Counsel, Banco Santa Cruz

The objective of this chapter is to highlight general concepts of applicable regulations in relevant financial derivatives markets and how the use of smart derivatives through distributed ledger technology (e.g. blockchain) can be beneficial to, or useful for, derivatives market participants to automate deal execution and, at the same time, comply with such regulations. The content of this chapter is not exhaustive and it does not constitute a legal opinion.

Regulation of the Financial Derivatives Market in the European Union

In November 2007, the Markets in Financial Instruments Directive (2004/39/EC) (MiFID) entered into effect in the European Union (EU). The objective of MiFID was to improve the competitiveness of financial markets in the EU through the creation of a single market for investment services and activities, seeking to ensure investor protection.

MiFID included important changes in areas such as conduct of business, market organization and market transparency. Regulation (EU) No. 648/2012, European Market Infrastructure Regulation (EMIR), refers to "over-the-counter" (OTC) derivatives, central counterparties and trade repositories. The objective of EMIR was to stabilize European markets through the requirement of stricter reporting obligations and a greater standardization of OTC derivatives.

EMIR requires the reporting of information for exchange-traded derivatives and for OTC derivatives. EMIR refers to the legal entity identifier (LEI), which is a unique alphanumeric code that identifies counterparties, central counterparties, brokers and beneficiaries. This regulation also refers to the unique trade identifier (UTI), which is used to identify specific trades.

Both the new Directive on Markets in Financial Instruments (MiFID II) (Directive 2014/65/EU), which repealed Directive 2004/39/EC (MiFID), and the Regulation on Markets in Financial Instruments (MiFIR), which modified the EMIR, were published in the *Official Journal of the European Union* in June 2014. These new regulations allow fewer exemptions than MiFID and are applicable to a larger number of market participants and products. The new requirements include increased transparency through detailed reporting and auditing of transactions.

Regulation of the Financial Derivatives Market in the USA

The Dodd–Frank Wall Street Reform and Consumer Protection Act of 2010 introduced relevant changes in matters such as consumer protection, minimum capital requirements, as well as payment, clearing and settlement supervision.

Some of the provisions that can be found in the Dodd–Frank Act regarding derivatives trading include: (i) increased transparency, requiring market participants to register either with the Commodities Futures Trading Commission (CFTC) or the Securities and Exchange Commission (SEC); and (ii) counterparty risk and systemic risk reduction through the use of a central clearing model.

Risks Created by Central Counterparties in the Financial Derivatives Market

Similar to the law of conservation of energy in physics, risks are never eliminated, only transformed. This means that the increased transparency provided by central counterparties (CCPs) may come at a high cost. In periods of low market correlation (i.e. when risk-mitigation strategies are not really needed), CCPs are excellent at dissipating shocks and redistributing risks. During periods of high market correlation, CCPs may exacerbate economic shocks acting as channels for contagion in the market. In such cases, a CCP may present a loss waterfall similar to a collateralized debt obligation (CDO), offering a false sense of security in the market.

Considering the presence of information asymmetries, the parties would be exposed to the lemons problem,[1] resulting in the mispricing of risk and potential market abuse by market participants with privileged information.

A proposed alternative would be a decentralized system that allows market participants to enter into trades directly, while keeping the benefits of increased transparency and expedited settlement.

Smart Contracts

In a paper published in 1997 by Nick Szabo entitled "Formalizing and Securing Relationships on Public Networks",[2] he proposed the use of robust cryptographic protocols allowing the creation of computer protocols that could operate as contractual clauses, binding the parties of a transaction and reducing the chances of any one of such parties defaulting on its obligations.

The financial cryptographer Ian Grigg introduced the concept of Ricardian contracts, describing them as contracts that are readable by both machines and humans. Also, Associate Professor of Law at the University of Colorado Law School, Harry Surden contended that the "contract-as-data" approach is not just a theoretical construct and that the parties to a contract can express their agreed terms and conditions using highly structured data, not just written words.

In many aspects, smart contracts are very similar to traditional contracts. The parties must decide the terms and conditions to apply and must memorialize them in some written form, which may then be executed depending on future events that may be foreseeable or not. If one of the parties defaults on its contracted obligations, there may be an additional set of clauses that would apply in such cases.

Smart contracts differ from traditional contracts in that they are written in computer code and can allow for automated execution of the terms and conditions agreed by the parties. Also, smart contracts can incorporate external information using third-party providers, called oracles. Oracles allow the smart contract to interact with real-world data and to evaluate the execution of the obligations. Additionally, oracles can deliver decisions made by another person, different from the parties, such as a private dispute resolution service.

A distinction must be made between a smart legal contract and smart contract code. A smart legal contract refers to the actual legally enforceable contract that is represented, completely or in parts, by computer code. Smart contract code refers to the code designed to execute conditional tasks that may be part of a smart legal contract.

---

[1] G.A. Akerlof, "The Market for 'Lemons': Quality Uncertainty and Market Mechanism" (1970), *Quarterly Journal of Economics* 84(3), 488–500.

[2] N. Szabo, "Formalizing and Securing Relationships on Public Networks" (1997), *First Monday*, 2, 1.

Limitations of Smart Contracts

Some traditional contracts or clauses may be too complex to be expressed in computer code. In some cases, some room for interpretability may be positive for the parties.

Consider the case of the Napoleonic Civil Code of 1804, which still applies in many parts of the world with relatively minor changes. Article 1385 refers to the obligation of the owner of an animal to repair any damages caused by it. In current times, judges have interpreted this article, extending it to the obligation to repair damages caused by inanimate things, such as motor vehicles, even though these didn't exist in 1804.

Implementation of Financial Derivatives Smart Contracts Using Blockchain

Many of the operational clauses present in derivatives agreements are suitable for automation using smart contracts, and these can be implemented through blockchain technology, using a Turing-complete language.

Considering the complexity of many derivatives contracts and the limitations of current technologies, an immediate solution could be obtained with the use of the external model of smart contracts, in which the legal contract maintains its current form and is executable through smart contract code.

Blockchain technology is proposed for implementing smart derivatives contracts. When evaluating the architecture of the blockchain, compliance with regulations must be considered. The immutability of the data is a natural advantage, and reading access for supervisory entities would be critical. Another thing to consider is data privacy regulation and security issues. Cryptographic security is constantly evolving, so the level of security obtained in the blockchain must be considered.

PayTech and Blockchain: Adjusting for Security and Risk

By Georgios Raikos
CEO, Talk on Strategy Ltd

Risk Estimates Rise Out of Proportion

In cyberspace, the risk of a security attack is increasing by the hour. The following year-on-year statistics, released for the period ending December 2018, paint a grim picture for the effectiveness of cyber-crime and the growing attack surface:

- Attacks to corporate web servers grew by 50%.

- 10% of URLs on a global scale carried some type of malware.

- Ransomware hit 1 in 3 of mobile devices in just one year.

- Malicious emails increased by another 50%, with phishing attacks still providing very high success yields for cybercriminals.

- Crypto-mining/crypto-jacking continued to infect millions of victims' CPUs, usually via browser-based coin miners with injected scripts.

- Attack groups became more consolidated and aimed at large – even sovereign – targets, with the aim of destroying the infrastructure. At times, their attack vector included 50+ simultaneous targets, making it almost impossible to defend.

- *WannaMine*, a sister malware of *WannaCry* – employing the *MSH.Bluwimps* crypto-jacking script – successfully entered large enterprise networks with the dual scope of DDoS attacks and near 100% CPU crypto-mining utilization.

The Decentralized Nature of Blockchain is Also its "Achilles Heel"

The initial crypto-mining of blockchain has attracted diversified uses, with a somewhat inadequate proof of concept. PayTech and FinTech have already made heavy use of blockchain technology in search of ways to spread the single data-rest-point and the risk of data breach via the high level of granularity embedded in blockchain. PricewaterhouseCoopers, during 2018, named blockchain "*the next evolutionary jump in business process technology*". However, in this new environment, the historical track record is neither long enough nor rich enough to provide actual statistics regarding the level of risk attached to blockchain implementations.

Every blockchain relies on nodes/endpoints, both as transaction blocks as well as appended hash records accounting for the integrity of the blockchain as a whole. This decentralized nature of blockchain is the system's "Achilles heel" at the same time.

Blockchain nodes often participate as endpoints within one or more IoT (Internet of Things) ecosystems. Endpoints are persistently under attack and can be corrupted by malware. Such destructive malware can infiltrate the blockchain via one of its nodes and corrupt the distributed database (e.g. the accounting ledger of a bank or the payments transaction log of a crypto-coin wallet provider). Encryption is a good way to make the breached data unreadable by outsiders, but corrupted data cannot be read by legitimate users either. At the end of such an attack, the blockchain will either have to "hard fork" (divide into two live versions) into one rogue chain and a second legitimate one (if possible), or simply "die" (either in value or by the sheer number of users massively abandoning the platform).

Cyber-Insurance Against Cyber-Attack

The insurance industry has stepped in to lend a hand when the data breach is too large to contain or the "brand shake" too big to ignore. Cyber-security premiums are very high, though, precisely because both the cost of a data breach and its probability are very high. There are ways to monitor risk and adjust insurance premiums in real time. Yet the adoption of similar methodologies across industry verticals is still not broad enough and standards have some way to go before consolidating into working documents for regulation.

Regarding blockchain, the only way to provide effective cyber-security against unknown breaches that threaten the value of the system is to be able to monitor the level of intrinsic risk within the blockchain in real time. The strategic vantage points for future blockchain implementations are:

- adjust cyber-insurance premiums proportionally to risk, or
- modify the structure of the blockchain in order to defend against attack.

Blockchain and the IoT

Taking for granted that every endpoint can be attacked both at the physical and virtual level, it is of particular importance to be able to safeguard all blockchain platforms that operate on top of these nodes from attacks that threaten blockchain integrity and, therefore, blockchain intrinsic value.

In the IoT (machine) world, we can view the hardware part of endpoints that carries intelligent firmware using heuristics and sandbox technology to sense an incoming attack, as intelligent devices, able to shut down or "pull-off the grid" before water-holing the contamination to their adjacent nodes. In practice, the low-level code sitting as firmware on the nodes should be universal and patchable across the entire blockchain, so that effective defence can be deployed and maintained at all times. Considering the market fragmentation, the hardware devices and the vendors that already participate in thousands of live IoT environments, it seems a little late to level up universal standards upon which regulators can enforce compliance. In that sense, the market has fully accepted unknown levels of systemic risk on the promise of quick profit and narrow slices of marketing strategy typically preferred by investing shareholders.

The "Cognitive Blockchain" Perspective

In a novel proposition for future blockchain structures, machine learning could be an integral part of the platform. The scope of machine learning algorithms, running as scripts on top of the original source code on all kinds of participating nodes, would be to feed the "intelligence" of the system as it grows in time and through time in order to become a "cognitive blockchain". This resembles the neuron structure within the human brain, which not only passes data but also absorbs information in order to "learn".

Within such a "cognitive blockchain", nodes will be able to "perceive themselves" and exchange between them crucial information about the integrity of the system. In other words, blockchain contracts will be made if both the participating nodes perceive the transaction as mutually beneficial. Otherwise, the transaction will keep delaying till further nodes downstream finally decide that the transaction is acceptable by the ecosystem's existing cognitive capacity (i.e. legitimate and non-threatening to all accepting nodes).

Letting Go – a Single Blockchain Economy

From the investors' point of view, only one thing is clear: capital has to keep flowing into R&D and university classes, where fresh minds will perceive their own interests and rules for "a single blockchain economy".

Someday in the near future, we may feel bold enough to let the algorithms produce the artificial intelligence that will drive blockchain, which in turn will run anything from public infrastructure to the global economy or yet more complex functions, like governance and socio-political systems. In such a highly decentralized environment, legislation and regulation – as we know them today – may no longer have reason to exist.

Under the overarching cybernetics dogma, "purpose, intention and function" of the system will have to juxtapose in order to best serve the human community. The risk though still persists that things can go completely wrong with no-one to blame and nowhere to roll-back. At the end of the day, the element of trust, which is so much valued and yet so rare among us humans, will somehow have to be instilled in such a cognitive blockchain, so that "systemic choices" will also be "ethical ones".

Cryptocommodities: An Essential Element of Decentralized Payments

By Steven Dryall
CEO, Incipient Industries Inc.

Decentralized payment systems have revolutionized how people and organizations can transfer value. To fully realize the functionality of a decentralized digital economy, we need to ensure an equilibrium of that value. Cryptocurrencies have enabled decentralized value transfer, but where does the value come from and how can that value be assured?

Cryptocommodities are an essential element for bridging the gap between traditional and decentralized economies. Crypto-commodities contribute to digital economic stability while maintaining an optimized level of decentralization for functionality.

A cryptocommodity is defined here as a decentralized digital asset that is used to represent the value of a standardized physical asset. Cryptocommodities can be exchanged in open markets but are also convertible to a correlated physical asset at a fixed-rate quantity. Quantity is measured in units which can be based on weight, volume, size or any standardized metric.

Some simple examples could include: one digital coin equal to one physical ounce of a certain metal; one digital coin equal to one physical litre of a specific liquid; one digital coin equal to one physical gemstone of certain characteristics; or one digital coin equal to a physical cookie, of a certain flavour, perhaps chocolate chip.

A cryptocommodity is an asset-based cryptocurrency,[1] applied to a specific type of asset with homogenous value. Specificity is important, as is consistency in the nature of the associated asset type. Assets with varying quality parameters can exist as a cryptocommodity so long as a base conversion value is established. The base value can be used for pricing of quality variants using ratios.

Expanding on the example: one coin equal to one litre of milk would have different resource requirements than one coin equal to one litre of juice. The exchange value of these two different coins would also be affected by the markets in which they are traded.

Separation of digital and physical assets with direct value association creates market opportunities. Value correlation enables manageable metrics. Cryptocommodities can exist for asset pools of any type. Asset pools can be distributed geographically.

Deployment

A cryptocommodity achieves viability through a specialized application of the three pillars of a viable cryptocurrency (Figure 1). The cryptocurrency software is the technology that enables the functionality of open-market exchange. The community is built by the users of both digital and physical assets. The liquidity is provided through open markets but also the conversion of the cryptocommodity to the physical asset. The conversion uses a predetermined value established during digital asset initialization.

Asset Initialization

The deployment of a cryptocommodity requires the creation of a cryptocurrency system combined with the administration of direct conversion of digital assets to physical assets. The creation of the digital asset requires predetermined quantities for both digital and underlying physical asset quantities. The technical requirements of the system must meet the criteria of a decentralized crypto-currency system to ensure stability of the digital asset. Provider(s)

---

[1] *WealthTech*, Chapter 5: "Blockchain Applications in Asset and Wealth Management".

national currencies (e.g. USD, CAD, GBP, etc.) or other physical assets (e.g. gold, silver, jellybeans, cookies, etc.).

Physical asset conversion is typically facilitated by entities that are distinct from those who handle equivalent asset conversion. Physical asset conversion is often handled by the source of the asset. Equivalent asset conversion is typically handled by currency exchanges.

Asset Redemption

Asset redemption refers to when a cryptocommodity is converted to the physical asset it represents. This is akin to redeeming a voucher, since the digital asset is a convertible claim to a physical asset.

Conversion Steps

There are specific steps involved with acquiring or redeeming a cryptocommodity. To complete the transaction, steps in the process have points of access that may vary in nature.

Points of Exchange

Cryptocommodities can be exchanged for other assets based on their inherent value when compared to their physical asset counterpart. The nature of this access point is determined by the type of desired exchange. Exchanging national currency for a cryptocommodity may require a different access point than the exchange for another cryptocurrency.

Points of Redemption

A cryptocommodity is redeemed when it is exchanged for the physical asset it represents. Redemption of a cryptocommodity requires the fulfilment of an order that includes delivery of the asset. Order fulfilment is handled by a redemption provider. The

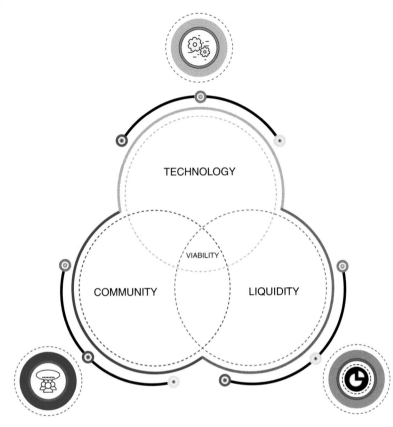

Figure 1: Three pillars of a viable cryptocurrency

of physical asset conversion must be established before the initial distribution of digital assets.

Asset Conversion

Digital assets can be converted into two types of assets: physical assets or equivalent assets. Physical asset conversion is when the cryptocommodity is exchanged for the physical asset that it represents. Equivalent asset conversion is when the cryptocommodity is exchanged for a value other than the physical asset, such as digital assets (e.g. Bitcoin, Litecoin, DASH, etc.), redemption of a cryptocommodity also potentially involves the return of the digital asset to the initial issuing entity and affects the overall economy of the cryptocommodity.

Redemption Providers

A redemption provider provides special liquidity for a cryptocommodity. Redemption providers are physical asset exchangers who directly support the fixed-rate digital asset to physical asset conversion. A redemption provider's commitment to the exchange of the digital asset is generally synchronous with the onset of the digital asset. This collateralizes the digital asset while also allowing the type of velocity and liquidity associated with cryptocurrencies.

If a redemption provider is a single entity or solitary exchanger, then the collateral is centralized. Centralization increases risk of losing viability. Multiple redemption providers increase access to the conversion process in addition to increasing the viability potential.

Redemption Administration

Administration of redemption ensures there are redemption points in place to provide liquidity for the cryptocommodity beyond open asset markets. The amount of established redemption administration will affect the viability of a cryptocommodity.

Redemption administrators are responsible for redemption enforcement. Redemption administration can be handled by one or more entities, each with distinction in their capabilities. Redemption administration with strict conversion enforcement is beneficial to hypercollateralization and is required for viability.

Hypercollateralization

A network of redemption providers increases viability and can lead to hypercollateralization. Hypercollateralization is achieved when a network of redemption providers supporting a cryptocommodity has more combined units of inventory available for redemption than there are digital asset units in open circulation. When a cryptocommodity has more physical assets available for exchange than there are digital assets in circulation, it is "hypercollateralized". Hypercollateralized cryptocommodities offer the best stability and confidence for users.

Summary

Cryptocommodities provide price stability in decentralized economic environments. Where other categories of digital assets may be difficult to analyse or quantify in value, cryptocommodities provide manageable metrics and analytics through their direct correlation with a specific underlying asset. Because cryptocommodities are tied to a fixed physical asset, it is possible to achieve transaction types that may not otherwise be possible with other cryptocurrencies or tokens. These are unique capabilities that make them an essential element of decentralized payments in the global economy.

Payments in Practice

5

PAYMENTS IN PRACTICE

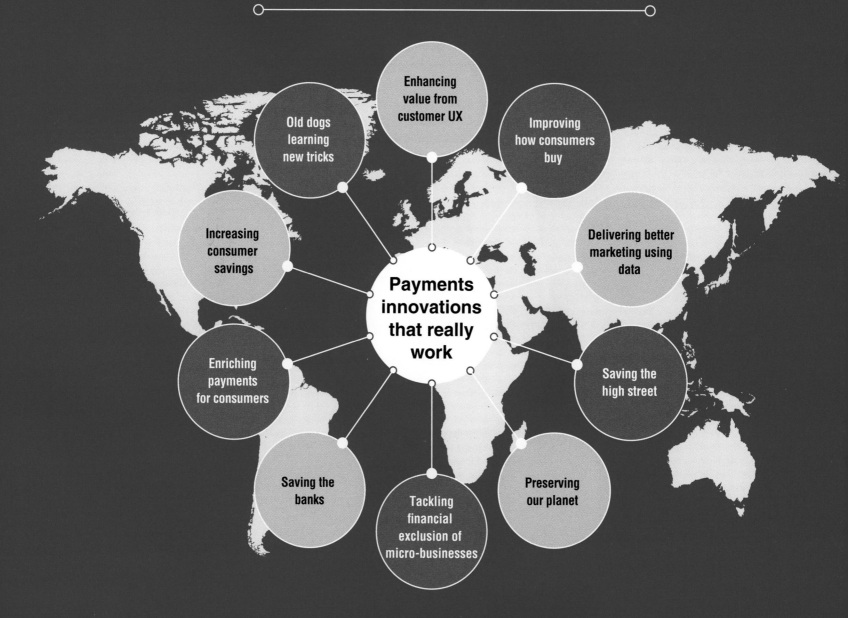

Payments innovations that really work

- Enhancing value from customer UX
- Old dogs learning new tricks
- Improving how consumers buy
- Increasing consumer savings
- Delivering better marketing using data
- Enriching payments for consumers
- Saving the high street
- Saving the banks
- Tackling financial exclusion of micro-businesses
- Preserving our planet

Executive Summary

Armed with a colourful historical, technological and regulatory backdrop from the first four parts of the book, this part provides insights into examples of payments innovations that really work.

A seasoned executive opens with case study-derived insights about the changes taking place across the spectrum of payments, for the benefit of consumers. The way in which mobile self-checkout can help retailers enhance the shopping experience at the point of sale, and quite possibly as a result save the high street, is described by a payment service provider marketer. While Alipay and WeChat Pay have got a lot of attention recently, a new arrival, UnionPay Quick Pass, has been making the headlines recently, and two FinTech academics explain why, and what this means for the whole payments ecosystem in the world's largest country.

By applying some revolutionary thinking, an investor and sustainability expert describes a fresh approach to preserving our planet using payments and cash-for-carbon. An influential operations and legal specialist then outlines how changes in payments have led to widespread adoption of some great products, and how the best are yet to come. A dose of realism is injected from an entrepreneur with experience of how payments innovation in asset finance came so near to, yet so far from, transforming saving rates in India. A data specialist then helps us understand the impact of the network effect in payments, and how overlaying data-driven insights enables more effective brand marketing at the point of purchase.

By seeing the customer experience as a continuum, and not neglecting how consumers feel in the after-purchase phase, we can provide a better experience that drives great value for the merchant, according to our next author, a leading marketer. A PayTech visionary then introduces the concept of "payments touchpoints" and explores how, in an open banking-enabled world, account aggregators will prevent banks from becoming providers of commodities. Next, an evangelist for change describes how consumers will in future benefit from rich insights into the impact of their purchasing decisions before the purchase is made, through the integration of personal financial management into the user journey. And we conclude by hearing from a product leader how in Africa, a fresh approach can help microbusinesses become integrated into the financial system, and in this way help solve problems of financial exclusion in the world's poorest continent.

The Perspective of a Passionate Payments CEO

By Andrea Dunlop
Chairwomen of the Emerging Payments Association, Angel Investor and Non-Executive Director; formerly CEO, Merchant Acquiring (part of the Paysafe Group)

Change Seen from Inside a Payments Company

As the Divisional CEO of a global payments business, I see payments as a highly creative sector and it is this creativity that is driving rapid change. I see new FinTech players emerging to deploy technology that reduces friction, adds convenience, resolves pain points and creates great consumer experiences. I see intermediaries disappearing or getting marginalized, unless they discover new ways of adding value. And I am seeing how scale and network effects in this brave new world can be a source of competitive advantage and sustainable growth.

Meanwhile, new business models are emerging that come from technology-driven innovation and profit-driven entrepreneurs, blurring the lines between banks and FinTechs, PayTechs and RegTechs, challenger banks and bank challengers. Companies providing new digital banking solutions – such as Monzo, Starling and Revolut – are being built with a mobile-first approach, while some traditional players are struggling to keep up with these new consumer-led propositions.

Growth and Failure

Hundreds of new companies have entered the payments market in the last decade. Many have business models dependent on continuous investment to support consumer acquisition in what has become a very highly competitive space. Not all of these businesses will survive, as they will not be able to navigate the obstacles ahead and find a path to profitability. Some will thrive and succeed on their own, while others will be acquired by traditional players to bolster their own offerings.

The Open Banking Secret Driving Change

I believe that open banking is our best opportunity to enable money to be moved cost-efficiently in real time and at near zero cost, allowing all users to benefit.

Open banking, and the new standards associated with it, requires banks to share data with third-party providers (TPPs) and enable them to initiate payments from their customers' accounts. This will transform the entire payments landscape. With open application programming interfaces (APIs) deployed within the open banking ecosystem, consumers can access multiple accounts through a single service provider, making it easier for them to manage and track their finances. This changes how consumers access their accounts and make everyday payments.

Changes to the Value Chain

We will see new intermediaries providing a one-stop shop for connectivity to all the banks. I believe this new ecosystem could undermine the major card schemes. But the business model for account information service providers (AISPs) is challenging. They need creative business models to generate revenue, because someone has to pay the company to cover its costs and generate a profit (albeit investor funds can support a company for some time). Either the business charges the consumer directly for the new service, or the company is rewarded by cross-selling another product to that consumer.

Meanwhile, open banking will help large online retailers and companies in niche high-risk verticals. If they have high charge backs and high decline rates, or are just looking to reduce their payment processing costs, then companies may take advantage of the new regulation to achieve these objectives.

Payment Initiation Makes Consumers Into Winners

By enabling TPPs to provide payment initiation services, the management of money is automatically completed through intelligent software. This requires banks to adapt in order to remain relevant, rather than becoming "dumb account managers managing dumb pipes". Open banking will have a wider impact than just in payments, particularly in how we use our financial data. What will be interesting to see is if the big tech players like Amazon, Apple and Google look to exploit this opportunity, along with the likes of Alipay.

It seems to me that we are finally in the era where the customer wins. The new FinTechs have seen the opportunity to be entirely customer-centric and the incumbents are waking up to it. For example, consumers now browse physical stores but then may purchase online from a cheaper or more convenient retailer. In many stores the browsing experience, the queue to the checkout or accessing customer service isn't easy – or acceptable to most consumers. In a multi-channel world, consumer choice is greater than ever and it's no longer necessary to visit a physical store to buy most things. For many retail products, shoppers can also "click and collect" from multiple outlets using their phone or computer and track progress of deliveries in real time online or on mobile. Conventional retailing no longer matches up to what consumers need or expect, and as a result, traditional retailers are suffering.

With a good example of what's to come, M&S Bank became the first mortgage provider to enable open banking-assisted mortgage applications. Customers will no longer need to source and supply copies of bank statements to support their mortgage application. Using the open banking-assisted journey, this documentation will be immediately and securely provided via an open banking

platform, making the process not only simpler and easier, but also faster and more secure.

Simplifying what is a painful and bureaucratic process for all consumers, open banking has the means to transform consumer experience across all of payments.

Raising the Retail Game

I believe the consumer experience in a physical store needs to be improved and the friction of payment needs to be removed to help reverse this trend. Retail brands need an omni-channel mindset, such as those of Apple and Nike, that have put this at the heart of their in-store experience.

One way of delivering a positive experience is by offering a personalized touch. One of Nike's latest in-store innovations allows you to customize a shoe in-store and pick it up within an hour. Such value-adding experiences allow stores to differentiate themselves and build loyalty. Engaging the consumer through personalized and relevant experiences is the key to attracting and keeping consumers happy.

Burberry also has a customer-centric approach that uses technology to enhance their customers' experiences before, during and after payment occurs. Consumers are recognized when they enter the store, with shopping assistants equipped with the mobile tools that can personalize the experience based on consumer preferences, purchase history and what's in their closet, all based on real-time information and personalized to create a real connection with the consumer.

Online Innovators Setting the Offline Pace

Sometimes e-commerce models like MatchesFashion.com started in e-commerce and then invested in bricks-and-mortar stores.

They have showrooms so consumers can touch and experience the products. They are similar to car showrooms, giving access to helpful and knowledgeable staff, but their sales are not reliant on in-store purchases. They do this to enhance their customers' experience and better connect with them.

I believe that consumers – especially those with the greatest potential lifetime value to retailers – want and expect a more personal experience tailored to their shopping habits. For the high street to survive, retailers need a relevant, omni-channel, insight-enhanced approach that delivers a seamless transaction every time.

The Future is Invisible

One of the terms I love is "making payments invisible", and I believe this will become the norm. For example, Uber's frictionless payments platform is at the centre of the company's disruptive business model. You order your taxi, take your ride and payment occurs automatically once you reach your destination. A less sexy but equally invisible payment is a direct debit or standing order, where the payment is triggered automatically without the consumer having to do anything other than set it up.

We are bringing the customer payment experience to the next level. Amazon Go's "just walk out" shopping experience, which uses the Amazon Go app to enable consumers to shop and pay without a checkout, is setting a high benchmark. Alexa is enabling consumers to order from Amazon by simply speaking a request. Capital One has partnered with Amazon to enable voice-activated payment of credit card bills. Tesla drivers can buy using an integrated in-car app at petrol stations and drive-thru's for coffee and food. In time, we will see automated insurance and car tax based on usage, with payment being

triggered invisibly and illustrated on a dashboard smart meter on your payment card.

Sorting the Settlement Problem

While many transactions are cleared in real time, the actual movement of money today can take anything from 2 to 10 days (or longer in some cases). A new dimension in payments is "instant settlement", which guarantees that the seller is paid, helping businesses and consumers better support cash management and liquidity pain points. The liquidity element has become very important to businesses, because releasing liquidity has a positive impact on cash flow, reduces liabilities and risks, and provides working capital.

Looking East for the Network Effect

In the last 50 years, Visa and Mastercard have benefited from a powerful network effect on their processing platforms. But in the last 5 years we see innovations from China and other parts of Asia taking centre stage. Platforms from Ant Financial (Alibaba), Tencent (WeChat) and Baidu have built dominant positions by removing friction. Their platforms also benefit from a powerful network effect to provide an enhanced consumer and merchant experience.

For example, Tencent's main business model was built on the social media platform WeChat. This has been a springboard into other areas, such as payments from TenPay, online banking from WeBank and even on-demand dining services. This "apps for everything" model is offering consumers access to a multifaceted, digital ecosystem whoever they are and wherever they are. These companies use the network effect to make super-profits, and they are investing these to take their models to the rest of the world.

Cranking up Crypto

So where does this leave cryptocurrencies in our consumer-centric world? My sense is that the real market for crypto is still undetermined. The heavy volatility of cryptocurrencies like Bitcoin, Litecoin and Ethereum does not help. But it does seem that the emergence of new "stablecoin" offerings, whereby a $1 digital token is matched by $1 in a trusted bank account, could succeed and overcome the limitations of assurance, stability, value and trust in a pure crypto model.

PayTech is the Future

The payments market is increasingly competitive and complex but by harnessing insights from understanding payments, adopting a consumer-led strategy and using invisible payments cleared and settled in real time, companies will benefit from the mass adoption of new payments solutions. And they will enable transformational change in the payments that have been dominated by banks and payment cards for the past 30 years.

Plugging the Data Black Hole: How Mobile Self-Checkout Can Help Revive the High Street

By David Grenham
VP Marketing, MishiPay

Challenging Questions for Retailers

The high street is under attack. News outlets are disseminating stories daily about decreasing retail footfall and the falling store sales that follow. Meanwhile, sales made online are continuing to rise. How can the high street fight back? What tools are available to help retailers revive their stores?

Stores are Not Delivering

Several factors have combined to diminish the performance of high street stores in their battle with the Internet, but the main factor is that physical retail stores are failing to deliver on the customer promise of an enjoyable, engaging experience. And nowhere is this clearer than in the in-store checkout experience. Customers have come to expect a frictionless, personalized experience. This is, after all, what Amazon and online shopping have trained shoppers to expect. This experience is the norm online, but the exception in-store.

Using Data to Enhance Experiences

How can high street stores offer the same personalized, frictionless experience as their online counterparts? One of the biggest

disadvantages that high street stores face versus their online cousins is the amount and quality of data to which they have access. Online stores are built on a wealth of data; they know precisely what products their customers view, the items they put in and take out of their basket, how long they spend browsing and how frequently they visit their sites. And they have been building these analytic engines for many years.

Online retailers use this data to create a more personalized experience for their users, with tailored communications based on each individual customer's shopping habits and preferences. Relevant, personalized content is delivered to the user throughout their journey. This increases engagement, which in turn increases the likelihood of conversion into a purchase being made.

Customers have become so used to this level of personalized experience that they miss it when it is absent from their shopping experience in physical stores. Indeed, most high street stores have a data "black hole" when it comes to insights about the behaviours of customers in their stores. This leads them to provide disappointing experiences as a result. So, embracing technologies that allow retailers to collect, harness and utilize information from in-store visits will allow high street retailers to transform their in-store experience, plugging the in-store data black hole to create a more tailored, personalized customer experience that benefits each individual shopper.

Transforming the In-Store Experience

There are a range of technologies on offer promising to transform the customer's in-store experience. Which have the biggest impact? Mobile self-checkout is one of the most impactful options available today. It is highly effective in allowing stores to embrace omni-channel retail and capture priceless data that can be used to improve the journey for their shoppers and ultimately shape their brand offer. Mobile self-checkout allows shoppers to scan products, receive enhanced product information – such as product reviews and ratings – pay using their mobile phone, then simply exit the store, with no need to wait in a queue at the checkout.

And shoppers using this technology typically scan two to three times as many products as they buy. This means that mobile self-checkout generates priceless data about shoppers' in-store behaviour. This can be used to improve the customer experience, personalize marketing and create the kind of frictionless retail journey that shoppers expect. When retailers offer scan-and-go, they can find out not just what their in-store customers purchased but what they didn't purchase, and why. They can understand how often their shoppers visited their stores, how long they stayed and their journey in-store. Just like online, this data can then be interpreted and utilized by the retailer and used to offer tailored content to the shopper, from discounts and stock information to product recommendations and invitations to relevant events. Shoppers within a specified radius of the store can also be re-targeted when the item they scanned but didn't purchase is reduced in price, or when the size they wanted has come back in stock.

Benefits Beyond Data

Data is not the only significant benefit that scan-and-go technology gives to retailers. According to a recent report, 72% of shoppers aged 18–44 use their phones in store (Salesforce Mobile Shopping Focus Report, 2018). Ensuring your shopper has a valuable reason to engage with your content and service, and not with those of a rival supplier, is therefore vital. Using mobile self-checkout to offer the shopper additional product information, purchase suggestions, how-to guides, product stock/location information and loyalty bonuses enables stores to make use of the smartphone that almost all of their customers carry with them daily.

As Salesforce notes: "As more shoppers turn to their phones in both the digital realm and the physical store, retailers need to focus on creating connected experiences in the mobile context" (Salesforce Mobile Shopping Focus Report, 2018).

Mobilizing the shopper's phone and enabling it to function as a mobile point of sale also means that less floorspace in stores needs to be devoted to checkouts and their associated equipment and materials. This allows stores to create additional fitting-room space, capacity for stock storage or the creation of new experiential zones. Perhaps more importantly, it also facilitates increased staff engagement with customers. A recent PricewaterhouseCoopers report stated that 59% of consumers feel companies have lost touch with the human element of customer experience.

Through their sales associates, high street retailers should be perfectly positioned to address this need and deliver personal, tailored interactions with their customers. Mobile self-checkout enables associates to be liberated from the disconnected realm behind the till and be repositioned on the floor to assist customers, provide useful service and add that invaluable human element.

Mobile self-checkout has another valuable benefit to offer in the battle to revive the high street: instantaneous, frictionless purchase. When making a purchase in a conventional retail store, the moment a user decides to purchase a product is not the moment they actually buy it. In fact, there is a significant disconnect – the shopper has to locate the checkout (which can be difficult in larger stores) and then, when they reach the checkout, they often have to wait in a line for service. Each of these points of friction reduces the chance of the consumer completing their purchase and increases the chance of some or all of their basket being abandoned. Once again, this drawn-out experience is something that has become undesirable to many shoppers who are now familiar with shopping online, where a transaction is made swiftly with a single click.

Instant Gratification

Mobile self-checkout allows customers to buy their chosen item as soon as they have made their decision, at the peak of their engagement with the product, at the point they are most likely to buy. What's more, they can make the purchase from anywhere in the store because the checkout is now, effectively, in the shopper's pocket. This means that the likelihood of purchase is increased, and that multiple transactions in the same store can happen at the exact same moment – rather than in the linear fashion in which they occur via a conventional checkout system.

Saving the High Street

The high street is able to offer customer experiences that online retail simply cannot successfully replicate. But "bricks-and-mortar" retailers are currently hamstrung by the lack of data to which they have access, and their subsequent inability to effectively personalize the journey for shoppers. Mobile self-checkout gives retailers the tools with which to fight back, to plug the data black hole in-store to offer improved experiences to their visitors. Those retailers that embrace this technology will find themselves armed with the best of the online and offline world, and will be poised to win the battle to revive our high streets.

How UnionPay Quick Pass is Beating Alipay and WeChat Pay in China

By Zhaoben Fang
Professor in Department of Statistics and Finance, USTC

and Junpeng Zhu
Doctor, Hefei iFlybank Financial Technology Co., Ltd

China UnionPay is a financial services corporation established in 2002 and headquartered in Shanghai. UnionPay operates an inter-bank information exchange network for bank cards in mainland China, which has now extended to more than 170 countries and regions around the world.

From 10m to 120m Users

Quick Pass is UnionPay's contactless payment product, relying on the People's Bank of China chip technology. It is a contactless payment product that conforms to the standard of EMV (the technical standard behind the smart IC cards formulated by Europay, Mastercard and Visa), using HCE (host-based card emulation) to generate virtual card numbers for each transaction. In May 2018, the logo of UnionPay Quick Pass was unified in the standard style of EMVCo's contactless indicator. The red Quick Pass app is free software released by UnionPay in December 2017. With the unified entrance of mobile payment in the Chinese banking industry, the number of users soared from 10 million to 120 million within one year (as of 24 January 2019).

Full Integration

In the current Chinese mobile payment market, UnionPay Quick Pass has become an important part of the payment ecosystem, with market share and penetration rate of 9.75% and 11%, respectively, ranking it third in China. UnionPay embraces the new types of business with an attitude of innovation and openness. It integrates the resources of bank card settlement management, point-of-sale terminals, ATM machines and QR codes. It coordinates the interests of banks, businesses, third-party payments and customers. It provides services to industry and commerce, transportation, health care, education and so on. It connects the card issuer and acquirer; the domestic and international. As a result, UnionPay Quick Pass continues to improve and optimize its user experience.

UnionPay Quick Pass uses the slogan "Quick Pass First When Paying". It can realize offline non-contact payment of mobile devices such as mobile phones, bracelets and watches, and online payment via apps. It also supports small-amount payment without passwords and with quick payment. Its user growth has been phenomenal: more than a million new users signed up on just one day, 12 December 2018.

Fighting Strong Competition

With the Alipay and Tencent Finance (WeChat Pay) duopoly of the Chinese payment market, why is UnionPay Quick Pass growing so rapidly? There are eight reasons.

1. The Chinese government provides policy support and supervision regulation safeguards. In 2017 the People's Bank of China launched the "Demonstration Project of Convenient Mobile Payment for the People" programme. UnionPay put forward "Ten Convenient Payment Scenarios for the People" together with banks, supermarkets, bus lines and subways, markets, catering, self-service vending, campuses, canteens, health care and traffic fines. This made Quick Pass permeate people's daily lives. Public transportation is the most prominent use case for Quick Pass. By the end of 2018, Quick Pass had been launched in 21 urban subways and bus lines in nearly

600 cities and counties. During a promotion, people could take buses for only one cent. UnionPay has also opened QR code services for connecting to banks and other partners.

2. Quick Pass integrates the unified mobile payment app entrance to the Chinese banking industry, which can be integrated in all UnionPay cards. This is safer and is an effective way to promote the use of Quick Pass.

3. Unlike Alipay, which relies on an e-commerce platform, and Tencent Finance, which relies on a social platform, the promotion of Quick Pass mainly relies on a variety of offline discount activities. For example, in the Spring Festival of 2019 there will be eight red-envelope activities including scanning of the UnionPay or Quick Pass logo, new user signup, repayment, transfer, checking in, friend inviting, consumption and app store consumption, aimed to reach a broader group of users.

4. UnionPay Quick Pass constantly improves its app functions to improve user stickiness. Functions including balance checks, payment, inter-bank transfer, multi-bank card management, investment and finance, etc. are provided to people for convenience.

5. The UnionPay Quick Pass app is secure and convenient. Quick Pass has multiple security guarantees, such as dynamic key and cloud authentication. The real bank card number is hidden during payment, and the cardholder's privacy is effectively protected. Relying on near-field communication technology, Quick Pass is more convenient than other payment products, and this technology is unique to UnionPay in China. At the same time, the high stability of UnionPay's inter-bank clearing system also provides a security guarantee for Quick Pass. For example, on Chinese New Year's Eve 2019, UnionPay processed 261.7 billion yuan of inter-bank payment clearing. The success rate of the network system was 100%, and the average transaction response time was 220 ms.

6. Relying on the innate advantages of UnionPay as a bank card union organization, it can benefit from the process of internationalization. There are more than 50 million merchants, 12 million point-of-sale terminals and 2.6 million ATMs using the UnionPay system around the world. Its coverage in Southeast Asia is more than 70%, and the percentage of European merchants supporting UnionPay cards is 60%. The Quick Pass app has been deployed in the Guangdong–Hong Kong–Macao Greater Bay Area, and the incidence of small and high-frequency payments is constantly growing.

7. UnionPay attaches importance to the reasonable distribution of social benefits. In accordance with the latest pricing mechanism, UnionPay distributes a profit-sharing proportion according to the General, Preferential, People's Livelihood and Public Welfare categories, so that card issuers, acquirers, third-party payments and customers have the initiative to participate.

8. The growth of Quick Pass would not have been achieved without its powerful marketing products. The Quick Pass app marketing product is a comprehensive, accurate, open-display and one-to-one whole-process closed-loop marketing product for banks, acquirers, merchants and cardholders, based on the China UnionPay marketing value-added service platform and the UnionPay card inter-bank network.

A Fully Integrated and Balanced Strategy

There is a long way to go from being a newcomer to being a key player in the payment ecosystem. It's not easy to catch up. There are some big questions to answer, such as how do we:

- Obtain customers at low cost?
- Change the payment habits of consumers?
- Improve customers' loyalty?
- Avoid the vicious "bonus hunters" in our promotional activities?
- Expand the market under the new policy environment of establishing NetsUnion Clearing Corporation?

Quick Pass is addressing all these questions right now. But there are still some growing pains. To respond to the competition, UnionPay Quick Pass might adopt the following strategies:

- Paying more attention to digital marketing in the digital era.

- Making full use of social media to attract new customers.

- Designing cartoons and games relating to Quick Pass to attract young customers (especially the post-2000 generation).

- Providing customers with more personalized services using artificial intelligence and big data analysis.

- Widely using voice recognition, face ID and other new technologies to make Quick Pass change with the times.

- Enhancing the service capabilities by acquiring startups (like Visa's merger with Simplex).

- Cooperating with FinTech companies to increase service capacities (e.g. cooperating with JoyinTech to design asset-backed security products to solve the problems of consumer credit receivables).

UnionPay Quick Pass sets out to balance products for businesses and consumers, connect domestic with international, and balance innovation and security. This will lead to healthy growth of Quick Pass alongside a variety of new products in the payments ecosystem.

How Payment Agility and Cash-for-Carbon Can Solve a Global Problem for Mankind

By Alessia Falsarone
Managing Director, PineBridge Investments

PayTech Solutions for Carbon Markets

Global payments technologies are likely to become important enablers of effective policy-making in advancing one of the most pressing issues in society today: climate change.

Since the first carbon trading scheme was launched in 2005, financial innovation has continued to expand the participation of both the public and private sector in international exchanges of carbon credits – in a similar fashion to how commodities such as energy, metals and agricultural products trade in organized markets. The Kyoto Protocol, the leading international effort to advance nation-level dialogue on the need to curb carbon emissions, will expire in 2020. It will be followed by the Paris Agreement, which, although not fully ratified, aims to establish measurable emission targets.

Over time, active interest in carbon markets has led to the customary use of an internal price for carbon by government entities and private-sector enterprises to guide scenario planning across production, distribution and procurement decisions. This was a much needed first step. However, critics of carbon-trading schemes continue to point to the voluntary nature as well as to its decentralized jurisdictional oversight to argue that policy-making may never contribute meaningfully to lower-carbon economies. Instead, payment technologies are best suited to help bridge the gap between short-term economic interests and the societal need to secure a state of climate resilience.

The Missing Link in Carbon Markets: Payment Agility

As reported by the World Bank, carbon-trading schemes are present in over 70 national and subnational governments. They have emerged from a fascinating history built on many attempts to design financial incentives with the purpose of tackling climate change. The term *carbon market* is utilized loosely to encompass carbon credits (allowances for carbon emissions under cap-and-trade schemes) as well as carbon offsets. There are two types of benefit here:

- As a tradable unit of carbon in the form of a certificate, carbon credits afford the holder the right to emit one metric tonne of GHG (greenhouse gas). With total available permits expected to decline over time, the net effect on market participants is the incentive to adhere to a direct reduction plan for their carbon-emitting activities and become less dependent from a capped trading plan.

- Carbon offsets are also linked to direct investments in projects that are designed and implemented with carbon reduction in mind. These include land and forest preservation, renewable energy and energy retrofit projects which are subject to official verification of both processes and outcomes. In recent years, the increase in popularity of offsets has been primarily due to the additional time they afford buyers to organically redesign their organizational footprint across geographies while minimizing the "internal" cost of carbon-emitting activities.

Multi-Year Horizons Require a New Solution

With emission-reduction outcomes taking a multi-year time horizon to materialize, the lack of an agile mechanism to assign a fair and comparable financial evaluation of both offsets and credits is likely to result in fewer transactions taking place in global carbon markets. To

doodleToonz.com

address this, technology advances in "payment agility" would lead to a consistent real-time tracking of carbon emissions by geography and economic activity, all the way to the underlying emitters.

In addition, by establishing a market-driven pricing strategy, traditional pay-as-you-go models would suggest a simpler recipe for carbon markets to gain vast scale and a measurable record of impact than traditional commodity exchanges. Pay-as-you-go platforms linked to the internal price of carbon would allow exchange participants to calibrate their willingness to pay to decrease their outstanding carbon balances and move the internal price to an equilibrium vs. other counterparties in the exchange.

Early adopters of this are most likely to include airlines, transportation and shipping companies looking to lower their pollution burden by directly establishing a virtual wallet for carbon balances per route and length of travel segment and digitally exchanging their carbon credits with other interested parties.

The Benefits of a Payments Model for Carbon Pricing

From a policy-making perspective, the benefits of adopting a payments model to determine carbon price targets are twofold:

- **The establishment of an agile marketplace**
  The ability to consistently assign financial value to positive or negative externalities from carbon-reduction activities will build trust in the future viability of carbon markets. In fact, what appears to be missing in the evaluation of the impact of traditional cap-and-trade schemes is a measure of carbon intensity per unit of transacted value. Pay-as-you-go wallet technologies provide the necessary backdrop to build a systemic management of carbon budgets through collaborative efforts among market participants, as opposed to addressing instances of policy failures among the myriad of national and international policy programmes.

- **Computational efficiency and digital ledger potential**
  Although digital payment authentication is still coping with the low adaptability of existing infrastructure alternatives for merchants and financial institutions, it has become easier to envision a digital ledger solution that integrates payments technology and carbon market dynamics. In order for international efforts such as the Paris Agreement to succeed, significant granularity at the regional, sector and company level is required, in the same way that payment providers follow transacted value. The launch of the Task-Force for Climate-Related Financial Disclosures in 2017 points directly to the importance of tracking and reporting carbon emissions in financial terms by linking carbon emissions to transaction-level activity the same way payments technologies are designed to deliver.

The difference between traditional carbon markets and their virtual wallet alternatives is the seamless tracking of carbon removed in aggregate from the system. A virtual wallet is also a more transparent mechanism where participants are incentivized to disclose their own willingness to pay to lower their exposure to carbon risk across their operational or geographic reach. In addition, from a risk management perspective, the likelihood of default vs. pre-committed carbon targets set by corporate or governance bodies would be easier to monitor and recalibrate as a function of the changing range of activities in which they engage.

Cash for Carbon – A Look Into the (Near) Future

The integration of alternative data (the non-financial data used to support decision-making) through payment mobility apps is introducing a number of use cases, including compelling business-to-business and business-to-customer carbon tracking solutions. The ability to reduce the carbon footprint of daily activities of businesses and of individuals as consumers and employees is a key trend to watch. While a variety of economic sectors are likely to augment their environmental and social stewardship through the integration of payments innovations, the biggest benefit is likely to be realized in streamlining supply chains in countries with the highest exposure to adverse carbon-emitting economic policies.

In the case of emerging markets, a growing number of small and medium-sized enterprises have been the primary advocates of payment solutions to leverage direct access to everyday capital while also creating a direct stream of measurable economic value from emission reductions. As payments' solutions are built to address the financial needs of a fully functional circular economy, they are positioned as the most efficient channel to direct and manage carbon sequestration payments, cash-for-carbon municipal programmes and congestion-charging schemes. The integration of mobility payments to address the need of a low-carbon economy transition is set to create the next generation of pay-for-good business models.

Sources:

https://www.brookings.edu/research/the-paris-agreement-and-its-future/.

https://www.weforum.org/agenda/2017/09/everything-you-need-to-know-about-carbon-trading/.

https://openknowledge.worldbank.org/handle/10986/29687.

https://www.belfercenter.org/sites/default/files/files/publication/establishing-a-global-carbon-market-shell-version.pdf.

Note: The views expressed by the author are personal and may not reflect those of a particular company or board of directors.

Revolutionizing the Retail Industry Through Integrated Payments Systems

By S. Elif Kocaoglu Ulbrich
FinTech Consultant and Author

"FinTech" is already more than a buzzword, liberating today's consumers from the siloed and limited banking options they previously had available. FinTech has created radically new experiences for consumers' banking and purchasing routines, turning cumbersome and generic procedures into convenient, real-time, tailored and relevant ones.

FinTech and PayTech

Payments companies are the rising stars of FinTech. Take Klarna, Stripe, Square or Transferwise – it's not a coincidence that the most successful and globally distributed FinTech companies have a focus on payment technology, or PayTech companies, carving out a whole new experience for consumers.

Long before it was possible to tap on a smart watch to buy a metro ticket, there was a time when even online money transfers were an *out-of-this-world* kind of experience. It's now a distant memory, but in the early 1990s we had to complete double-sided forms to authorize a payment, then drop it in at the nearest bank branch. The cards bearing bank account and branch numbers ranked as important as IDs, and invoice payments were the cheapest and safest e-commerce payment option for consumers until credit card acceptance rates improved.

PayPal Paves the Way

In those days, online payments were bureaucratic, slow and expensive. That's why, taking customer experience seriously for the very first time, PayPal was able to grow quickly and globally. Introducing a brand new concept of sending money electronically, to a person or a merchant, with a simple and free protocol, changed the way consumers saw their shopping experience forever.

Although it was considered a risky move at first, through its strategic acquisition and integration of PayPal, the online marketplace eBay was able to scale fast. This proved that payments were not just about sending money from A to B. Payments had become a crucial part of the ideal user journey. Seeing the network effect sparked by a good user experience, incumbents were challenged to invest more in services and functions to enhance their own customers' experience, even if they did not produce obvious additional value for the company itself.

Widespread Adoption

As a consequence of the "improved payment experience" mindset that developed over time, today's customers expect to be able to pick the fastest, most convenient and personally preferred payment option for themselves, without paying any additional fees. This is irrespective of whether they are in a restaurant, a petrol station or a church. Visionary retailers accepting that integrated, omni-channel payments are a necessity already feel the pressure to outsource payment functions to PayTechs, to be able to take the shopping experience a step further.

For example, Uber and Eat24's integration of Venmo's person-to-person (P2P) cost-sharing functions within their app is a good example of a complementary payment service. It has the potential to ensure customer retention and loyalty on top of a seamless customer experience. In-vehicle payment technologies, such as those developed by partnerships like Jaguar and Shell, integrating PayPal and Apple Pay into the car dashboard, enable consumers to buy and pay without having to leave their car.

The Amazon Go concept allowed us to take a peek into the future, changing the way we check out in a physical shop. Taking this a step further, we increasingly expect our household appliances to order and pay for their maintenance services automatically.

Keep Raising the Bar Across Retail

There are many new payment tools to which consumers now have access. This is "raising the bar" for payments experiences. Soon, all retail players (online or offline) will be forced to provide a full set of payment options. The good news for retail is that, although the area of payments is maturing, the potential for the underlying technology still hasn't been exhausted. The user journey can be enhanced further by experimenting with alternative technologies such as tokens, biometrics, distributed ledger technology, machine learning or the Internet of Things. In future, there will be individually branded currencies for all retailers; perhaps iris-scan payments could be adopted.

From PayPal to Alipay

Some companies are slow to change. Even PayPal persisted with its core product for longer than necessary and, as a result, was excluded from some regions. Markets like Korea and China created their own local PayPal alternatives, which actually ended up raising the bar for retailers too. Among these local pioneers, Alipay, the subsidiary of the Chinese retail company and online marketplace Alibaba, is peculiar for being one of the first traditional retail companies to invest a significant amount in PayTech for the sake of improving overall retail customer service.

Alipay was ahead of the game and created considerable user loyalty by offering utility bill or traffic ticket payment assistance, creating extra value and comfort for consumers, on top of more social services such as P2P transfers. Whilst the local market is not entirely competitor-free (WeChat Pay has over 1 billion adopters),

Alipay keeps on stirring user interest through constant refinement and development, and by emphasizing customer loyalty both locally and globally.

Relying on the Chinese consumer's purchasing power, Alipay has also taken steps to ensure acceptance from high-end retailers outside China. If a user of Alibaba would like to buy a handbag from Harrods in London, the obvious choice of payment would still be Alipay. At the end of the day, once a customer becomes familiar with using a payment instrument, it is hard for competitors to steal that user back.

Alipay follows users everywhere, offering the same scope of services around the world and cooperating with local service points, ensuring it stays a part of the user's daily routine, no matter what they are doing and where. There appears to be a silent race between retailers following in the footsteps of Alibaba, but until their user experience becomes as unique and as sticky, they will struggle to compete.

The Revolution Ahead

In the end, no matter the vertical, retailers that are slow to blow away the cobwebs will be threatened with loss of market control. As integrated payment systems become the next important milestone for revolutionizing retail, the distinction between PayTech and retail will become blurred. We will see more retailers jumping onto the PayTech bandwagon for improved user experience, and to see PayTechs cooperating with retailers for access to their customers.

All in all, embracing complementary skills and offering consumers the right end-to-end experience will be the only way to turn short-term popularity into long-term success. Integrated, seamless, omni-channel payments can and will turn the tables for all kinds of consumer-facing businesses in the long run, and will become a bigger part of our lives in the years ahead.

Asset Management and Payments in India – So Near and Yet So Far

By Rajesh Krishnamoorthy
Vice Chairman, iFAST India Holdings Pte Ltd

As the asset management industry in India has found out, not all innovations in payments work. But there have been valuable lessons learnt for all participants, in India and elsewhere.

Let's start by defining the payments ecosystem that powers the asset management industry in India. It has three main participants:

- **National Payments Corporation of India** (NPCI), a not-for-profit umbrella organization for operating retail payments and settlement systems in India. This is an initiative of the Reserve Bank of India (RBI) and the Indian Banks' Association (IBA) under the provisions of the Payment and Settlement Systems Act 2007 for creating a robust payment and settlement infrastructure in India.[1]

- Any **sponsor bank** (mandated by the NPCI) that allows an asset management company/platform/broker dealer/payment gateway (referred to here as **service providers**) to access the NPCI services.

- The licensed **scheduled commercial banks** where millions of customers have their **individual savings or current accounts**.

The Business Pitch to a Billion People

Consumer investment is an important component of a modern economy. Mutual funds help to capture consumer investments and channel them into businesses, but the penetration of mutual funds in India (as calculated by the proportion of GDP that are "assets under management", AUM) is significantly below the global average.[2]

As one of the most populous[3] (almost 1.2 billion) nations in the world, asset management funds represent a valuable potential source of inward investment in India in the years ahead. However, the concepts of mutual funds or AUM are still little known among uninitiated consumers in India. Therein lies the biggest opportunity for India and the asset management industry: to initiate the uninitiated such that they can benefit from wisely investing their money in the future of India.

To achieve this, the industry has been searching for the right message and a simple solution. It has found its mojo in the "Mutual Funds Sahi Hai" campaign. *Sahi Hai* in Hindi is a layman's term for something that works, something that is good, or something that is beneficial, besides its literal translation that it is right. The pitch is that one should start investing early, even if it be in small amounts, and continue to invest in a disciplined way over long periods of time without worrying about the ups and downs of the market. In other words, the concept of "rupee cost averaging" is being promoted using the Mutual Funds Sahi Hai campaign.

The goal was for an investor to be able to sign a simple, standardized payment instruction that allows their service provider to initiate systematic debits to his or her bank account. The payment instructions would then follow a standardized industry practice, reducing error, reducing friction and reducing cost. A fine objective. But how could 39 different asset managers, 1,000 different banks and a plethora of other participants pull this standardization off?

[1] https://www.npci.org.in/about-us-background.

[2] https://economictimes.indiatimes.com/mf/mf-news/mutual-fund-industry-aum-to-hit-rs-50-lakh-crore-in-next-5-yrs-deepak-parekh/articleshow/65516938.cms.

[3] http://www.censusindia.gov.in/2011-prov-results/data_files/india/table_1.pdf.

The PayTech that Powers a Billion Dreams

India developed a new PayTech that enabled systematic investment plans (SIPs) to be set up in India, and 26 million had been set up by January 2019.[4] SIPs are (largely monthly) payments made from an investor's bank account to a mutual fund, and around 26 million payment instructions are made every month. The individual payment amounts range from as low as INR 50 (approximately US$0.7 cents) to as high as INR 10 million (approximately US$140.8 thousand).

This was made possible with the help of the National Automated Clearing House (NACH) under the NPCI.[5] The NACH was created to rationalize and standardize the multiple electronic clearing systems that existed in India and systemically migrate all such customer instructions on these systems to the NACH. The main thrust was to make sure that repetitive or periodic payments could be initiated without any local barriers, and that all participants could be provided with a single set of rules (operating and business), open standards and best industry practices for electronic transactions.

This system is processing significant volumes of transactions: for the period April 2018 to February 2019, 2.47 billion credit and debit instructions have been presented with 2.33 billion successful transactions. The value of final credits from Indian consumers into SIPs is INR 10,710 billion (approximately US$151 billion).[6]

[4] https://economictimes.indiatimes.com/mf/mf-news/mutual-funds-collect-rs-8064-crore-via-sip-in-january/articleshow/67941641.cms.

[5] https://www.npci.org.in/product-overview/national-automated-clearing-house-product-overview.

[6] https://www.npci.org.in/product-statistics/nach-analytics-18-19-ytd.

Innovations Riding on the NACH Stack

Platforms which had tied up with all 39 asset managers came out with solutions riding on the NACH stack. The stack authorization that would have otherwise powered a repetitive debit were used to create a mandate that would be honoured by the investor's bank as and when it was presented or at a defined frequency of debit or a combination of both.

This simplified the process for consumers and the industry too. What would have required a one-to-one mandate being set up for each investor for each asset management company, and as a result many individual mandates, got crunched into just one NACH mandate. An Internet banking authorization was also not required, as the mandate could be used for one-time payments for a non-SIP investment as well. Simple, secure and inexpensive.

Further Innovations Enabled by FinTechs

Further innovations on this stack solution were introduced by the FinTech players. One was a built-in option to pause payments at will and resume later. This meant that if faced with any cash flow issues for subsequent investments, investors could simply pause the instruction – compare this to how it was done originally, when the only option was to cancel or terminate the investment.

A feature that enabled consumers to increase their monthly investments was the next big innovation that took place. Stepping up a SIP over time adds a tremendous business boost to the asset managers, whereas for the intermediaries – they could show proof that merely by stepping up your monthly investment by 10% every year over 10 years, you can shorten your timeframe to reach a million rupees from 13 to 10 years at an expected return of 10%.

Instant Investments and Redemptions

Instant investment and instant redemption were made possible with the unified payment interface (UPI) of NPCI. An investor could either use the NACH mandate to pay or get a "collect from" instant request from a service provider using the UPI and approve this on his/her bank's mobile application (or the stack UPI application published by the NPCI). As a result, using the same infrastructure, asset managers came out with money market funds that allowed investors to redeem their units and receive the settlement in as little as 2 minutes.

The Pain of Paper, and of Regulatory Flip Flop

The original NACH mandate was paper-based. It allowed for debits as high as INR 25 million (approximately US$375 thousand). However, problems such as the quality of the handwriting, signature mismatches and physical wear and tear during transit of the paper forms was increasing the costs of setting up a mandate. When volumes of mandates surged, banks were unable to manage defined turnaround times for setup. Investor experience suffered due to this unpredictability. Paperless was the only scalable solution – an electronic signature-based mandate setup, or eNACH.

So, FinTech players specializing in providing e-sign solutions sprang up.[7] These entities provided application programming interfaces (APIs) through which service providers could get investors to e-sign the NACH mandate. The mandate was signed using an API-based solution provided by the Unique Identification Authority of India (UIDAI) called Aadhar e-sign. Within a few days there was a huge surge in mandates, with near zero rejections.

It's Not All Plain Sailing

The Indian government tried to make UIDAI identification of every citizen mandatory. This would allow them to access bank accounts and securities accounts and make utility connections. Unfortunately, this attracted protests, in the form of litigations against the government, from many activists who claimed this was a breach of personal data and privacy. The ensuing policy "flip flop" and lack of an adequate legal framework dragged this matter into the Supreme Court of India.

The Supreme Court's ruling prohibited the use of the UIDAI API in the creation of eNACH, which led to the withdrawal of eNACH mandates from November 2018. PayTechs were back at the drawing board to find a solution that enables investors to contribute to asset management funds efficiently and cost effectively in a way that satisfies the requirements of the regulator. The only respite has come in the form of an interim solution from NPCI[8] that allows for the creation of eNACH up to INR 100,000 (approximately USD 1,400). It allows usage of Debit Cards / Internet Banking along with 2FA (two factor authentication) to create eNACH as against the previous method of using e-sign. Technology, and the entrepreneurial PayTech industry, are not going to get in the way.

---

[7] http://www.cca.gov.in/cca/?q=service-providers.html.

[8] https://www.npci.org.in/sites/default/files/circular/Circular%20no.003%20 Implementation%20of%20E-Mandate-%20approval%20of%20RBI.PDF

Exploiting the Value of Data Embedded in Payments Systems

By Suramya Gupta
Fund Manager, SBI Holdings – Japan

Capturing Insights About Offline Customers is Hard

We live in a world where online behaviour of consumers is tracked and analysed to an increasingly intrusive extent. The ongoing debate in the USA regarding the role that online platforms like Facebook might have played in the previous American elections is a clear indication of the growing ability to track online customer behaviour (and increasingly guide it).

However, despite the rapid growth of online retailers, the majority of global retail purchases continue to be offline. And in the offline space, brands have always struggled to figure out which customers are buying their goods, which are not – and what incremental steps could help drive the second set of customers into the first set.

Profiling and Organizing Offline Shoppers

With the level of fragmentation in physical retail and the vast number of retail brands, there is no easy way to profile and organize access to offline shoppers. This has led to the growth of a global advertising industry which struggles to measure the real impact of promotions. There is no easy way to measure the impact of targeted promotions on offline shoppers, and the direct purchase value delivered.

In the online space, this question is addressed by Google and Facebook, both of whom have attracted customers by enrolling them through information (Google Search & Maps) and social interactions (Facebook, WhatsApp). The resultant data collected has been monetized by providing curated access to brands. However, neither of these two platforms are able to directly track offline consumer purchase behaviour. Tweets, Likes and Forwards are used to measure "social engagement" as a proxy for this.

How Many-Sided "Payments Platforms" Can Help

Traditional payments systems were designed to enable settlement of transactions with a limited focus on the nature and context of transactions. Banking payment channels are good at moving money, but are not effective at moving information related to the transaction. A new type of payments organization, called a "payments platform", has recently started aggregating payment channels and integrating with enterprise resource planning (ERP) systems, helping businesses reduce costs and increase sales.

However, across Asia, we are now seeing the emergence of new payments platforms focused on solving "strategic" problems for businesses. These payments platforms add real-time intelligence to traditional payment channels, making them more valuable. These channels are delivered through offline point-of-sale terminals that allow the payments platform to build a large merchant network. Merchants, who are the anchors of such offline payments platforms, join the payments platform to add billing information to the channel that helps reduce back-office operation costs and human errors.

Merchants are also attracted to the value-added payment services provided by the payments platform's partners (purchase finance solutions, loyalty programmes and employee benefit programmes, for example). These value-adding partners are attracted to the payments platform because they get access to merchants at a lower cost than would otherwise be possible. Such access is enabled through intelligence inferred about a merchant's business and through data gathered by a deep integration of the merchant's ERP with the payment channels.

New Asian payments platforms that have been built as many-sided networks as described above can then combine intelligent payments data of multiple businesses to create powerful data aggregates, which are then used to infer a lot more about the offline customer (e.g. their demographics, what, when and where they buy, and the characteristics of their buying behaviours).

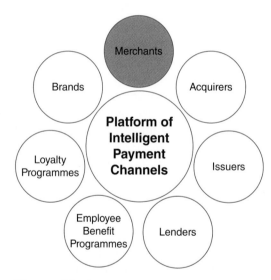

Figure 1: Many-sided payments platform

The Intelligence-Enabled Network Effect

The capability to add intelligence creates a network effect that drives increasing adoption among a broader group of businesses:

- **Brands** who sell their products to these **merchants**.

- **Merchants** join to drive preference through tightly controlled **loyalty programmes**, driving better returns on their marketing investments.
- **Acquirers** who want to access payment transactions happening at these **merchants**.
  - **Acquirers** join to save on their fixed-infrastructure investments by participating in a shared infrastructure at a variable cost. They also benefit by being able to select which transactions they would like to process to improve their profitability.
- **Issuers** offering e-wallet and **employee benefit programmes**, who want to access customers coming to these **merchants**.
  - **Issuers** join to access and drive preference for their products with the customers buying at these **merchants**.
- **Lenders** such as credit card issuers, banks and non-banking finance companies.
  - **Lenders** join to offer attractive loans against purchases to customers buying from these **merchants** at a lower cost and risk.

Each of these participants joining the platform in turn benefits the merchant by enhancing their sales, creating a flywheel network effect.

How Many-Sided Payments Platforms Can Help Brands Capture Insights on Offline Customers

A many-sided payments platform (as described above) can combine the intelligent payments data of multiple businesses to create a powerful data aggregate. This can be used to infer a lot more about the offline customer – their demographics, what they buy, where they buy, purchase frequency and even ways to access them. The payments platform can then provide this information back to a brand to help increase wallet share or retain customers better.

In addition, the platform can also provide insights about customers not shopping with the brand. This enables them to identify customer segments that need better targeting. Furthermore, for every campaign run to target a specific segment of customers, the payments platform would be in a position to accurately measure the impact of the campaign through future payments data from the brand.

Such insights drive more efficient customer targeting and accurate measurement of the impact of brand initiatives. We have seen live use cases in Asia, where these kinds of insights from payments data have allowed brands to make decisions on store location and advertising (location of digital hoardings), to be able to target customers based in specific areas of a city.

These payments platforms can thus help brands acquire new customers in more accurate ways, help brands know more about their customers to retain them effectively and increase wallet share, and help brands try out new product and marketing innovations quickly and cost-effectively. In other words, payments platforms can help businesses monetize their payments data to provide better goods and services to customers, faster and more cheaply.

It is important to caveat that payments platforms will need to keep all privacy laws in mind and ensure that the data analytics is conducted on macro-consumer cohorts and not on specific customers.

Conclusion – Payments Platforms as the Google and Facebook of the Offline World

We believe that some of the payments platforms emerging in Asia are uniquely positioned to develop into many-sided networks. With a strategic approach, these networks could emerge as the Google and Facebook of the offline world. As payments platforms benefit from network effects, they will drive more business participants to the network, and increase the volume and richness of the transactions data. This enables the payments platform to derive increasingly sophisticated insights regarding offline customers and enables brands to deliver a genuinely multi-channel proposition to consumers for the first time.

Reinventing the Customer Experience by Focusing on the After-Payment Emotional Experience

By Dr Christine Bailey
Chief Marketing Officer, Valitor

The customer experience is vital to success in the retail sector and represents a continuous battleground for retailers. Omni-channel retailers have the added challenge of delivering a great customer experience across all of their channels. By rethinking the customer experience to focus on the after-sales experience, retailers can stand out, increase customer retention and even gain new customers.

The After-Payment Emotional Experience

At the heart of this new approach is the concept that retailers need to view the customer experience as a virtuous circle, containing three core elements: pre-, during and post-payment. Currently, retailers have focused on and seen success in the pre-payment element. However, for the modern customer this is only part of the journey. Following an independent research report into customer experience, it is clear that consumers have an after-payment emotional experience (APEX) that is being overlooked. This should worry every business leader, as APEX is the key to unlocking customer experience success.

APEX is the emotional feeling that customers have, both immediately after making a purchase and throughout their post-payment interactions with a retailer. It particularly affects areas such as returns, refunds, target marketing and promotions. The cyclical nature of the customer experience means that it also plays a crucial role in the pre-payment and during-payment elements as well.

Right now, retailers are largely ignoring APEX. They are letting their customers down and losing them in the process. This is at odds with the work brands are doing to win customers and it makes the process of customer retention much harder. Consumers are keen to establish trust and loyalty with a retailer, but will not hesitate to move to a competitor if they feel let down. The future of retail will be won or lost in the post-payment experience.

Start the Right Way

It all starts at the beginning of the relationship. Get it right and you can quickly foster trust and loyalty that can grow into a beneficial relationship for both parties. The first touchpoint with a customer will often set the tone of the relationship and the likelihood that the customer not only returns, but shares their positive experience with their own communities.

The results of a survey of over 2,000 consumers in the UK indicated that in this area, retailers are succeeding. When asked how much they enjoyed the customer experience, across a range of five different product categories, on average over three-quarters (77%) of consumers said they enjoyed it. Researching a product (60%), visiting a store or website (59%) and paying for a product (42%) were highlighted as the most important parts, emotionally, within the buying process.

But despite retailers getting off to the right start, they cannot afford to take their eye off the ball during the pre-payment experience. Rude staff (55%), long checkout processes (38%) and difficulties in finding the right product are the most likely issues to repel a customer. It's essential that every part of the customer experience lives up to customers' ever-increasing expectations. If they feel let down, they will vote with their wallets.

Customer Insights vs. Data

Getting marketing and promotional materials right from the start is important for the customer experience. Wasting time (33%) and delivering irrelevant offers are the biggest turn-offs for consumers with email marketing. However, omni-channel retailers already have the ammunition at their disposal to solve these problems, in the form of data. Having data on a customer's habits and preferences means that retailers can develop personalized and tailored offerings to entice consumers back without jeopardizing the relationship.

To do this effectively, retailers need to ensure they have an omni-channel payment solution that combines all the different online and in-store payment methods into one, connected system. With regulations such as the General Data Protection Regulation (GDPR) and Payment Card Industry Data Security Standard (PCI-DSS) making it critical to keep customer information safe, omni-channel retailers need secure systems for doing this. One way to do this is via tokenization. Tokenization is a simple yet secure way to collect information from multiple payment methods and connect them together. In essence, it replaces a customer's bank or payment details with a unique identifier (a token) that can then be shared across different payment systems, while at the same time the actual customer data is safely and securely stored.

Using tokenization, retailers can quickly start to build up a picture of a customer, and use these insights to develop marketing, promotions and offers that are relevant to them. Tokenization also reduces the burden of PCI-DSS compliance, providing a dual benefit to retailers and their IT and compliance teams.

Think After…Before

Payment, while important, is not the end of the customer journey. Over half (54%) of consumers expect at least a basic level of support from a retailer post-purchase. In fact, 22% view a payment as a contract or agreement and rightly expect a certain level of care after making a purchase.

It is at this transition that the story begins to change. Once payment has been made, many retailers are failing. This is risking not only customer retention, but also the chances of gaining new customers. For example, a negative APEX experience will mean nearly half (47%) of consumers will be less likely to pay attention to a brand's marketing in future. And once lost, a customer is even harder to win back.

A key sign of this failure is visible in how consumers view their experience of returning a product, with over a third stating that the process to do it is "rubbish". This is in addition to the 40% of consumers who see the complaints procedures as "rubbish" too.

Improving APEX Doesn't Need to be Expensive

The good news is that improvements don't need to cost the earth. In fact, half of the consumers surveyed reported that the biggest annoyance with returning an item was simply the lack of free returns. This is in addition to the quarter of consumers who see a badly explained returns policy as the biggest reason for them to not return to a retailer. For any retailer looking for a competitive edge, reviewing these processes and policies is an easy win. Making a few small changes and having the right technology will have a positive effect on APEX and as a result, customer profitability and lifetime value.

It's Time to Act

The first step for those looking to change is to rethink the customer experience as a continuous cycle that needs attention at each of the three key stages of pre-, during and post-payment. Think after, before.

Next, retailers need the right omni-channel payment solution that features tokenization technology to help them gather and consolidate data for a 360° view of a customer. Leveraging data from a customer's actual purchases and habits will quickly lead to the APEX that they now rightly expect. If retailers don't put the customer first at every stage of the buying process, they will have to watch their customers go to a brand that does.

How Open Banking and Payment Touchpoints Will Save Banks

By Anna Maj
FinTech Leader, PWC

The Big Questions Facing Banks Today

Most customer interactions with a bank end up with a payment. But payments have traditionally been a domain dominated by banks. Now, under the EU's second Payment Services Directive (PSD2), the role of traditional banks could change, as new players attacking that segment – such as challenger banks and other FinTech and PayTech companies – see payments as a bridgehead into customer relationships. Banks risk becoming providers of commoditized products, running the "dumb pipes" behind the payments network. So, can banks make payments the primary customer touchpoints? And can payment-driven value propositions be a remedy for banks seeking to avoid becoming the commodity providers of financial services?

Making the Change

The challenge is how to prevent banks being reduced to back-end processors and make them first-choice front-end service providers. The payments services layer sits on top of the banking services layer, so the digital banking front-end naturally becomes an entry access point, the first touchpoint for consumers, a sort of "payment gateway" to the open banking ecosystem.

Under open banking, banks are obliged to grant access to bank account data through open application programming interfaces (APIs) for non-banks registered as third-party providers (TPPs). To maintain the balance in the payments ecosystem, the incumbents should not only deliver, but also consume, the APIs provided by other stakeholders. Open banking is a game of APIs, but not in a quantitative sense. Both Token and Klarna claim to onboard 4,000 banking APIs.[1] No matter how many APIs have been aggregated and integrated into the platform, the real value of API banking lies in the quality of the use cases that can be built and commercialized.

The Role of Account Aggregators in Preventing the Commoditization of Banks

On the one hand, account aggregation is the solid building block for creating value-added services. On the other hand, it is the tip of the iceberg within the entire finance ecosystem.

As a standalone entity, an aggregator doesn't bring either much value to the end user, or a fully monetized opportunity for the bank. But 70% of the revenue of retail banks derives from their customers having more than one banking relationship.[2] For example, BNP Paribas Fortis Bank in Belgium has been partnering with Tink, a Swedish FinTech and API enabler. Tink provides account aggregation services that include a multi-banking application for retail customers launched in February 2019. One in four of BNP Paribas' customers has an account at other banks (KBC, ING, Belfius).[3]

---

[1] Based on the company's information (as of February 2019).

[2] Based on the PwC 2018 analysis.

[3] According to the BNP Paribas Fortis Bank announcement: https://www.finextra.com/newsarticle/33426/bnp-paribas-fortis-rolls-out-multi-bank-account-aggregation-app/mobile.

This is just one of the powerful use cases showing how incumbent banks can grasp the opportunity of being the first-choice providers of multi-banking services, with the payment initiation function embedded. They can drive an enhanced customer value proposition with the primary payment touchpoint at a preferred bank. Another example is ING Bank, which has been building an open banking proposition with payments as its focus with various FinTech partners, including Payvision in the Netherlands and the Czech startup Twisto in Poland, for online payments and instant crediting.

Banks Must be Open to Open Banking

Banks should demonstrate their deep understanding of how consumers want to send, share, save or spend money and come up with a range of features and functionalities based on the specific customer payment behaviour. Bill payments, cross-border, foreign exchange payments, subscriptions, person-to-person, in-store or mobile payments are all in the scope of open banking. Furthermore, various payment-related services – such as merchant deals and retail offers, crediting, lending and insurance – should be showcased and built into the open banking engine. Powered by the use of data-driven APIs, these can be a real game-changer.

Businesses Benefit Too

This does not only hold true for consumers. Open banking unlocks a great business-to-business (B2B) opportunity too. Small and medium enterprises (SMEs), large corporates and merchants can all play the same game, particularly SMEs that have been underserved by banks so far. This is still a relatively uncrowded space compared to consumer payments, that will soon explode with a wave of innovative use cases within the collaborative open banking ecosystem.

Platform Banking for SMEs

SMEs want tools to help them run better businesses, and this can be obtained from platform banking providers. Platform banking provides a marketplace where SMEs can build more relations with potential partners and clients. Payments are a core component of the SME open banking proposition.[4]

Seamless Multi-Banking Experiences for Large Corporates

In addition, large corporate clients want a seamless multi-banking experience, with payments and treasury services integrated into the background. They are well positioned to benefit from dedicated APIs in a "Bank as a Service" model enabled by open banking.[5]

Big Banks are Embracing Open Banking Too

Commercial banks serving SMEs or merchants are rapidly grasping the opportunities of open banking. Account-to-account (A2A) payments using payment initiation functions (from payment initiation service providers, PISPs) are game-changers too. For example, in February 2019, KLM airlines, powered by the Dutch payment platform Adyen,[6] launched a service that enabled bank account payments to be made available for UK consumers. The International Air Transport Association (IATA)

---

[4] Based on the "It's Now Open Banking", Accenture for Open Banking Business Survey 2018 (February 2019).

[5] Ibidem.

[6] Adyen aggregated 90% of UK consumer banking accounts (according to The Paypers, February 2019).

also partnered with Deutsche Bank to better serve its B2B clients and merchants thanks to the PSD2-enabled A2A transfers. And in October 2018, mBank in Poland launched a B2B platform for e-commerce merchants focused on payment and credit using APIs.

Embracing Payments to Embrace Change

Payments are at the heart of the banking ecosystem. That is why payment solutions built and integrated by banks in the frame of open banking platforms, including A2A payments, are emerging across the marketplace. A2A payments accelerate the adoption of low-cost, real-time instant payments without the costs and rules of the familiar payments schemes. They are non-repudiable, irrevocable and more secure due to the strong customer authentication (SCA)-compliant component, resulting in no charge backs and limited fraud. They are healthier and safer for all stakeholders, from users to banks, merchants, acquirers and payment service providers.

Banks Will Use Open Banking to Remain First-Choice Providers – and Avoid Becoming Commodity Providers

Incumbent banks will become first-choice providers of banking, payments and financial services for users in many different verticals. Sometimes this will be integrated under one umbrella platform (e.g. insurance, retail, telco, entertainment, travel or automotive) and become a one-stop shop for most payment activities.

This is how the customer shopping experience arrives at the point where a personalized consumer journey within the financial ecosystem begins. Digital transformation will continue through the use of a conversational user interface, a voice-powered technology being integrated into banking platforms. With such innovations, banks will not only create a new payment-driven, contextual customer value proposition, but also take the customer's payment experience to the next level: instant, seamless, hassle-free and invisible.

Why Personal Financial Management Will Be Embedded Into the Next Generation of Payments

By Szilvia Egri
Founder, Femtechlab Ltd

Innovative payment solutions have evolved at a rapid pace in recent years. As a result, even the card-based status quo is facing challenges. We found the following three trends to be the most significant driving forces behind this process:

1. BigTech and FinTech players are demanding a front seat in the payment innovation race.

2. The European Union's second Payment Services Directive (PSD2) regulation is stimulating competition in the market by creating new roles of financial intermediaries. To add more spark, instant-payment infrastructures are being built, setting out a new playing field.

3. Evolving technologies like computer vision, speech recognition, machine learning and biometrics promise a seamless shopping experience that makes the payment itself effortless and even "invisible".

This chapter will elaborate the last trend.

The best practices presented in this chapter will show you how payment is increasingly fading into the shopping experience. It also points out the potential drawbacks, and how the new ways of payment may deprive customers of financial control.

Finally, this chapter argues that the redesign of personal finance management (PFM) solutions is also required in a way which vests customers with informed decision-making power. This new generation of PFM not only tracks and structures payments and provides insights after purchase, but is also embedded into the payment process. It enables customers to consider alternative payment options and the financial consequences of purchase at the moment of payment.

Payment is Increasingly Fading Into the Shopping Experience

Invisible payment is the term used across several industries to describe the new generation of payment solutions where the payment itself is faded – seamlessly integrated into the end-to-end shopping experience.

Invisible payment solutions meet all of the following criteria:

- Service enrolment (onboarding) – as soon as the customer installs the app and registers a payment credential.
- Customer identification – at the beginning of the shopping experience.
- Transaction authentication.

Market players have designed a range of innovative approaches to meet the above criteria. Let's take a look at some prominent examples of invisible payment solutions in retail and transportation.

Invisible Payment in Retail

Barclaycard Grab+Go is a pilot project focusing on low-value payments. After creating an account in the app and registering payment details, purchases can be completed with a single click. The solution uses a smartphone camera to scan the barcode displayed on the packaging of goods.

Amazon Go went one step further and eliminated even the effort of scanning products. Customers can log in with their existing

Amazon account after downloading the Amazon Go app. Customer identification is completed while they pass through the entrance door by scanning the personalized barcode from the app. To provide the service, Amazon uses hundreds of cameras, weight sensors on the shelves, sophisticated image recognition software and machine learning technology. The Amazon Go solution is able to recognize and analyse customers' interactions. As a result, the customer can simply pick up the desired goods, put them in the basket and go.

BBVA started a similar experiment in 2018 jointly with its restaurant partner, Sodexo Iberia. BBVA and Sodexo enabled 1,000 employees to order coffee or make reservations in selected restaurants, eat and leave without asking for the bill. The next phase of the project is likely to be even more exciting: facial recognition and machine learning algorithms are planned to be integrated into the system to identify both the faces of users and the products on the tray.

Invisible Payment in Transportation

Ride-sharing companies carried out the first step into what is now becoming the mainstream customer experience in transportation. The next step in the invisible payment journey in transportation is likely to be shaped by the Internet of Things (IoT). Gartner predicts that there will be 20.4 billion connected products in the world by 2020. Vehicles will most probably be counted among the devices that substantially transform our daily lives.

Visa uses the IoT to integrate payments seamlessly into the customer experience. Visa connected-car experiments focus on shifting the "point-of-sale" into the car. They identified three IoT-based use cases for invisible payment: fuelling, parking and ordering take-away food. With the help of beacons and near-field communication technology the car is able to communicate with the bump at the fuel station, the parking meter or the fast-food merchant. The "in-car" application registers the payment credentials, displays the transaction details along with the relevant

offers of loyalty and reward programmes, and finally enables the customer to confirm and complete the transaction with one click.

Invisible Payment Solutions May Deprive Customers of Financial Control

Invisible payment solutions ultimately aim to minimize the effort needed from the customer to complete a payment. This aspect of the payment innovation process is certainly welcome – but in order to enable truly customer-centric redesign of daily financial transactions, we need to carefully consider the potential drawbacks.

Payment innovations are reflections of the consumer society itself. New ways of payment shorten the time period when valuable financial information can be effectively shared with the customer. This lack of insight is a problem, because it limits the ability to consider the financial consequences of the purchase.

What's more, customers are incentivized to make payments without stopping to think at all about the impact on their finances. If they are not careful, customers can actually run out of money more easily and faster than before.

With all the ongoing experimentation, raising financial awareness among consumers needs to be high on the innovation agenda. Control over spending and saving behaviour is a crucial factor for customers to retain their financial wellbeing. To get there, customers need to be adequately informed when making financial decisions – practically before or at the time of payment.

Existing PFM Solutions are Deficient

Most PFM applications – like Mint, Money Dashboard or Yolt – aim to provide control over spending and spur savings behaviour. The problem is that the current generation of PFM tools supports the customers ex-post. They track and structure spending, check cash flows and send alerts *after* the transaction is completed.

Emma and Squirrel took one small step further. Emma assists customers in finding and cancelling unnecessary subscriptions, while Squirrel helps to split the salary up into bills, savings and weekly spending allowance. Again, these tools will not solve excessive purchasing habits, but may at least enable a more controlled way of spending.

But in a world of innovative payment solutions, how do we make sure that the customer receives sufficient assistance *before* making an invisible payment?

"Embedded" PFM Solutions Empower Customers with Financial Control

To address the core issues of spending behaviour and incentivize customers towards a more conscious management of money, the next generation of PFM solutions needs to be even smarter.

To me, this means that specific information on the actual financial situation is offered to the customer *before* the transaction's authentication takes place. In practice, this would require the available balance to be presented to the customer along with the purchase amount *prior to* making a decision for payment. Accordingly, the next generation of PFM solutions would analyse the spending behaviour, consider the actual financial situation and send alerts *in advance* of payment if they were about to make a purchase exceeding the predefined spending limit or leading to debt.

To increase financial awareness and enable financial wellbeing, payment innovators need to consider and explore "informative payment" solutions rather than targeting "invisible payment" solutions only. As a society transitioning from limited consumer behaviour to a more advanced state of financial security, we need to look beyond the seamless shopping experience and help the customer regain control of financial decision-making before it is too late.

How Helping Microbusinesses Accept Digital Payments Could Transform Kenya's Economy and Enhance Inclusion

By Peter Gakure Mwangi
Head of SME Finance, Kopo Kopo Inc.

The Frontier Beyond Person-to-Person Payments

The next big frontier for mobile payments in Africa will be for micro, small and medium enterprises (MSMEs) to accept mobile payments. Enabling such enterprises to receive payments digitally using mobile payments would be both a major revenue opportunity for FinTechs and a way to transform the economic wellbeing of thousands of small business owners in Kenya.

In the 6 year period between 2011 and 2017, there were 135 live money deployments with 338 million registered accounts and a combined transaction value of US$20 billion. However, only 3% of that value was in the form of merchant payments.[1]

In Kenya, mobile payments have experienced rapid and widespread growth since the launch of the M-Pesa mobile money service, in 2007. By the end of 2018, Kenyans had cumulatively made about 9 billion transactions valued at US$220 billion. US$20 billion was transacted using M-Pesa in 2018 alone. Almost all of these transactions are in the form of person-to-person (P2P) transfers.[2]

But Kenyans Still Buy Most Things Using Cash

95% of Kenyan shoppers buy their goods and services from microbusinesses, especially dukas (small local shops), kiosks and pharmacies.[3] And almost all of the payments received by these micro merchants are in cash. Payments to suppliers are also carried out using cash, as they prefer cash to any other form of payment, and all payment transaction information is recorded on paper.

The majority of merchants in Kenya are MSMEs that mostly operate in the informal economy. There are over 1.5 million formally registered MSMEs in Kenya, and many more operating in the informal sector. The MSMEs make up 90% of all registered MSMEs in Kenya, and play a crucial role in Kenya's economic development. They are a source of employment for the majority of Kenyans in a country with 50 million inhabitants. They are mostly located in urban areas and along busy highways. Examples of these micro merchants include dukas, pharmacies, cosmetics stalls and Telkom outlets selling mobile phones and airtime.

These businesses have a maximum annual turnover of KES 500,000 (about US$5,000) and employ less than 10 people. The findings of a survey by the Kenyan government showed that these very small businesses accounted for 81.1% of employment reported for the MSME sector in 2016.[4]

The Opportunity for FinTechs and Kenya

How can FinTechs help convert cash payments to digital payments for these microbusinesses? How can FinTech companies provide

[1] GSMA Mobile Money Statistics (2011–2018). Retrieved from https://www.gsma.com/mobilemoneymetrics.

[2] Central Bank of Kenya Statistics (31 December 2018). Retrieved from https://www.centralbank.go.ke/national-payments-system/mobile-payments.

[3] The Report: Kenya (2016). Retrieved from https://oxfordbusinessgroup.com/kenya-2016.

[4] Micro, Small and Medium Enterprises (MSME) Survey Basic Report (24 October 2016). Retrieved from https://www.knbs.or.ke/2016-micro-small-and-medium-enterprises-msme-survey-basic-report-2.

a compelling value proposition to these micro merchants, encouraging them to adopt and use mobile money payments? And most importantly, are there profitable ways in which financial technology companies can serve these microbusinesses?

Building an Inclusive Payments Technology

Any payments technology targeted at microbusinesses must be:

- Inclusive – a system that works only for some businesses and not others will only end up creating a new digital divide within the economy.

- Usable by all businesses – even those at the bottom of the pyramid.

- Easy to understand and use by semi-literate users.

- Efficient to scale across all merchant segments.

- Resilient.

- Cost-effective.

- Simple – the transaction journey for the customer should have very few steps, especially if the user interface is on unstructured supplementary service data.

- Consistent, to ensure confidence and familiarity.

Network stability is also vital to ensure the success of merchant payments. If the network is unstable, customers will be unable to complete transactions and merchants will be unable to confirm payment from the customers as a result of delay in receiving payment notifications. This would hinder the adoption of the service by microbusinesses.

Ensuring Rapid Adoption

FinTechs need to understand the value proposition that will incentivize these microbusinesses to sign up for mobile payments.

This will determine how well they acquire new merchants in the market. This is easier said than done. Most of these businesses prefer cash, which is more familiar to them. The value proposition must offer more benefits than cash and be cost-effective.

In order to ensure robust user growth of micro merchants, FinTechs must consider the cost of merchant acquisition. Merchant acquisition, whether directly or through a third-party acquirer, can be very expensive. It is therefore paramount that a FinTech understands the average cost of acquiring a new micro merchant, and how long it will take them to break even.

The merchant acquisition costs are normally dependent on three main variables:

- *The nature of the business*. A FinTech may have higher average cost of acquisition compared to a bank, which can utilize its branch network to convert already existing micro merchants to mobile digital payments. A FinTech may also have to deploy its own merchant acquisition teams or work with third-party acquirers.

- *The size of the merchant*. Acquiring micro merchants is cheaper than acquiring larger merchants. The sales cycle of a small merchant is shorter than that of a big merchant which might require several sales meetings before the account is closed. Bigger merchants also require integrations with their core operating systems. This may hike up the cost of acquisition.

- *The sales channel used to acquire these merchants*. Direct sales tend to be more expensive than other sales channels. Online sales are the least expensive.

Using the Internet to Sign Up Micro Merchants

The Internet provides an opportunity to lower the cost of acquisitions and to scale the payments service to microbusinesses across Kenya. The Internet provides a huge opportunity for reaching out to these merchants, wherever they may be. At the end of 2018 there were 42 million active Internet subscriptions in Kenya, out of a population of 50 million people.[5]

Onboarding these micro merchants into the payment system must be quick and convenient, while ensuring at the same time that proper due diligence is carried out. In Kenya, government licences for microbusinesses are expensive. This hinders many micro merchants from registering their business. Some of these merchants may be tempted to fake their licence. The due diligence process should be automated and streamlined to ensure that at least the minimum know your customer process is carried out without locking any properly registered merchants out.

Ensuring Robust Revenue Growth from Micro Merchants

It is paramount for FinTechs to understand where their revenue is coming from. This will require segmentation of these merchants into various categories in order to have a deeper understanding of revenue growth and revenue retention.

Micro merchants have small transaction sizes. In Kenya, the average mobile money amount sent and received in 2018 was KSH 2,776 (about US$28). This is also likely to be the average transaction size received digitally by these microbusinesses.

These merchants are also very sensitive to pricing. The merchant fee in Kenya has dropped by 67% in the past 6 years and is likely to keep moving towards zero. Merchant transaction fees are currently at 0.5% per transaction. FinTechs have to find alternatives to lower transaction fees if they are to be profitable. Value will only be found in economies of scale in merchant acquisition, activation and engagement, as well as the launching of new value-added services. The most obvious of these is digital lending, because the biggest challenge of micro merchants is access to working capital. According to the World Bank, the financing gap for microbusinesses in Kenya is US$1 billion.[6]

Kopo Kopo Inc., the first mobile merchant payments FinTech company in Kenya, is currently offering short-term digital micro loans for stock financing and other use cases to its network of 40,000 merchants. Merchants are scored by their daily mobile money payments. The loans range from KSH 25,000 (US$250) to KSH 300,000 (US$3,000). Merchants with a good credit score can qualify for loans of a maximum of KSH 5 million (US$50,000). Merchants receiving loans are active users of mobile payments and have a longer customer lifecycle compared to those who do not take the short-term credit.

Acquiring and Maintaining Quality Users

Targeted acquisition of microbusinesses that are likely to be quality users of merchant payment systems presents a big challenge. The churn rate for these micro merchants is very high – 46% of all MSMEs in Kenya close their business within the first year of launch, and another 15% in the second year.[7]

However, with an inclusive merchant payment solution that simplifies the onboarding process of a diverse group of micro

[5] Communication Commission of Kenya Sector Statistics Report Q1 2018–2019 (21 January 2019). Retrieved from https://ca.go.ke/document/sector-statistics-report-q1-2018-2019.

[6] World Bank, MSME Finance Gap (27 February 2019). Retrieved from https://finances.worldbank.org/Other/MSME-Finance-Gap/ijmu-5v4p/data.

[7] Capital Business: 46pc of Kenya's SMEs Close Within a Year of Founding (15 May 2018). Retrieved from https://www.capitalfm.co.ke/business/2018/05/46pc-kenyas-smes-close-within-year-founding.

merchants into the payment system, one can observe trends over time, and learn which segments of merchants produce quality users. Maintaining quality users requires proper training and engagement over time. Micro merchants require several training sessions before they fully adopt the payment solution. Engagement with these merchants should go on throughout the course of their merchant journey.

Conclusion

Although there is a huge opportunity in working with the thousands of micro merchants in Kenya, great efforts must be made to understand the right business model and technology required to reach and serve these microbusinesses in a profitable way. Partnerships between different players in the digital payments ecosystem are required in order to reach scale within reasonable time and cost. But if these challenges can be overcome, this represents an attractive revenue opportunity for FinTechs and a chance to bring thousands of microbusinesses into the formal financial system in Kenya, with all the associated social and economic benefits.

How Decentralization Can Create a Customer-Centric Ecosystem

By Michael Boevink
Founder, Boevink Group

Consumers have to pay for the things they buy. This chapter explains changes in consumer behaviour, changes in how we are approaching payments and changes in how payments serve consumers.

Currently we are charged and pay through a centralized structure dominated by large payments companies. In the future, consumers will be charged and pay through a decentralized function using a ledger that gives the trust back to the consumer. A digital transformation to this new future will take time, but one day the consumer will be able to make transactions with digital currencies in a safe, transparent and trustworthy way.

The central question and theme is: "With technology, can we move to a consumer-centric ecosystem?"

Beyond Current Technologies

Mainstream consumers are not using the latest technology of digital currencies, because it does not fulfil their needs. Although technologies built on the Bitcoin network are very promising and soon we will be able to pay for a cup of coffee without even touching a card or payment terminal, we have to realize that this is purely from a technology perspective. Consumer behaviour and trust in the payment world is critical if it is to add value to consumers' lives.

Banks, open banking and FinTech companies are changing the way we have always done it, creating something new which consumers can embrace in their daily lives. Mass adoption only succeeds if consumers embrace the payment platform, which has been dominated by banks and payment cards for a long time. Bitcoin has already been available for 10 years and still has not reached mass adoption, nor will it until we have completed a full cycle of digital transformation.

A new consumer-centric ecosystem will be defined by players who are close to the daily lives of consumers. That is why Amazon and Google are becoming players in the financial services industry. Above all, they are engaging daily with consumers and that's a game-changer for banking and the consumer. As a use case you see, for example, Android Pay being seamlessly integrated into all Google and third-party services as well as being connected to loyalty programmes. They analyse what a consumer does online and can get really close to providing them with the right service at the right time.

Consumer Lifestyles

Consumers have routines and their lifestyles are built around a social, private and business circle. The consumer can be a parent at the weekend, paying for a sandwich in a sports club, an employee on Monday, buying a coffee or having a company lunch, and a retired person on a Friday evening, having a drink with friends or dinner with a partner. All around these movements there is a payment flow.

One of the challenges for banks is that by law, they have to serve every consumer. For example, the chequebook is still fully distributed in the UK market and the latest innovation is that a cheque actually settles in one day instead of five days. From a technical viewpoint you have to understand that challenger banks can cherry-pick more easily than the incumbent banks. These banks also have a much bigger impact in the global payments hierarchy, but are less flexible. We can expect lots of partnerships with banks within the FinTech playing field, except for the players who really centralize their business around the consumer.

Consumer Roles

Consumers have many different roles. For example, a woman can be a mother, an employee, a freelance worker and a member of a sports team, part of a social network club, alumni girls' society, wife and manager of the household. Around her life she has her payment flows, with different ways of paying and from different accounts. So, the more you know about the daily behaviour of this consumer, the better you can support her needs. Incumbent banks do not have that information and are currently not equipped to serve consumers' varied needs. Consumer-driven companies have a lot more access to this data, and there is trust to give more data for incentivizing them. In future, the payment flow will be integrated into these different roles with different participants, where all payments are interchangeable, and also better designed to satisfy needs.

The woman in our example has more than 10 payment flows from different budgets. Within the "bank rail" these can be interchangeable depending on need. If she has a minimum budget for groceries, but there is extra loyalty credit on the energy account, then she is able to use this credit to increase the grocery budget, instantly fulfilling the need. In an economy driven by market power and self-interest, there will be "power to the people" derived from an unregulated platform, which will function like this. It is a dream to think that new technologies – such as digital currencies with blockchain – will be able to offer this. However, consumer-driven companies are able to bring together a network of participants to combine understanding and access to influence consumer behaviour.

An Interchangeable Wallet

In an ideal world a player such as Google, which has a clear data profile of a consumer and is used by them daily, can offer a check-box with your energy supplier, favourite supermarket or work cafe. In these three places you can imagine all cards becoming interchangeable in one wallet. Every move a consumer makes is somehow registered or followed. The secret is to be consumer-driven and set the rules that add value to the consumer. Imagine that to pay for a child's education, additional capital is required. This could be obtained by issuing your own personal currency asset secured against your house, based on its value.

A "blockchain" that adds participants within a network of personal decentralized ledgers around your profile is a very elegant solution to this problem. Although Bitcoin is over 10 years old, we see that the current approach is still in its infancy. A "sharing the wealth" approach is silently being developed and grown, but it will be difficult to predict how fast consumers will adapt to this change.

Taking the Long-Term View

In the next 10 years we expect a lot of initiatives from new companies who will start the process. Within 20 years there will be a shift in the current way we are using payments. This is based on the fact that consumers do not like change and in the banking world it is a golden rule that a new service takes a minimum of 7 years to get to consumer acceptance. The change will happen gradually and the more consumer-centric services are launched, the easier the consumer will find it to integrate these into their lives. What we are seeing is that technology passes through phases, whereby it can truly support you as a consumer and empower you, as well as your financial needs, at any point in time. We know this change is happening, but only as fast as consumers are able to adopt and use it in their lives.

Blueprint for Change

6

BLUEPRINT FOR CHANGE

From: the "plumbers" of payments, working in isolation, dealing with the pipes of financial services

- Behind-the-scenes, unglamorous but necessary and skilled roles
- Usually operating at national level

To: Collaborative, forward-thinking innovators, with a wide range of skills to keep pace with the speed and complexity of PayTech on a global scale

- Designers
- Creators
- Engineers
- Technicians
- Mechanics
- Visionaries
- Customer champions

Executive Summary

You've read all about the fascinating world of payments. But what about the future? If you bring together consumers demanding change, regulators enabling competition and technology making change possible, what do you have?

In the last part of *The PayTech Book* you will hear from some of the leading thinkers in the world of payments. A director of one of the world's largest banks shares a vision for how the digital world will unfold, what this means for cash and the financially excluded, and how cooperation will allow the payments industry to satisfy consumers' growing needs for instant, convenient and secure payments. A professor of marketing who founded the Emerging Payments Association explains why some PayTech innovations fail to take off and provides some practical advice for innovators and investors creating the future of our industry.

A FinTech adviser explains why many startups fail to reach their potential and proposes a structured formula for success. An academic focused on emergent technologies, innovation strategies and policy describes the impact digital banking is likely to have on payments market infrastructures. An entrepreneur explains the changing role of money in our lives. He goes on to introduce the concept of programmable money and its adoption in a world of open banking, commonly accepted standards and digital identity – and how this could save the banks. Another entrepreneur highlights the changing requirements of gig economy workers and how payments can unlock open banking solutions to service the freelancer segment.

Cybersecurity and its importance in a world of increasingly sophisticated criminals is explained by a PayTech security and compliance specialist, and how data analytics and artificial intelligence can help reduce fraud and money laundering to acceptable levels. The concept of different networks and their current and potential roles in PayTech is explained by a FinTech Association leader. The ecosystem surrounding payments, so often opaque to many, is described clearly by an industry veteran, who goes on to explain what changes are taking place in a mature country to allow it to remain ahead of the game.

The future of mobile money in Africa is considered by a senior technology executive in light of the success of a widely adopted technology solution in Zimbabwe and the impact this could have on commerce, society and economies across the continent. We conclude with a romp through time, highlighting the changing nature of payments.

A Blueprint for Change

By Marion King
Director of Payments, NatWest

If someone was to tell you that the foundations of our banking system stem from a theological order of monks fighting a holy war, you would perhaps raise an eyebrow. Stick with me. In 1185, the monastics of the Knights Templar could deposit large sums of cash in return for a letter of credit. The Templar would voyage to Jerusalem with his letter, which would be exchanged to withdraw cash. Here we have an early example of an independent organization storing money for the benefit of its affiliates, using a payment mechanism of value exchange to prevent knights from having to transport heaps of cash across the world. This independent organization was, in effect, a primitive bank.

Fast forward to today and you will see that the banking industry has not deviated away from this core dynamic. Institutions continue to exist in order to serve the financial needs of customers, albeit through more complex and varied means. In payments, institutions collaborate and compete to facilitate the exchange of value between customers. As we look to the future, technological change will drive further collaboration and competition, generating more choice for customers. The UK saw 38.8 billion payments in 2017, a number which owes its size to technology.[1] Payments are faster, more frequent, more secure and larger in both quantity and value than ever before. In this chapter we explore the blueprint for change, analysing how the payments industry is embedding customer orientation into technological change in order to best serve the financial needs of people. We begin by exploring four themes.

Digitalization and the "Dash From Cash"

2017 saw debit card payments surpass cash as the most common means of payment in the UK in terms of volume. This momentous change poses questions about the roles of cash and digital currency in our society. While cash continues to be prominent, digital currency is unquestionably the talk of the town. In the eyes of the consumer, digitalized transactions offer numerous benefits. Payments can be made faster and often require only a card or smartphone. For many, gone are the days of digging through your pockets or purse for coins and notes.

Spending limits are no longer confined to the cash in your wallet, as consumers now benefit from immediate access to their bank balance, 24/7. On the other side of the exchange, retailers also stand to gain. Laboriously handling change and cheques creates inefficiencies and increases costs. Self-checkout tills enable greater volumes of customers to be served, and at a reduced cost. Portable card terminals and QR code technology mean that retailers around the world are increasingly able to sell their products with little else but an Internet connection.[2] And as we look to the future, the online marketplace will continue to disrupt the way we shop. Consumers can make purchases from their home and merchants can sell goods without a physical store. Companies that can leverage societal desire to use digital currencies stand to gain immensely in the years to come.

However, going digital isn't so straightforward, and the "dash from cash" must be controlled. The Independent Access to Cash review claims that 47% of people in the UK, or 25 million people, believe that "cash is not a choice, but a necessity".[3] Based on the current rise in debit card popularity, a straight-line trend would show cash ceasing to exist by 2026. There are a number of risks

---

[1] Summary UK Payments Market.

[2] Accenture Report Future Payments Tech.

[3] Independent Access to Cash Review.

associated with a cashless society that make this outcome unlikely. Firstly, a big proportion of our population is not digital-native. They do not have the digital know-how or access to benefit from many of the features of a cashless society. A sudden leap into a cashless society risks excluding those people, potentially causing a decline in consumer consumption. This is already the case in Sweden, where some merchants now refuse to accept cash. Secondly, many people rely on cash for their budgeting. Stripping this demographic of their budgeting tools risks depriving them of control over their finances. Finally, some of rural Britain is unable to offer cashless services. Poor broadband and a lack of desire are hurdles to this implementation. Banks have a responsibility to cater to the needs of all members of society. As exciting as digital banks are, the needs of society as a whole must be met. Traditional banks are proud to serve all members of society, including people and businesses that depend on cash and non-digital services. The dash from cash may be inevitable, but change must occur gradually, and there is space for innovators to lead the transition.

How We Pay is Changing

As society becomes increasingly open to digitalization, the industry is re-evaluating how we make payments. Traditionally, finance and technology have existed in a somewhat estranged dynamic. Current affairs in payments show that, today, this view could not be further from the truth. Innovation shows that we are experiencing a consolidation of erstwhile juxtaposed entities to yield a symbiotic relationship:

- Traditional players in the finance industry have infrastructure, end-to-end industry knowledge, an extensive customer base and, most importantly, trust.

- Technology-driven firms have agile innovation, adopting modern ways of working and proudly exhibiting disruptive attitudes.

The two mixed together have brought us FinTech or in some cases BigTech. The power of partnership is exploding in payments.

Innovation is taking many forms; some firms are looking at attaching QR codes to advertisements, creating apps that can scan these codes to take you straight to the payment window for that product. Others are creating unique single-use credit card details, trying to prevent fraudsters from stealing usable bank account details during online shopping. Here at NatWest, we are particularly enthusiastic about peer-to-peer technology, where customers can pay directly into other bank accounts without funds having to be held by an intermediary.

A key theme consistent across all of this innovation is that payments are being integrated into customer journeys. Customers no longer expect to swap mobile apps or enter their bank details to make a payment. With the push of a button or a nonchalant scan of a code, customers want to complete the purchase. The challenge for innovators will be to deliver this while guaranteeing security and efficiency.

Cooperation as a Catalyst of Competition

Cooperation will be pivotal as firms seek to innovate and disrupt the payments industry. In fact, it already is. Following the financial crash of 2008, the Financial Services Authority (now the Financial Conduct Authority) and the Bank of England collaborated to reduce the barriers to entry in the banking industry, enabling new challenger banks to enter the market. The consequent competition for customers has spurred innovation, encouraging firms to embrace customer-centric mentalities throughout their business.

More recently, the advent of the second Payment Services Directive and the roll-out of open banking means that traditional banks do not have an oligopoly over the data of their many customers. With the consent of the customer, regulated financial institutions can share data in order to facilitate the rapid development of products and services. Far from being nebulous, the sharing of data in a proper manner incentivizes firms to improve the customer journey. In a world where those with the best understanding of customers have the most success, there is no other way for firms to thrive. For example, some firms now provide artificial intelligence-enabled fraud tools, to analyse BACs data to detect malicious behaviour.

It is important to remember that the fraudsters are also innovative; however, cooperation and data sharing can help firms in the fight against crime. One such example is where firms provide biometric analysis – using data derived from typing patterns, keypad pressure and corporeal analytics can detect a change in user and hence is able to keep customers safe and secure online in the event that their device has been stolen or compromised.

It is essential that firms do not lose sight of the fact that they are merely custodians of data that is owned by the customer. When this relationship is appropriately harnessed by cooperative firms it can yield insight and a platform for new services. Cooperation between firms sharing data in a competitive environment stimulates innovation, which in an increasingly customer-centric industry will positively improve the customer journey in the payments domain.

Money that Knows Us Better than We Know Ourselves

The data derived from open banking has the potential to lead to ground-breaking behavioural analysis. For centuries, the fundamental neoclassical microeconomic assumption has been that humans operate in rational and predictable ways. Half of this assumption has been swept under the carpet by recent challenges in the school of behavioural economics. (i.e. how irrationality, personality, randomness, addiction, persuasion and quirks of the human psyche impact on economic decision-making).

The data collated from customers and shared openly between banks gives a better understanding of behaviour, and financial institutions can use this information to provide bespoke services to customers. For example, imagine a scenario where – using data – a bank knows that a customer makes many international calls. Assume also that there is a procedure in place that enables the customer to express that they'd like to continue doing so. Using this information, banks can provide excellent insights for the customer. What if a bank could find that customer a cheaper mobile broadband deal suited to international phone calls? What if, rather than just offering a cheaper deal, a bank could automatically swap a customer to that deal, automating the process and saving the customer from having to manually do it themselves?

In this scenario, is it necessary for customers to go through the payment experience themselves, or with consent should the bank be allowed to adjust direct debits on behalf of their customers? Such questions and ideas will become commonplace in the future, and will be the basis for considerable debate. The opportunities to use data to provide tailored services for the benefit of customers are plentiful, and we can be sure of seeing innovation in this space in the years to come.

However, in order to ensure favourable outcomes, it is important to consider the risks that technology surrounding data impose. By understanding customer behaviour using data modelling and by listening to the needs and wants of customers, unsupervised firms could instead harm customers. Mike McAteer, co-founder of the Financial Inclusion Sector, aptly warned that firms could use data to exploit behavioural biases, using confusing sales and marketing strategies to extract value from customers.[4] Vulnerable customers are particularly at risk. All firms must understand the risks, because inadequately tested algorithms could lead to erroneous conclusions about customer behaviour.[5] Improperly stored or transferred data could lead to unintended disclosure or identity theft. The key point here is that the market has a responsibility to

---

[4] The Raconteur Future of Money Special Report.

[5] CFI website.

proactively serve the needs of the customer and treat their data with respect, integrity and transparency.

Final Remarks

As was the case with the Knights Templar, the future of banks revolves around the needs of the customer. In the world of payments, the industry will use technological change to make the customer experience simpler and more efficient. By navigating through the digitalization of currencies, redefining the means through which we pay, cooperating as a means of competing and using data to provide bespoke service to customers, the payments industry will better serve the needs of customers.

Change will enable customers to do more things, and to do things they already do differently. Firms must embrace the challenges that will be brought about by an increasingly digitally enabled society if they mean to survive. They must be quick to adapt and determined to innovate. As we look to the future, the words of the Greek philosopher Heraclitus must remain permanently on the tip of our tongues: "Change is the only constant". And we are all the better for it.

Accelerating the Adoption of PayTech Innovations

By Dan Horne
Professor and Associate Dean, Providence College School of Business

Introduction

Beginning in the first several years of the new century, predictions were made that mobile payments would make up 20%, 30%, even 50% of all consumer transaction volume by 2015. Here we sit in 2019 with products that do everything they say on the tin and more, but penetration figures in the USA are still well under 1%.

This is by no means to suggest that the problem is restricted to mobile payments. This miscalculation, and the constant undershooting of targets for consumer adoption of new payment technology in general, is the result of three factors:

1. Some forecasts are simply attempts to create self-fulfilling prophecies. The reality is that predictions of revolution make headlines whilst predictions of evolution end up in the waste bin. However, in this information-saturated world, hype is hard to sustain.

2. Innovators fail to understand the core components of consumer adoption of technology. Despite claims of being consumer-centric, many operate in a manner that echoes the "if we build it, they will come" approach of the 1950s and 1960s. Unfortunately, demands on consumers' time and the flood of information make this approach ineffective even for truly new, hugely beneficial payment innovations.

3. Because financial products involve money, there is a heightened sense of risk that must be overcome before adoption will take place.

Below I outline the various consumer concerns that inhibit adopting new ways of paying and suggest ways of more confidently introducing new products based on better consumer understanding and better understanding of the internal processes and framing that tend to blind payment innovators to the realities of the market. The case is made that consideration of actual perceived benefits, the frank assessment of learning costs and the creation of trust are simple yet necessary steps in accelerating the use of a given payment technology.

Incrementalism is Not an Option for Startups

If you are Unilever selling in an existing market, then a "New and Improved" label and a marginal change are probably enough to generate some increased attention and sales. If you are a smaller or unknown brand, then what you offer has to be RADICALLY better at fulfilling consumers' needs than whatever it intends to replace. This may sound derogatory, but consumers are lazy and are unwilling to try something new unless it promises to really make a difference in how they live their lives. However, this change must be real to the customer and not just hype.

Harvard Professor John Gourville wrote about this phenomenon in a famous *Harvard Business Review* article[1] entitled "Eager Sellers and Stoney Buyers". Gourville correctly noted that entrepreneurs tend to view their products in isolation and overestimate the value of what they have created. Consumers, in contrast, view the benefits of new offerings within the context of their lives and relative to how they are currently dealing with their needs. As such, a new product may be better than an existing one, but the difference between the old and the new is not enough to overcome the risk of adopting something not previously tried.

Gourville's model suggests that sellers overestimate their product benefits by a factor of three while, because they tend to be risk averse, buyers underestimate to the same degree. The implication

---

[1] *Harvard Business Review*, June 2006.

is that new offerings must be perceived as offering a very large benefit over the incumbent. If the product is truly new, this hurdle may be cleared, but if it is simply an incremental change, adoption will lag.

Consumers Don't Have Time to be Guinea Pigs

More than 99.99% of people face two major constraints in their lives – time and money. The latter is really a choice of framing. Today's consumer-driven economies create demand for goods and services beyond what is necessary for survival. Time, however, especially in developed economies, is in serious short supply. Given all the alternative ways that we can spend our time, it, not money, has become the most valuable possession. It is easy to see this in the marketplace; as time has become increasingly rare, convenience has become the most sought-after product attribute.

Most PayTech innovations are, therefore, rightly built around speed and convenience, something that we'll address below. However, inventors of new PayTech products are so often caught up in the creation of bells and whistles that they fail to recognize that the customer often has to follow a long road to realize those benefits. Sometimes innovators actually know their products too well. They can't unlearn the hours of using and testing that accompany development, and so their ability to empathize is distorted. New users, however, have a learning curve to travel before they can make use of the features that differentiate the new product from its competitors. The coolest and best product will ultimately flop if the journey from first awareness to actual use is long and/or arduous.

Trust is the Not-So-Secret Sauce

In addition to the two substantial hurdles above, financial service providers face an additional layer of wariness from the end user simply because the products involve money. Especially when

dealing with people in the middle and lower economic strata, a mistake leading to the loss of money can have substantial, and potentially long-term, consequences. Thus, the perception of trust is an absolutely necessary condition for adoption of new PayTech products. Moreover, the perception of trust incorporates not only feelings about the individual firm, but also those about the industry as a whole.

The How-To Section

Taking the above into account, let me close by setting out the three ways in which PayTech firms can increase their chances of innovating successfully:

1. Dealing with the creation of value is a tightrope walk for some. How can a firm get attention in the market without hyping the differentiating characteristics? Foremost, the core product has to be great. Invest in the "must-have" components of the product and resist the urge to spend time and effort building features that are, however flashy, only useful occasionally or to a small segment of your customer base. Resist, as well, the natural entrepreneurial inclination to oversell. Yes, it's your child, but be confident presenting what it actually does well – not what you are bringing out next week, next month or next quarter.

2. Invest in making the user experience very fast and very easy. There is a tendency to want to capture all kinds of data from new customers because "well, data are important and we'll figure out what to do with it once it is in-hand". Unfortunately, this tactic decreases the probability that there will actually be any data to figure out. After the monumental task of getting someone on the brink of committing, having someone drop out is shameful. Capture what is absolutely necessary legally and to operate; the rest can wait.

3. Product or brand trust is important but tends to be related to time and personal experience, both missing for new products from

unknown brands. Some products try to build trust quickly through extensive marketing efforts. That can certainly work, but few have the resources to take this path. An alternative way to establish a perception of trust is to de-risk the user's experience. This can take the form of actual risk reduction through guarantees and excellent customer service, or strategies to create perceived risk reduction, such as partnerships with established brands or associations with credible industry groups.

How to Build a Successful PayTech Product

By Vasyl Soloshchuk
CEO, INSART

In recent years, we have observed an explosion of FinTech startups. Few of them manage to succeed and monetize their business. Very often they fail due to a lack of understanding of the industry, its challenges and its gaps. This gets in the way of innovative ideas and workable solutions.

So how can FinTech startups build successful payment products?

Find the Problem

Although the US and European payment ecosystems are already well developed, they are far from ideal. Many things have not significantly changed in the last decade. For example, all payments are always about bank accounts. A consumer can't use PayPal, Venmo, Zelle, or any other payment platform without connecting with a bank account.

There are several problem areas where opportunities lie:

- There's certainly a trend towards **seamless payment processes**. Great examples are Uber and the checkout-free Amazon Go stores, where the payment process is hidden entirely. Companies that provide services relevant to other areas of life will succeed if they use technology to make payments so easy that they are almost invisible to consumers.

- **Big data analytics** has been a buzzword for years; however, little has been done in terms of processing the data. Transaction data contains insights about consumers, their financial position and the goods and services they buy. Machine learning can be used to analyse customer experiences, preferences and behaviour. Based on the data, financial companies can improve the client experience and build loyalty. Such initiatives can help many companies increase their revenue, and thus are welcome.

- Another growing trend in PayTech is **open data**. Regulations such as the second Payment Services Directive are forcing banks to open their systems to third-party providers. This creates new opportunities for startups. Via application programming interfaces, many legacy banking systems are integrating with more flexible FinTech startups that are focused on front-end activities, efficiency and scalability.

- Changing customer expectations make it almost impossible for autonomous products to show significant expansion and monetization. Technological disruption encourages consumers to choose **all-in-one apps** where they can chat, catch up on news, find job opportunities, undergo self-development, buy, donate and invest. WeChat is a great example of such an app.

- Open data, together with data analytics, makes payments part of a person's identity. Thus, cyber-security has become critical. FinTech companies are developing solutions to use **artificial intelligence, machine learning, and the Internet of Things** to minimize violation risks.

- Back in 2016, leading Canadian banks started building a digital identity ecosystem. During 2018, several countries – including Thailand, Singapore and several West African states – initiated digital ID programmes aimed at protecting against fraud. Innovation in this area is highly necessary.

- In the **least developed regions**, such as Africa, Latin America and certain parts of Asia, there are even bigger opportunities for innovation. Here, the entire ecosystem is still under development. Considering the cultural context of the regions, the payment channels and client experience may differ significantly. This is where it's definitely worth looking for opportunities.

Check Out Your Idea

Above, I provided examples of areas where PayTech startups may look for ideas, whether the aim is to create a disruptive product or enhance the existing ecosystem. Nevertheless, having an innovative idea is not enough to create a really worthwhile PayTech product. Understanding the inner workings of the industry may become crucial to the success of a startup.

Unfortunately, many FinTech startups think about their ideas mostly from the consumer's standpoint, and make assumptions about how the system operates instead of discussing the problem with industry experts. Their assumptions may be wrong, and the product they create may not turn out to be viable. If the founders of a PayTech startup don't have expertise in the industry, they need to figure out all the details of the problem they want to solve.

Similar to any other industry, payments have rules and regulations; some of them are obscure for people outside of the business. From one side, we have observed a need for greater openness throughout the industry. From the other side, regulations require robust measures for identity data management.

To make things worse, regulations differ from country to country. Even within the USA, each state mandates its own regulatory body, and in many cases these conflict with each other. Very often, strict regulations make it difficult for startups to grow and monetize.

Some experts believe that disruptive technologies, such as blockchain, can replace regulations. As a step in this direction, JPMorgan has created the Interbank Information Network, a blockchainbased system.

Industry players say that regulations are always obsolete because it takes several years for regulators to make rules governing the ways new technologies are applied. However, there are instances when regulators have invited FinTech companies to propose changes to regulations. In Barbados, the central bank has created a "regulatory sandbox" in order to test unproven technology or products and services that don't fall under any existing legislation, and to determine regulatory issues and suggest alternative measures. Similar sandboxes appear in Latin America, the UK and Singapore. Such sandboxes allow PayTech startups to examine their innovative ideas and launch products in the payment field with lower barriers to entry and at lower cost.

Scale the Business

Once a PayTech startup has figured out the details of a problem they aim to solve, launched a minimal viable product and validated their business model, new pitfalls await them.

A disruptive product raises clients' expectations, and if the startup doesn't meet these, it will definitely lose. Many PayTech startups fail to scale their business. Their further growth depends mostly on their ability to rapidly expand the software functionality. However, at this stage PayTech startups generally experience significant difficulties due to technical debt and a lack of established processes in the team.

Inappropriate architecture, poorly documented code, performance issues, inability to "parallelize" software development – these are all examples of obstacles that prevent startups from creating new features at a rapid pace.

Takeaways

As you identify a problem and think about the solution, ask yourself the following questions:

- Does your idea harmonize with the existing landscape, or disrupt the industry?
- How does your payment product comply with regulations or pioneer changes?
- Will your product be autonomous, and if so, how will it succeed?

- If not, which industry players will be interested in integrating with you, and why?

When your business starts to become successful, the list of questions changes:

- To what extent should client feedback influence your further development so that clients aren't disappointed and your product evolves in a balanced way?
- What needs to change in the company to achieve exponential growth?

The Future of Digital Payments Market Infrastructures

By Jonathan Liebenau
Reader in Technology Management, London School of Economics and Political Science

Dana Lunberry
PhD Candidate, London School of Economics and Political Science

and Daniel Gozman
Senior Lecturer, University of Sydney

Introduction

Payment market infrastructures (PMIs) are facing considerable turmoil and are under a great deal of pressure to be updated. There are three reasons for this:

1. New attitudes towards regulatory scrutiny from central banks and regulators.

2. New business models associated with FinTechs and especially challengers such as Ripple.

3. New technologies that offer new control mechanisms and promises of cheaper, faster, more transparent and less risky methods.

Below we explore how the rise of digital banking, emerging payments alternatives and some aspects of the service economy are likely to lead to substantial changes in PMIs in future.

The Rise of Digital Banking

Digital banking is reinventing the financial industry as we know it.

Digital banking is substantially different from "digitalized banking", which involves updating legacy products, services and processes to become digital. Digital banking uses new business models and digital technologies that give more choice for organizations because they are more flexible and malleable than technologies of the past.

Digital technologies also enable organizations to integrate in new ways, allowing structures to cross-subsidize each other. They enable "track and trace" capabilities along with instantaneous flows of data and information. Such features of digital banking enable the development of new business models that provide increased value to providers and their customers. They level the playing field and reduce the organizational boundaries and bureaucratic institutional processes that were barriers in the past.

The development of new business models in financial services is gaining momentum. Some of the models being adopted are moving beyond financial services and into an open marketplace. Platform enterprises, for example, provide new sources of value to customers. From the development of multisided markets, these platforms can span industries, offering customers a broad range of products and services. Mobile and online platforms, such as the world's largest mobile payments platform – Alipay – are meeting a variety of customer needs from payments to insurance selection and digital identification services. At the other end of the spectrum, there are emergent business models geared towards closed payments systems. Niche payments systems are developing into the very modes of production, meeting specialized needs with high levels of efficiency.

The changes being observed in the market are affecting business practices everywhere:

- Financial institutions may have to broaden or diversify their businesses.

- Others may have to specialize and focus on a particular market gap.

- Some may move from satisfying consumers to focusing on businesses.

Those dependent on legacy systems are especially vulnerable to change. Unsurprisingly, an increasing number of large banks are launching standalone digital banks in order to bypass the hurdles brought by legacy systems and organizational cultures. Digital banking is the way of the future and the rapid adoption of application programming interfaces (APIs) means the shift towards new banking models based on multiplayer integration is well under way.

Emerging Payments Structures

As a result of today's technological possibilities, new payments structures are being developed:

- Among the most radical payments innovations are **peer-to-peer networks and cryptographic currencies** (e.g. Bitcoin), driven partly by frustration arising from shortcomings in existing PMIs. Cross-border payments are relying less on traditional banking infrastructures, moving beyond established payment rails (e.g. Visa, Mastercard, PayPal, etc.). Experimentation with newer technologies, such as Ripple's employment of blockchain, are facilitating new collaborations and removing unnecessary layers of intermediation. In the future, such alternatives may help solve some of today's major challenges – such as those involving liquidity, settlement and currency exchange.

- In **high-risk regions** of the world, and especially where bank accounts have historically been inaccessible to large segments of the population, payment alternatives have been sought and the structure of payments has become more diversified.

- Innovations such as **mobile money**, which is an account linked to a phone number, have started to mature and are permeating many societies – especially in developing and emerging markets.

- Globally, **mobile wallets** are on the rise as mobile network operators, retail and tech giants venture more prominently into the payments arena.

Innovations in domestic payments have also begun to strongly influence cross-border payments. Increasing demand for mobile payments (payments through mobile phones) and real-time payments (known for their speed with messaging and tracking capabilities) are challenging payments networks and providers to rethink and redesign systems for all types of payments.

Because of such improvements, customers have become accustomed to instant and transparent payment services. Consumer demands are driving incremental technological developments in such a way that affords them a frictionless, integrated and comprehensive payments service experience.

Dynamics of the Service Economy

The service economy presents other drivers of change across industries which are causing ripples in financial services – including cross-border payments. In this do-it-yourself era, financial institutions can close more of their branches and rely more heavily on online and mobile banking as their primary mode of customer engagement.

Some institutions are shifting the burden of service onto the customer without compensating them. Others are expected to improve services in order to compete in today's rapidly evolving financial landscape. By leveraging large volumes and a productive use of customer data, institutions can provide greater value to customers through a diverse suite of end-to-end services which enable customers to fulfil their needs without focusing on sales of proprietary products.

Fostered by recent regulatory changes, such as the General Data Protection Regulation and open banking, and the need to diversify business portfolios, institutions are developing data-rich services to differentiate themselves in the market and gain customers' valuable trust.

The Future

In the future, the role of digital technologies will become increasingly prominent and will be particularly important for improving customer relationships and redistributing risk.

As customer expectations evolve, and as the demand for greater speed, transparency and convenience continues to rise, technologies will enable new business models that can meet these demands.

Technologies will help reduce risk by disintermediating the layers of legacy systems which we have today. They will enable enhanced methods for detecting and tackling cybercrime, which is becoming increasingly sophisticated. In today's context – with changing regulations that tend to push for open APIs while placing more responsibility for security onto the providers – technology will become critical to the chances of survival for many institutions.

It's Money, Jim, But Not As We Know It

By Marten Nelson
Co-Founder and CMO, Token Inc.

Money. Few other social systems play such an important role in helping us get on with our lives. Even fewer systems can claim to be on the brink of such fundamental change, driven, of course, by the rise of digital tech in payments.

PayTech innovations are challenging some of the most sacred premises in banking. What is money? What are payments? Do we even need currency anymore? Moreover, do we even need banks? Heck, what even *is* a bank these days?

So different is this new world that pretty soon we're going to need to find new ways to talk – and think – about payments.

Programmable Money

In time, this simple concept will completely transform the global financial services industry.

In essence, money is nothing more than a shared set of rules for exchanging value. A €20 note is only worth €20 because it has been assigned that value by the European Central Bank, according to rules enshrined in law. Everyone who uses the Euro participates in these rules and agrees to abide by them.

Programmable money is just the same. The only difference is that here, the rules which define when and how value can be exchanged can be reimagined according to how the payer and the payee want to transact.

For example, banks and their customers can use programmable money to hardwire terms and conditions (T&Cs) into their transactions, securing and verifying them using a combination of cryptography and tokenization technologies. This means that transactions can only ever be authorized when all the T&Cs are met. This also makes the transaction virtually impossible to hack, since the data transmitted between the transacting parties is meaningless to everyone else, so it can be sent freely over the Internet. This happens instantly and – crucially – enables the bank to reduce its dependence on third parties who would conventionally charge a fee for verifying the authenticity of the transaction and those performing it.

By using programmable money, banks in particular have a huge opportunity to transform how they operate. Many of the transaction-based services banks provide – like inter-bank and intra-bank transfers, cross-border payments, direct debits and bank-to-bank payments – all require third-party validation. Today's external checking process costs the bank and slows everything down.

Open Banking: The Dawn of a New Pay

Open banking – the idea that an individual's bank account data and payment facilities can, through public application programming interfaces (APIs), be accessed and managed by customer-permitted third parties – is a beachhead into the mainstream for a variety of new PayTechs. These include programmable money and smart tokenization.

In Europe, the second Payment Services Directive (PSD2) is forcing banks to cede control of their accounts and data to customers. It will create an ecosystem that fosters both collaboration and coopetition between banks and FinTechs. This promises to deliver more choice, more intelligent services and a better customer experience to end users.

Two-Sided Ecosystem

Open banking creates a two-sided financial ecosystem. Banks sit on one side and everyone seeking API access to banks – including merchants, developers, other banks, consumers and payment and data third-party providers (TPPs) – sit on the other.[1]

The middle ground – conventionally inhabited by clearing houses, payment schemes, processors and other authorizing service providers – is no longer needed. "Bank-direct" engagement is the order of the day and transactions, in the form of both payments and account information, can occur automatically and instantly.

That's the idea, at least. The reality in Europe has been somewhat different: banks are struggling to get going.

Why? Because success in open banking is contingent on the banks' APIs being two things:

- interoperable, and
- easy for third-party developers to write to.

The lack of a European open banking API standard means that neither of these conditions is being met and, as a result, the mass interconnectivity that PSD2 was designed to generate isn't yet happening. Instead, the widespread development of proprietary APIs is causing fragmentation and integration pain for both banks and TPPs, and holding back the development of the market.

Of the APIs that are available, only a handful of banks in the UK, collectively known as the CMA9 (Competition and Market

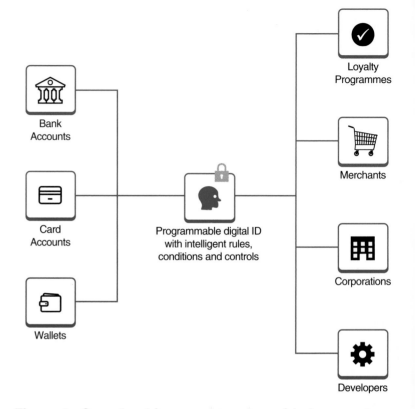

Figure 1: Open banking creates a two-sided ecosystem

Authority 9), are using the same one. They are only doing so because the UK regulator required them to and, even then, each bank has implemented the standard differently.

This is bad for everyone: it increases costs and complexity at each bank, opens the door to insecure solutions, which expose banks and their customers to unnecessary risk, and hinders adoption by software developers who only have bandwidth to write to one or two APIs.

History has taught us that developers will not write to more APIs than this. If there were as many operating systems as PC or smartphone manufacturers, it would be cost and time prohibitive

---

[1] For more information on the economics and strategies of multi-sided networks in banking, see the academic work by M. Zachariadis and P. Ozcan (2017) "The API Economy and Digital Transformation in Financial Services: The Case of Open Banking". SWIFT Institute Working Paper No. 2016-001. Available at https://ssrn.com/abstract=2975199.

for developers to build apps. This is why there are two platforms each for PCs and mobile devices; it's the maximum number the developer market can sustain.

Only when the standards are established, and developers are supported, do things really take off. The global success of Google Play and Apple's App Store are testament to this. An enabled and well-supported community of developers has delivered more and better apps for iOS and Android than either Apple or Google could achieve in isolation. In the same way, by supporting TPPs with easy API integration and data availability, banks have a chance of being the architects of their own transformation.

Token has created a single API that connects to all banks for payment and account information requests. This enables banks and TPPs to sidestep the problem and, in time, aims to become the *de facto* platform used across the open banking ecosystem.

What are the Opportunities for Banks?

It's worth keeping in mind that the primary driver of both technology and regulation in open banking comes from customer demand. The end-game – to deliver a more comprehensive, powerful, convenient and secure digital banking user experience – is a *response* to the expectations of today's increasingly impatient digital consumer.

In this context, PSD2 ceases to be a compliance issue for banks, and instead becomes a business development opportunity. A big one. When open banking is "done right", banks can deliver more and better services that deepen customer relationships and establish market differentiation. And those that provide the best support to third-party service providers will gain significant early-mover advantage, the kudos of cutting-edge positioning and many new customers.

As the financial services API economy takes shape, new business models will also emerge along with a whole host of new payment and data aggregation services, providing revenue opportunities for banks that haven't yet been identified.

Customer Centricity

The introduction of open banking puts the customer firmly in the driving seat – after all, it is now up to them to decide which services to connect their account to. It stands to reason then that the banks which reposition themselves to align with this new customer-centric dynamic will prosper the most.

Given that banks' portfolios of (previously uncontested) products and services will need to compete alongside the rest of the market, here's a key question:

> *What else can banks do for their customers that can't be done better, faster or more securely by a third party?*

Bank-Grade Digital ID

At the heart of the open banking revolution is the business of transaction authorization. Banks operate to a tightly regulated and long-established model of trust: the bank verifies your identity and uses it, confidentially, to enable you to securely engage with the transacting world. Bank cards are already widely accepted as forms of ID, so why shouldn't a bank also apply that identity verification to digital use cases?

The model is already up and running, but is provided by other stakeholders. Google and Facebook take a cut every time you choose to associate a new authentication gateway with the login credentials you use for their accounts; a process known as "federated authentication" or, more commonly, "login with Facebook" or "login with Google".

Their offering is flawed, principally because Google and Facebook continue to underpin the service with the same "shared secrets" model as old-world bank security. Lose your root password to a hacker and you automatically gift them access to your other associated web accounts as well. Its reliance on password credentials makes it badly insecure.

Using modern, secure authentication solutions based on public-key cryptography, bank-grade digital ID verification that has been set up for open banking can sit behind the federated authentication service just as easily. Then, banks can use this service to generate new revenues or monetizable data, either from their customers or from the service providers whose gateways they secure. Maybe from both.

Self-Sovereign Identity

The model of self-sovereign identity (SSI) builds on this idea and, usefully, also marries it to the new age of customer centricity. SSI is the concept that people and businesses can store their own digital identity on their own devices, and provide it efficiently to those who need to validate it, without relying on a central repository of identity data. Essentially, it does in the digital world what we do today with passports, drivers' licences and ID cards.

Here the opportunities for banks are just as significant: thanks to the depth of their know your customer processes, they have a chance to become (for a fee) enablers and validators of SSIs, for their customers to own and control, using their APIs as the systems interface.

Completing the Journey: Total Digitization

Having established that the advent of the open banking infrastructure has far-reaching implications for banks, it is also important to note that, to date, open banking APIs only really take care of the front-end messaging part of the transaction. As far as

the customer is concerned their money moves instantly, yet the actual back-end processing of the payment still requires the bank to utilize traditional payment rails.

What, then, if these rails could be bypassed too, and the entire process digitized? Banks could accelerate the whole end-to-end transaction process, axing costs and ridding themselves, finally, of the legacy system inefficiencies that have held them back for years.

This is another tremendous opportunity for banks, and can be seized by using "stablecoins".

Stable What?

A stablecoin is a cryptocurrency that is either pegged directly to a fiat currency, backed by another asset or programmed to ascertain its stability. A stablecoin's "backer" could be a fiat currency (or currencies), or a commodity, like a barrel of oil or a bar of gold. The aim of a stablecoin is to provide a cryptocurrency that will always maintain the same value; it was originally conceived to provide a safe haven for cryptocurrency traders seeking to protect their investments against market volatility.

Cryptocurrencies are increasingly falling under the scope of financial services regulations (e.g. the European 5th Anti-Money Laundering Directive – AML5). This is gradually lowering the barriers to entry for banks by providing the regulatory protections they need to confirm the legitimacy of their engagement in the crypto world.

A New Digital Rail for Open Banking Transactions

A stablecoin that is backed by a centrally issued fiat currency (or currencies) can be used to provide a secure, instant and low-cost "tunnel" through the Internet, via which banks can send and receive digital funds without reliance on the traditional payment networks. Think of it as a virtual private network for transactions.

Achieve this, and banks will command a level of agility never before seen from regulated financial institutions. They will be able to both comply with regulation and operate globally. Authorizing and processing transactions will occur simultaneously, enabling the flow of financial data and services to and from customers without friction and at a fraction of today's costs, creating new possibilities for revenue.

Conclusion

A set of new innovations that could save the established banks is on the horizon. The cloud of FinTech disintermediation will evaporate, Jim, meaning that banks may once again live long and prosper.

Payments as Open Business Banking Enabler for the Gig Economy

By Conny Dorrestijn
Founding Partner, BankiFi Ltd

and Mark Hartley
Founding Partner, BankiFi Ltd

Small and medium enterprises (SMEs) need and deserve better banking services than they have experienced for decades. In Europe alone they contribute to more than half of the value-added income, employ more people than all the large corporates put together and by their very nature nestle in the heart of society. In truth, they are not "SMEs" but people with real lives and a beating heart for their enterprise. They are business customers that behave like retail customers and everything they do in their business life is entwined. Business has an impact on private wealth; the payroll and paying creditors, although residing in the business, impact their private liquidity too. And this goes even further for the so-called "gigs" or freelancers, the self-employed, a very fast rising – literally – untapped market. Do we really think they want to meander through a jungle of apps to mix and match the financial support they need? Or should we as banks embrace this open banking era to serve those customers first and best?

SME and Freelancer Banking Today

Meet Chris. He left his job 2 years ago as creative director with a large tech firm and set up a social media agency for brand activation. He is on the go 24×7 and capable of serving small local companies as well as the large international technology firms he still counts in his network today. He knows that sales is a contact sport, chasing new business in the UK, but also in Singapore, Amsterdam and Berlin. He works with Amy and Jeff – self-employed top-end designers – and has a base production and account team of five. The business plan projections he went through with his business banker when he opened an account for a first loan mean very little today. If that one big project comes through the door he needs to hire contractors for 4 months and buy in supplies to a count of £200,000. If the deal does not happen, or not now, the picture is very different. When all goes well he has to either go back to the bank for a good conversation with his helpful (but rigid) account manager, or spend the better part of the weekend figuring out if any of the crowdfunders in the app store can help him with some short-term money at an affordable rate. He wants to spend every single minute on the projects and not on figuring out where he stands financially. At the same time, he is responsible for his staff, his customers and his family at home. So, queueing up for another long round of "painful" conversations to get a line of credit he taps into occasionally is what he must do – but in fairness, based on irrelevant data before the ink is dry.

This is not an odd story; this is a very normal business day for millions of entrepreneurs around the world – people with a high sense of responsibility, eager to "do their thing" and truly disliking any distraction (read "doing accounts" and "payments"). This is, however, also the everyday life of the frustrated and very willing bankers who would love to treat their clients in a human and holistic way. Bankers who are tied up by compliance on the one side, yet on the other side hear every day that they have to go "all the way" for their clients, think like they do and be creative. Both parties want to do it differently and, in an open banking world, "we can".

Imagine…

The same Chris now gets up in the morning, checks his iPhone watch and sees the signed contract. He onboards the customer and sends the first invoice for the 30% downpayment. He has given the bank access to his accounting package and their "nudges" system sees the outstanding amount and also the incoming invoices of suppliers. Later that week he gets a notice on his mobile: "Chris, congrats but this means you will be short of some 75K for about 10 days, do you want to sell some invoices to us, alternatively here is our offer for a 12-day line of credit. In the meantime we will pay your bills (payments on behalf) from either this or your other bank accounts to which you have given us access."

Relevance is the New "Black"

This is just one example, but what we see here is that the bank has moved from a position of necessary time-consuming "evil" to a financial partner who is able to look at and deal with a wider picture. Here we see the bank in a starring role as true business-enabling partner – there at the right moment and the relevant occasion. Relevance has overtaken delight in customer experience.

Bank Account-ing for Freelancers

For Chris's self-employed team members the world has changed too. Whereas before they would subscribe to a cool cloud-based accounting package of which they only used the invoice generation and VAT functionality, they are now "bank-accounting". They use their bank account to enter relevant invoice data and in the open banking remit, the bank is able to generate and send the invoice by mail or SMS and better still, collect the monies and put them in the right virtual account. Having done that, it is easy to submit the VAT return at the end of the month or quarter through the same bank account channel. Freelancers often issue a single-digit number of invoices per month and need nothing more than an "open business bank". "Get them early – keep them for life" is a mantra that rings (very realistically) true here.

The Bank as a Third-Party Provider

So far, the bank takes as much centre stage as the customer in this story. Why? Why not the masses of third-party providers[1] and FinTechs that "are about to take away payments first and then all other business from the banks". Well, there are a few impediments besides culture: first they need to be regulated as account information service (AIS) or payment initiation service (PIS) providers; second they need very large marketing budgets to attract volumes of those (low-margin) customers; and third there is the issue of trust. As the data breaches and flagrant data abuse cases tumble over us, factually correct or not, we feel and think that most big techs are after the same thing – our data is their business and therefore they do not have our best interests in mind as they focus on monetizing our data.

Through open banking, banks can put their experience and customer insight to work, see what their customers do with other banks and apps in their app store, and so develop a role of true financial orchestrator in their busy lives. Banks, because they are used to strict compliance rules, might even be better guardians than big techs when it comes to fine-grained consensus around data and respect for General Data Protection Regulation, whilst at the same time building relevant services around it.

---

[1] A third-party provider (TPP) is an authorized online service provider that has been introduced as part of open banking. They exist outside of your relationship with your bank, but may be involved in the online transactions you carry out. There are two types of TPP: PISP (payment initiation service provider) and AISP (account information service provider).

Open Banking is Open for Business – Today!

Business customers appreciate value for money. Gaining time and insight is valuable to them; no-frills instant payments are better than fee-levied card payments for e-commerce. Flexible lending rates are important too, or qualified introductions to apps in the bank's app store that might serve them better. Banks need fee income and lower costs. This is open business banking 2020 – delivered by your bank today.

The Financial Arms Race: The Game With No Rules

By Ekaterina Safonova
Director of Partnerships and Training, Technical Advisor, Cybertonica

We are living in an era of revolution in payments. In the past 20 years, different and novel types of payments have burst into our lives and transformed the industry beyond all recognition. Competition between financial institutions, the appearance of new technologies, changing customer demand for new services, growth in the use of mobile and other devices, new laws and regulations, and more have shaped payments from every angle.

Some changes took us years to adopt, some just days to make new payment technology an inherent part of daily life:

- Internet payments
- online banking
- mobile payments
- PayPal
- contactless payment (cards)
- Bitcoin
- micro payments
- Chip & PIN
- biometrics
- wearables (watches, rings, bracelets and more).

2018 was a crucial year for financial institutions and merchants due to the adoption of open banking initiatives and new regulations such as the second Payment Services Directive and the General Data Protection Regulation requiring total compliance and increased transparency. In these changing conditions, the financial industry is moving towards real-time payments and one-click services, as customers want fast and frictionless payment experiences.

Fraud Landscape

In a new world of super-speeds, the fraud landscape continues to develop, with more complexity and sophistication. New technology's appearance always opens new horizons for criminals to exploit, challenging them to make fraudulent schemes more effective and creating new opportunities to test their tactics against fraud prevention and detection capabilities. Faster payments in all their new forms are also coming on stream, and this will increase the fraudulent activities that financial institutions (FIs) and businesses are going to have to face.

There are always two active groups of users of any new technology:

1. advanced customers, hunting for new technologies, and
2. fraudsters, waiting to test new payment products and exploit them.

The Priorities

In light of this, the priority is for FIs to improve how they distinguish between legitimate users and fraudsters before allowing them to use their payment products. And the same should be true for individual customers and businesses. From the outset, all faster payments transactions should be processed through a fraud-detection platform, where all suspicious activities can be monitored and anomalies detected before a serious fraud occurs.

Continuing data breaches have become a perfect personal information source. Stolen data such as government IDs, social security numbers, credit cards and account credentials (users' ID/password pairs, secret question answers and much more) sits in criminals' databases.

How Criminals Exploit Systemic Weaknesses

Identity Theft

Sometimes, IDs can be chosen by customers, but often the system autosaves an email address as an account ID and this creates a very specific problem: fraudsters, with the help of "bad bots", can carry out a credential-stuffing attack, whereby they go through websites and try those stolen pairs to see if an account exists or not. According to the 2017 Bad Bot Report published by Distil Research Lab, bad bots were found on 96% of websites with login pages. Fraudsters are very persistent and systematic in their attempts, and they continue attacking until they hit a jackpot. Then they log in, having undertaken an account takeover (ATO) to perpetrate the planned fraud.

Compromised Future Accounts

Another dangerous problem is that fraudsters compromise not only existing accounts, but also accounts that could possibly be opened in the future, because customers will normally use their email address as user ID.

Compromised Business Email

And this is not the end of the criminal circle, unfortunately. Stolen email addresses can be used in business email compromise (BEC) schemes to add more headaches for FIs and businesses. Due to this, fraud and risk specialists have to keep in mind that ATO, identity theft and BEC often go together.

Data is the New Oil

In our digital era it's not oil, but data – and especially our personal data – that is becoming the strategic asset for businesses and a fruitful source of enrichment for cyber criminals. According to

Data Breach Index data, records lost or stolen between 2013 and 2017 totalled 9,230,693,578 (4% encrypted). In the first half of 2018 only, we lost 3,353,172,708 data records (2.2% encrypted). This amount of breached information is double that in the first half of 2017.

So, account takeover and identity theft will continue to grow in scale and complexity. Fraudsters bring all their resources and modern techniques on board, including advanced machine learning and artificial intelligence to attack with sophistication on a huge scale, hunting for our data and monetizing it in all possible ways. They focus their attention not only on existing accounts – to drain them or use them to commit account fraud – but also discover new destinations, where FIs and businesses haven't adopted new fraud prevention and detection techniques yet.

And smaller businesses are at higher risk than businesses at scale. They have to pay attention to their customers' accounts, but also protect themselves from falling victim to commercial ATO.

The Danger of Biometrics

Acuity Market Intelligence predicts that by 2020, biometrics will be fully ingrained into our life – 3 billion smartphones with biometric functions, 5.5 billion biometric apps downloaded every year and more than 800 billion transactions with biometric authentication proceeded on mobile devices annually. Demand for biometric technology is super-high among the young generation, who are already used to transacting via mobiles.

But fraudsters have a great chance to attack, because biometrics, being convenient and fast, have serious drawbacks. What if your biometric data is stolen or forged, perhaps using a 3D-printed image using a bioprinter with stem cells? Our businesses are facing new and completely novel types of payment fraud and security risks, while our workplace is being transformed into a dynamically changing battlefield, where it is extremely hard and sometimes even impossible to detect our enemies.

A 2018 Javelin Research study on identity fraud revealed that 16.7 million identities were stolen last year. Distinguishing between a login from a legitimate user and that of a fraudster in these conditions has turned into a major challenge.

Rising Costs, Rising Risks

Companies invest heavily in cybersecurity and fraud prevention, but despite that, the situation is getting worse. Payments-related fraud costs the global economy US$600bn a year. We have to admit that there is something wrong with how we are fighting fraud. Our consumers demand a fast, modern and seamless experience but to satisfy their expectations, businesses, especially medium and small, unintentionally weaken their control processes, creating perfect conditions for fraudsters to take advantage of their vulnerabilities.

Sophisticated Criminals – KYC Redefined

In a digital world, why are the bad boys always a step ahead? Because they are dynamic, expansive, adaptive, persistent and sophisticated in their actions. To achieve their goal, fraudsters quickly adapt their approach and technologies to attack a specific business model, knowing exactly which business type has its individual vulnerabilities and what they are.

KYC (know your customer) is important for building loyal long-term relationships with customers, but how about KYF (know your fraudster)? Only by analysing fraudsters' behaviour, "cracking" their mindset and connecting this knowledge with individual business models will we be able to fight fraud and identify fraudsters.

Fighting the Forces of Fraud

It's necessary to keep in mind that the forces of fraud are constantly changing; in order to understand and identify them

and their interactions, we need the power of machine learning. Even the best of humans fail in this arms race due to its scale and dynamics; rules are not relevant anymore, because they are all based on the past.

Companies have to invest wisely into the new products that suit their individual business needs and provide stronger authentication based on behavioural biometrics, which is dynamic. While you surf the net, the platform knows who you are. The technology behind it is driven by AI and ML algorithms that constantly learn customers' behaviour patterns, being able to spot any abnormalities and create a 360-degree view of every transaction happening in real time.

Blending Art and Science in Fraud Prevention

Making cybersecurity and fraud detection systems successfully fight fraud is an art and science, because when done wrong, it wastes time and money, distracts customers, gives too many false positives and ruins businesses. While many focus on providing frictionless omni-channel customer experiences, they neglect the fact that modern fraud is also happening through all these different channels, complicating prevention and detection.

In order to stay competitive and a step ahead of fraudsters, to create a perfect balance between a frictionless, fast and fraud-free customer experience, FIs and modern businesses need a solution that is instantly adapting to an ever-changing payment/fraud landscape. A solution that uses very high-velocity data synchronization of many channels and types of data; running advanced machine learning in real time to understand the behaviour and riskiness of every transaction helps to achieve this blend of art and science, to prevent fraud in a game with no rules.

How Network Paradigms Can Lead to New Payments Innovations

By Zeng Ziling
Fellow, Sichuan Association of FinTech, China

By considering the characteristics of different networks, the PayTech industry can learn what is required to become more efficient and productive. Below I will show the payments paradigm of the past; the paradigm behind most of today's payment innovations; and the direction of future PayTech innovations, using value networks.

There are different types of value networks in payments.

Payment Platforms

As a same-side network, a platform is the most common paradigm in the world of the Internet. With a platform, all users enjoy economies of scale due to the network effect.[1]

Platforms are also the most common paradigm in retail payments. A platform connects payers and receivers through multiple channels, remotely or nearby. Examples are PayPal, Alipay and WeChat Pay, where users remit money to each other. One important issue for platform-type business models is the large scale of users required. One payment platform is

---

[1] J. Hendler and J. Golbeck, "Metcalfe's Law, Web 2.0, and the Semantic Web" (2008).

Chain shape
Industry participants form a chain shape relationship
e.g. Letter of credit, CMBC's factoring

Same-side network
When transfer cash to each other, the platform server connects numerous clients
e.g. PayPal, Alipay

Discrete network
Industry participants form a discrete network
e.g. organizations with no consensus,
        heterogeneous systems

Tree shape
Industry participants form a tree shape relationship; financial intermediaries play most roles
e.g. financial instrument issuance
        group company treasury, securitization

Cross-side network
The platform connects two very different groups of clients
e.g. Stock Exchange DvP PvP

Mesh network
Industry participants form a mesh network relationship
e.g. central bank monetary policy regulation,
        SWIFT GPI

Figure 1: Illustration of different network paradigms

not usually compatible with another, for both competition and regulatory reasons.

In a multi-sided platform (MSP)[2] there are several distinct groups of users. Marketplace platforms like Amazon and Taobao include buyers, sellers, couriers and other service providers also playing roles on the platform. Similarly, in financial markets, a stock exchange is a marketplace that connects a buyer and a seller, and also includes a financial intermediary, a securities company and their banks on the platform.

The purpose of such an exchange platform is to guarantee the delivery of money and value. In securities this is by delivery versus payment (DvP) and in foreign exchange it is by payment versus payment (PvP). With the help of distributed ledger technology (DLT) and smart contracts, the payment instruction and the delivery of any consideration are synchronized through all possible participants with shared status in the blockchain. The need for a cash guarantee may become obsolete, and the settlement speed can be much faster, using such an approach. The Bank of England, Monetary Authority of Singapore (MAS) and Singapore Exchange (SGX) under Project Ubin, and the Shanghai Stock Exchange (SSE) of China, have been exploring the utilization of blockchain in the exchange settlement.

Chain Shape

A letter of credit (L/C) in trade finance is one classical chain shape paradigm. It includes applicant, beneficiary, advising bank, issuing bank, nominated bank and others. Though a uniform electronic data interchange is used in transmitting the L/C message, the inability of interoperation of those participants' systems prohibits enhancing the efficiency of the L/C transaction. This multipartition is a classical use case for blockchain technology. The first L/C

powered by blockchain from Barclays Bank in 2016 proved the viability of blockchain in such a scenario. The exchange of documentation shortened from 7 days to less than 1 day.

The China Minsheng Bank[3] created a tool for financial institutions and their clients dealing with trade receivables, but they could be just financing the channel. A real liquidity provider uses them as compliance channel. The money provider cares about controlling the money through this chain. So, the liquidity provider, compliance channel provider, borrower and borrower's trading partner form a chain of four nodes.

Another significance of this service is that the bank outputs the capability to control accounts to the clients, so that the nodes of clients on the chain can control the payment of funds in both directions of financing and repayment.

The importance of managing the payment activities of participants in a chain shape is that traditionally, a centralized service could only touch the topologically nearest participants. The inclusion of more participants beyond the nearest layer is the foundation for more innovation.

Tree Shape

In a financial instrument issuance procedure,[4] it may take days or weeks to raise funds. Too many intermediaries in the financial market fragments into logical layers and vertical segments and geographically. These players form a logical tree shape.

The market needs solutions to enhance the efficiency of the financial intermediary. Vertically, the financial institute uses one

---

[2] A. Hagiu and J. Wright, "Multi-Sided Platforms", *Harvard Business School*, October (2011).

---

[3] China Minsheng Banking Corp, Cash Management and Settlement Dept, 2019

[4] Also discussed in *The WealthTech Book* (Wiley, 2018), p.181

financial instrument to create another. Horizontally, the fundraising process needs to aggregate pieces of money into one. Upwards is the fundraising process and downwards is the repayment process. An interoperative payment solution will significantly increase the efficiency of these processes.

Many group companies with complicated subsidiary structures often use a financial shared services centre to increase the financial management efficiency of their organization. This includes the treasury of the group companies in different business functions and jurisdictions. A centralized treasury needs to move cash among the holding and branch entities in planned payment and receipt. A payment solution provider needs to adapt the requirements of the accounts of the group companies, forming a tree shape.

Mesh Network

Many businesses establish relationships at a very small logical scale, creating isolated ecosystems. Any information or value transferred among these isolated ecosystems faces many problems (e.g. inter-operation, application programming interface socket standard, trust and recognition of value).

These are discrete networks without consensus among each other. Payments players may form a mesh network organization that could be the combination of the above. Blockchain/DLT with smart contracts provides the key to heterogeneous or incompatible solutions and ecosystems which lack consensus.

In traditional payments, SWIFT uses a mechanism of agent banks for any two banks without a direct payment relationship. The

transfer cost, time and route are unknown in this case. It could be as slow as several days in some extreme cases – much slower than human couriers. SWIFT GPI and Ripple show what blockchain can do to revolutionize international payments.

Sometimes, the capability of private businesses is limited. The negative externality effect causes the need for public goods. For economic activities within and across jurisdictions, a public infrastructure could be established to solve the negative externality effect problem. The central bank needs to execute and monitor its monetary policy – how cash is used in the transactions among all its regulated banks. The US government also regulates all USD transactions, both foreign[5] and domestic. The public department of different jurisdictions needs such infrastructure to realize its own policy goal and to provide services to the public.

Conclusion

With PayTech's innovative solutions of payment financial technologies, the use case of payment solutions will expand beyond the two parties of payer and receiver. The above paradigms are just some of the most intuitive cases with their extracted features simplified for discussion. In real cases, it may be a combination of paradigms. For business entrepreneurs seeking a breakthrough, it is important to notice the need for managing the complicated relationships of payment participants. These paradigms could be the guidance or blueprint leading to the next wave of innovation.

---

[5] IEEPA 1977, US Patriot Act 2001, National Defense Authorization Act for Fiscal Year 2012, etc.

It's the Ecosystem, Stupid! Keeping Ahead in a Payments Ecosystem

By Simon Hanson
Head of Public Affairs, BACS

Payments underpin the UK economy and ensure our competitiveness internationally. It's generally accepted that the UK enjoys one of the most technically advanced and secure payments ecosystems in the world. But what is required to make sure this leadership position is maintained? And what is the future for the UK's payments ecosystem?

What is a Payments Ecosystem?

Broadly defined, a business ecosystem is a network of related and interlinked businesses that interact with each other to supply complementing components of the value proposition offered to prospective customers.

So, an ecosystem is the network of organizations – including suppliers, distributors, customers, competitors, government agencies, and so on – involved in the delivery of a specific product or service through both competition and cooperation, as with every ecosystem.

Classic ecosystem theory suggests that each entity in the ecosystem affects and is affected by the others, creating a constantly evolving relationship in which each entity must be flexible and adaptable in order to survive, as in a biological ecosystem.

And therein is the problem. An ecosystem is a closed system, clearly defined and governed by rules and laws. And as it is in an ecosystem's very nature to be stable and secure, it supports its constituents in a networked value chain, making access to new members difficult unless they play by the ecosystem's self-defined rules. We can see this very clearly in UK payments.

So how difficult does this make it for innovation to influence the way that the ecosystem supports the delivery of its services and products? And is there likely to be a conflict within the ecosystem between protecting existing ecosystem members and promoting new entrants? The answer is "probably"; without changing the ecosystem rules and therefore the existing relationships within it, new innovative delivery approaches will always struggle to become established.

This is bad news for the industry, its regulators and consumers. Without recognizing the restrictions that the current relationships between members of the ecosystem create, the industry will always be slow to develop innovation and become more efficient and cost-effective. Without enabling innovation with the right balance of protective and innovative regulation, officials will not see the development that their policies expect for consumers. And consumers will not enjoy the freedom of choice that developments in data use should offer.

The Challenge in UK Payments

The UK payments ecosystem, underpinned by real-time gross settlement (RTGS), delivers secure, instant, bulk and high-value payments which have stood the test of time. The industry and its regulators, led by the Bank of England, and including the Financial Conduct Authority (FCA), Payment Systems Regulator (PSR) and Competition and Markets Authority (CMA), ensure that it is safe, secure and rarely breaks down.

However, on the one hand we hear about the problems of old obsolete banking infrastructures that desperately need revitalizing for the future. We see news of banking outages stopping people from accessing money and hear of people suffering at the hands of payments fraudsters who find it all too easy to dupe us.

But on the other hand the UK must be doing something encouraging to be such a cauldron of financial innovation. FinTech is worth £6.6 billion to the UK economy and accounts for 11% of the global FinTech industry. Around 76,500 people are employed in this sector.

So, while the UK payments ecosystem is a successful example of how to deliver things well, it is becoming its own dead-weight. Without ecosystem change it cannot hope to develop the innovations that are expected in the future.

Change for the Better?

Of course, the UK payments system is currently being overhauled; the Bank of England is redeveloping RTGS and Pay.UK is delivering the new payment architecture (NPA). These are planned to enable the new technologically based payments services to connect to the core payments structure.

These steps are essential; without changes, the UK may well become a less attractive place to do business. International businesses require the most up-to-date infrastructures and that includes payment systems – the ability to move money safely, securely and in a timely manner.

But the full opportunity won't be realized unless the potential restrictions of the existing ecosystem are removed. As new providers come closer to delivering alongside "mainstream" providers, the carefully balanced payments ecosystem must develop to accommodate their new change and innovation imperatives. Because true beneficial change is impossible without recognizing that it is change in the ecosystem that is critical. And this will lead to a need for change across the established end-value chains and the business models of the current ecosystem members. This will lead to some ecosystem members thriving whilst others fail. Will it be a question of "adapt to survive", or will the established ecosystem members resist change?

A Bigger Ecosystem?

So how will the ecosystem adapt to new, faster-moving and more innovative elements without compromising its inherent security and safety? What rules and laws will be required? And who has the responsibility to govern and lead the required frameworks for success in the new ecosystem? Is it the government? Regulators? Ecosystem members? Who?

Recently, the CMA's Retail Banking Reform package led to the delivery of open banking standards in the UK, which in turn offer opportunities to deliver data-enhanced services for consumers. This should be an enabler for consumers, but the risks need to be mitigated as well as the opportunities taken. Each new opportunity could bring a challenge to current ecosystem members. How will all these entities react?

Is the Future International?

In PayTech, the ecosystem and its ability to adapt to new technology, new services and new consumer expectations will determine its future. The way we all access and use financial services is changing and will continue to do so, and those organizations that gear up to the new technological and data revolution will best be able to capitalize on them.

But how we succeed in ensuring we can use these innovations and stay safe and secure is ultimately up to the entire ecosystem; not only the large financial entities that dominate activity today. As commerce and trade become even more international, businesses and consumers will require not a national ecosystem but one that can capitalize on international opportunities.

And in this context, the future for the UK payments ecosystem is only assured if it can become more internationally focused. Is the future in pan-nation payments ecosystems? Will this create greater opportunities? As trade becomes more international, payments ecosystems need to do so too.

Mobile Money: Creating a Cash-Light Africa to Solve the Financial Inclusion Problem

By Srinivas Nidugondi
EVP and Chief Operating Officer, Mobile Financial Solutions, Comviva

and Mohit Bhargava
Deputy General Manager, Product Marketing, Mobile Financial Solutions, Comviva

The USA and Europe are, without a doubt, at the centre of any discussion pertaining to mobile payments. And why not? From credit cards to online banking, the very genesis of digital payments took place in these regions. Mobile payments, though, are altogether a different ball game. In this context, Sub-Saharan Africa takes centre stage, with services like M-Pesa, EcoCash, Airtel Money and Orange Money in the fray.

An Overview of Mobile Money in Africa

The 2007 launch of M-Pesa in Kenya marked the debut of mobile money in Sub-Saharan Africa. Since then, the service has grown in leaps and bounds in the region. So much so, in fact, that there are 142 mobile money services in 42 Sub-Saharan African countries currently. This accounts for approximately half of the world's mobile money services and active users.

To illustrate further, one in every five adults in the region actively uses the service, according to the World Bank Findex. In fact, in 12 African countries, the number of mobile money accounts surpasses bank accounts, facilitating financial inclusion for millions of unbanked customers. Mobile money has become an integral part of the region's financial system.

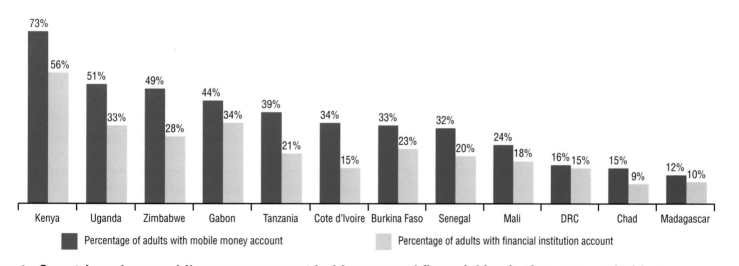

Percentage of adults with mobile money account
Percentage of adults with financial institution account

Figure 1: Countries where mobile money account holders exceed financial institution account holders

Source: World Bank Global Findex Database 2017

Drivers Behind the Growth in Mobile Money Adoption

Mobile money is a viable alternative to conventional banking for unbanked and underbanked customers. It is readily accessible via the unstructured supplementary service data (USSD) channel on both feature-phones and smartphones. Agents, who offer last-mile services, also play an important role by enabling customers to register and convert cash into e-money (cash-in and cash-out). Several telecom operators offer mobile money to leverage their extensive recharge agent network. In many countries, operators have created an expansive agent network, much larger than bank branches or ATM networks.

From Money Transfers to Micro-Loans: A Phased Growth

Mobile money didn't attain success overnight. It was a two-phase process. In the first phase, mobile money providers focused on acquiring customers and growing the agent network. The services on offer were person-to-person transfers and airtime recharge. Once these gained traction, the scope widened to include payments for bills, merchants and salaries.

Once these services reached critical mass, micro-loans, savings, savings clubs and insurance become available, followed by international remittance, financial aid payments and tax payments. Mobile money providers forged partnerships with banks, money transfer operators and government agencies to build a comprehensive digital payments ecosystem.

The Impact of Mobile Money

The impact of these services has to be considered in the context of social and economic aspects, such as financial inclusion. In Kenya, M-Pesa is used by at least one person in 96% of households. According to *Science Magazine*, M-Pesa has lifted an estimated 2% of Kenyan households (numbering approximately 194,000 people) out of extreme poverty.

These services have also played a key role in conflict-affected economies. For example, in Somalia, a World Bank report states that mobile money has superseded the use of cash. In Sierra Leone, during the Ebola crisis, mobile money shortened the payment time to Ebola response workers from over 1 month to 1 week, according to a United Nations study.

Case Study: EcoCash Zimbabwe

EcoCash Zimbabwe is an interesting case study to highlight the success of mobile money in Africa. After a decade of hyperinflation, Zimbabwe switched to using the American dollar in 2009. Currency change mitigated the economic crisis, but led to a cash crunch.

Zimbabwe's largest telecom operator Econet Wireless introduced EcoCash in 2011 to eliminate cash. EcoCash was designed to be accessed by both feature-phones and smartphones using USSD and the EcoCash application. Additionally, EcoCash established an expansive agent network of 40,000 agents for cash-in and cash-out of digital wallets, reaching almost the entire population of Zimbabwe, which banks were unable to do.

EcoCash focused on three strategic elements – service innovation, distribution (agent network) and marketing – to create Zimbabwe's largest digital financial service, used by 9.8 million subscribers, or approximately 90% of Zimbabwe's adult population.

Service Innovation

EcoCash's services started with person-to-person money transfers, expanding to bill and merchant payments and then to collateral-free mobile savings and loans. A total of over 25 services were

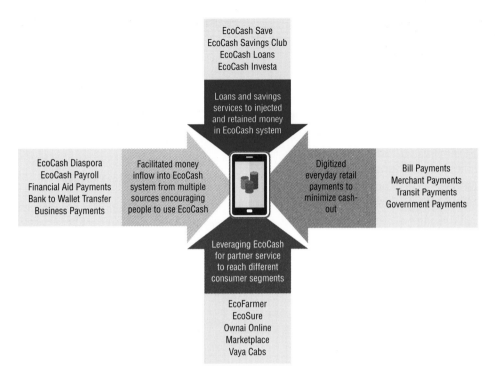

Figure 2: The four pillars of service innovation strategy

launched over 9 years. This "break-the-cash-cycle" approach was built on four strategic pillars.

- **Services that facilitate the inflow of funds**

  - **EcoCash diaspora.** EcoCash partnered with Western Union, MoneyGram, WorldRemit, etc. to enable over three million Zimbabweans in diaspora to send money to a customer in Zimbabwe. Digitizing remittances has made them significantly faster, cheaper and more convenient for consumers than conventional methods. US$300 million has been remitted through EcoCash diaspora since its launch.

  - **EcoCash payroll.** EcoCash has partnered with multiple organizations including SSB which disburses salary for government employees, NSSA which makes pension payments, City Councils and National Parks to facilitate the digitization of salary payments.

  - **Financial aid.** Aid organizations like World Food Program, Save the Children, Oxfam and Plan International have switched from cash disbursements to EcoCash.

  - **Bank to wallet transfers.** While unbanked consumers require agents for cashing-in, banked consumers have the option of topping up their wallets directly from their bank account. EcoCash has partnered with 12 banks to facilitate this.

  - **Business payments.** Vendors and businesses receive payment via EcoCash.

- **Digitized retail payments to minimize cash-out**

  - **Bill and merchant payments.** Over 50,000 merchants and billers in Zimbabwe accept payments via EcoCash. Customers can pay by simply entering the biller or merchant code and payment amount. The service has gained tremendous traction, as merchants only require a basic handset for payments. For merchants having POS, EcoCash partnered with Mastercard, launching Africa's first Mastercard companion card. Branded EcoCash Debit Card, it can be used at 15,000 points of sale (POS) in Zimbabwe and 47 million Mastercard access points worldwide. For small and medium-sized businesses who cannot afford POS, EcoCash introduced EcoCash Scan & Pay and EcoCash ta. These services leverage QR codes and near-field communication technology for contactless payments.

  - **Transit payments.** Customers can buy flight tickets and pay bus fares using EcoCash.

  - **Government payments.** EcoCash has partnered with government agencies, enabling customers to pay taxes, duties and tolls.

- **Loans and savings**

  - **EcoCash Save.** Launched in partnership with Steward Bank, EcoCash Save is a micro-savings account for unbanked customers. No document or opening balance is required to start it. Accessible via a mobile device, it is used by 1.5 million customers.

  - **Savings Club.** A group savings service which digitized traditional savings clubs Maround and Mukando.

  - **EcoCash Loans.** Customers can take advantage of short-term micro-loans without documentation. The loan amount is calculated on the basis of Econet/EcoCash service usage.

  - **EcoCash Investa.** Customers can purchase bonds and trade shares via a mobile device.

- **Reaching different consumer segments**

  - **EcoFarmer.** Farmers can pay premiums for crop insurance.

  - **EcoSure.** Consumers can buy various insurance services.

  - **Ownai online marketplace.** Customers can buy goods online using EcoCash.

  - **Vaya.** Customers can book cabs online using EcoCash.

Distribution Strategy

EcoCash has established a network of 40,000 agents, 97 times bigger than the network of any commercial bank in the country.

EcoCash pays out a significant portion of its revenue to agents as commission. This has motivated agents to invest more in the business. EcoCash also provides US$1 additional commission to agents when a customer's total transactions reach a particular limit, encouraging agents to motivate customers to transact actively. Moreover, EcoCash has set lower investment requirements for agents in rural areas, compared to those in urban areas. This has ensured consistent growth across both areas. As a result, 70% of the rural population is using EcoCash.

EcoCash has employed Steward Bank to offer low-cost floating loans to EcoCash agents, helping them to remain liquid despite a cash crunch.

Marketing Strategy

EcoCash has opted for a mix of above the line (ATL) and below the line (BTL) marketing activities. ATL activities – like TV and radio commercials, print advertisements and billboards – create awareness about the service. As a part of its BTL strategy, EcoCash recruited 2,000 brand ambassadors, to educate people about EcoCash and register them. In the initial days, approximately three-quarters of customers were registered by these brand ambassadors.

To drive transactions, EcoCash provided contextual promotions based on services. For example, employees subscribing to EcoCash Payroll benefited from free EcoSure Funeral Cover. The most successful of these initiatives were loyalty programmes like Chaka Chaya ("It's happening or trending"), which encourages customers to transact more to earn points and eventually win rewards. In 2017, during Chaka Chaya the number of EcoCash transactions increased by 800%.

Helping to Solve the Financial Inclusion Problem

The results of the above strategies speak for themselves. Since its launch, EcoCash has transacted over US$78.4 billion, increasing financial inclusion from 32% to over 90%. It processes 70% of national payments by volume, making the economy cash-light. In Financial Year 2017-18, EcoCash processed US$13 billion, equivalent to 73% of Zimbabwe's gross domestic product.

Conclusion

Mobile money is helping to make Africa cash-light, and in this way solving one of society's most important problems, the inequity of those falling outside the financial, economic and social system.

Back to the Future: A Miraculous Time-Trip Through the Future, Present and Past of Payments

By David Gyori
CEO, Banking Reports

BLUEPRINT FOR CHANGE

2220 AD, Asteroid "3361 Orpheus"

A deep, calm, divine and peaceful voice loudly and authoritatively echoes through space: "Payments are primarily social interactions, special forms of communication as well as exchanges of information; payments are only secondarily representing exchanges of value."

Peggy and Victor are sitting in their privately owned space cave carved inside asteroid "3361 Orpheus". Since the beginning of the 23rd century it is trendy to have your own asteroid. Peggy and Victor purchased "3361 Orpheus" recently. The previous owner was a robot who recently moved to a larger asteroid-cave. Peggy and Victor now have to pay this robot using **intergalactic gravitational wave payments**. Robots started to have their own assets and liabilities and pay their own taxes since "deep learning" merged into "deep earning" during the second half of the 22nd century.

2119 AD, Proxima Centauri

Peggy and Victor are newcomers to Proxima Centauri. They are learning **NPP (neural proximity payments)**. NPP is a technology transmitting funds by thought. Neurons emit weak magnetic signals that are perfectly readable by another person's brain.

2049 AD, Helsingborg, Sweden

Peggy and Victor are attending the *Cashless Society Decennial*. The mayor is giving a speech: "10 years have passed since our Minister of Economy has placed the last 100 Krona bill into the museum. 10 years in the first **fully CBDC (central bank digital currency)-based society**, a blockchain-based immutable monetary machine."

The mayor continues the speech by listing numerous advantages of their cashless society. Let's listen in: "One of the unexpected advantages of CBDC is the blessing of negative nominal interest rates. While physical money existed, the monetary toolbox was restricted to positive nominal rates. The tool of negative nominal rates was absent from the monetary arsenal while cash was around. Why? Because at negative rates below approximately minus 0.75%, entities would remove money from their bank accounts and store it in cash instead. This could destroy the entire banking system."

"Luckily, in our age of fully digital central banking, the entire monetary arsenal is at the disposal of decision-makers. This makes the system of base rates symmetric, giving equal weight and relevance to both negative and positive base rates. This has boosted the power of expansive monetary policy and reduced the severity of crises." The mayor raises his voice: "My dear cashless citizens, I am happy and proud to report that we will never have to go through a crisis like those in 1929, 2008 and 2033 again."

2039 AD, Palo Alto, CA

Peggy and Victor are smiling at each other: they are both wearing their smart contact lenses and they immediately saw that they received some money. Their account balance is written in the bottom right corner. Smart contact lenses have driven smartphones and smart watches completely out of business. Smart lenses use the micro-electricity of the human body as well as energy from the sun. **Smart contact lenses** are creating an **augmented reality** environment, where users see additional digital information on top of physical reality. People are also buying things through their smart lenses. You just have to focus on the bottom right corner for more than 1.5 seconds and blink, and this triggers a payment.

2029 AD, Shenzen, China

While walking along a pedestrian superhighway of the world's largest city, Victor remarked: "Peggy, look at these empty skyscrapers, they belonged to the once mighty payments companies of Mastercard and Visa. As we are living in an **exclusively QR code-based payments environment**, they have now become obsolete."

"But why did they have to go out of business, Victor?", replies his partner.

"Because those companies thought that people would use plastic cards and carry them all the time."

2020 AD, London, UK

Peggy and Victor are on the tube, travelling on the Elizabeth Line and each reading a copy of *The PayTech Book*.

"Victor, I've just read that **WeChat Pay** in China has over 900 million monthly active users."

"Yes, that is mind-boggling", he replies. "But Peggy, did you know that PayPal had to acquire **Venmo** in December 2013 through the acquisition of Braintree?"

"Victor, this is news to me but really, why is this relevant to WeChat Pay?"

"Because Venmo is a payments app that deliberately and proactively shares with your friends what you buy, when, where and how much you pay for it. This is ideal for the youngest generation, Gen Z. For Baby Boomers, financial transactions are meant to be private by default, but for the young generation of Millennials and Gen Z, the role of payments has shifted and evolved into a natural social interaction", Victor adds with great confidence.

"Yes, this book is full of exciting things. Have you read the part about VR Pay?" asked Peggy with curiosity in her voice.

"No, tell me more" replied Victor.

"**VR Pay** is designed for young people playing computer games and watching sports multiple hours per day online, wearing their virtual reality headsets. Alibaba found that these people prefer to shop online wearing these headsets. So, the Chinese technology giant decided to launch VR Pay, a solution where young people can, by nodding and focusing their facial expressions, enter 3D online department stores and buy the goods and services they desire, while comfortably wearing their VR headsets."

"WOW, thanks Peggy, *The PayTech Book* keeps surprising us. I'll definitely give it a five-star review on LinkedIn."

1971 AD, Washington, D.C.

Peggy and Victor are watching live TV as President Richard Nixon is announcing the termination of the Bretton Woods international monetary system.

"Peggy, we are now entering uncharted territories", said Victor. "By removing the guaranteed and fixed exchangeability of the US dollar with gold, we are entering the era of **fiat currencies**."

"What are fiat currencies?" replies Peggy, interested by a new phrase entering the language.

"Fiat currencies have only nominal, and no intrinsic value. Their acceptance is guaranteed by government regulation. And they are legal tender and therefore have to be accepted."

"Do you think it will work, Victor?"

"We will see. At this point it is an open question." Little did they know…

1295 AD, Venice, Italy

Victor and Peggy are excitedly listening to the speech of the famous explorer Marco Polo: "I have now returned to you from China. I have returned bringing you the blessings of representative money. **Representative money** is the concept of paper money. Instead of paying each other using impractical cattle or heavy precious metal, I will teach you what I learned in China: to utilize **paper notes** in order to create an easy and frictionless payments experience."

9000 BC, Damascus, Syria

Peggy and Victor are talking to a farmer who is proudly explaining to them: "Our advancements in agriculture, producing more and more surplus, have helped us to use **livestock and grains** as universal mediums of exchange. Vegetables, plants and animal skins now all have their own exchange rates."

100,000 BC, Neander Valley, Germany

Peggy and Victor are sitting in a cave. Peggy is offering **fruits in return for the piece of meat** Victor is giving her. In the background a deep, calm, divine and peaceful voice loudly and authoritatively echoes: "Payments are primarily social interactions, special forms of communication as well as exchanges of information; payments are only secondarily representing exchanges of value!"

Fifteen Ways in Which Our Digital Future Will be Shaped by PayTech

By Tony Craddock
Director General, Emerging Payments Association

Rapid changes in technology, consumer behaviour and regulations are creating a new digital economy in every part of every country in every region of the globe. Inspired by reading over 60 chapters of *The PayTech Book*, and conversations with many of the Emerging Payments Association's passionate payments people, I am excited to share three "Big Ideas" – and a further 12 – in this chapter, which are a sample of the fresh thinking and original perspective in the Emerging Payments Association (EPA)'s community of entrepreneurs, thought leaders and innovators.

The Three Big Ideas From the EPA

Unnecessary friction will almost disappear but will be added back in where valuable

As in the telecommunications industry, the dominant pricing model in payments will move from a per-transaction basis to a subscription basis. In time, technology and competition will drive the cost of processing a transaction down towards zero. Other sources of friction, such as the time taken for a transaction to be completed or the need for users to learn different ways to buy things across different payment platforms or at different stages in the buying process, will also be significantly reduced.

But friction in some transactions is both necessary and welcome. Rules will be adopted that help to ensure there is the right amount of friction in every transaction. This ensures that buying things is not too easy for some people or for some types of transaction. The challenge for the regulators is to ensure there is the right balance between specifying such rules through regulation and allowing the market to decide and police such rules through schemes, banks and other players.

Banks and the nature of banking will change completely

In delivering on the promise of technology and satisfying users whose needs and expectations are rapidly changing, there will be a shift in the underlying technology and systems deployed by all service providers, especially large banking institutions.

The challenge faced by the largest companies is that the majority (sometimes over 90%) of their IT spend is on maintenance, whereas for their new competitors and suppliers it is mostly spent on development. To remain competitive, the largest will buy payments technology from the smallest – especially in the back office – even if they are their competitors.

The traditional banks (in the UK, this means the nine members of the Open Banking Implementation Entity's CMA9 group of companies that provide current accounts for 80%+ of consumers and 85%+ of businesses) will have to redefine how they serve customers. By 2030, these banks will look completely different to how they look now. Some will become platform businesses that take deposits and manage customer experiences using products provided by FinTechs. Some will use payments platforms provided as white-label services from FinTechs such as Alipay. Others will become the plumbers that run the core banking systems while leveraging the power of their trusted brands to deliver other people's products.

Most will learn to cannibalize their core businesses to ensure they remain competitive. Those that do not will die.

Central banks, led by the Bank of England, will get digital

Most central banks are neutral to methods of payment. They do not seek to promote any payment method above any other, but do believe that the public should have a choice.

However, a few central banks, such as those in Denmark, Finland, the Netherlands and Sweden, have all adopted a progressive pro-digital payment stance. They have recognized that coordinated market intervention is needed to ensure that consumers are not left behind in a new digital economy where market forces alone may not ensure this.

To support the transition to a low-friction, largely digital payments ecosystem, while preserving stability and ensuring the competitive nature of the UK on the world stage, the Bank of England must become pro-digital and adopt a digital-preferred payments strategy.

If this happens, the bank will also maintain a supervision regime that understands biometrics, artificial intelligence, machine learning, distributed ledger technology and other digital technologies. This understanding will help guide the adoption of these new technologies safely and securely. It will also allow us to manage the needs of the adopters and ensure that no one is excluded due to their income, disability or vulnerability.

And maybe central banks could set up and run a Global PayTech Advisory Council, where its representatives encourage adoption of PayTech. Many EPA members – such as Barclays, Mastercard, Starling Bank, FCA, Visa, Monese and Omnio Group – will welcome the move and cooperate enthusiastically to make this happen.

Another Dozen Digital Ideas

Identity will become digital – at last

By building a framework that allows for digital ID on a regulatory basis, the UK will enable more access for the excluded and more people to switch to better services from both banks and non-banks.

A new way of reducing money laundering will be adopted, involving a complete re-engineering of anti-money laundering activities.

By 2022, the UK government will open up Companies House, the driving licence agency DVLA and the Passport Office to support this digital identity framework. This will enable straight-through processing for efficient onboarding of new customers.

And by 2023 the regulations on the Joint Money Laundering Steering Group will change to enable digital ID to become the norm and set the standard for digital identity globally.

All this will require something that is readily accepted but very hard to do well – collaboration. The EPA's "Facing up to Financial Crime" white paper explains how to make this happen.

The rise of FinTech will lead to the fall of FinTech

The magical mix of investment, talent, proximity and collaboration is attracting an increasing number of FinTech and PayTech companies around the world to the UK. While we are seeing more mergers and acquisitions and new investment (Monese, Starling, Banking Circle and Omnio Group alone have raised £500m+ since July 2018), we will also see more failures.

In time, however, FinTech will evolve, become more pervasive and just be seen as "integrated technology used in financial services and banking" rather than a separate industry segment. But its absorption back into the mainstream of financial services will happen only when financial services themselves can achieve the same magical combination of factors that made FinTech happen in the first place.

Central banks will roll out a global 24/7 real-time settlement system

While the obstacles to 24/7 real-time settlement are well known, the apparent reluctance of central bankers to overcome them aggressively is not understood. The Bank of England will solve this problem by 2025, and the development of "settlement synchronization" will stimulate a whole new industry segment that can take this capability around the world, in the same way in which Faster Payments and companies like Vocalink have done before with real-time clearing.

The industry's use of the term "access" will change – and rightly so

"Access" will no longer refer to access to settlement for non-banks or access to bank accounts for FinTechs or businesses.

It will be about access to better payments services for everybody. Inclusion will become a theme of payments in the next decade, and the UK will become a global leader in enabling the adoption of payments innovations that improve lives everywhere.

Business banking will boom and the boundaries to consumer banking will blur

The move to a freelance economy will lead to more individuals opening business accounts, which in turn will create innovation in the sector, as the demands of that audience will be very similar to those of traditional banks' customers. It is likely that those challenger banks providing flexible consumer banking services will be best qualified to provide micro-businesses with feature-rich, low-cost banking services. In time, business bankers will no longer be seen as the innovation laggards, as they start to set the bar for consumer banking very high.

"Current accounts" will become indistinct from "bank accounts"

It will not matter that non-banks cannot refer to their e-money accounts as "current accounts" under the current regulations. Consumers cannot tell the difference, so will soon refer to their everyday accounts as current accounts regardless of what licence the account provider holds.

The payments industry will continue to be invisible to consumers – as it should be

Consumers do not want to know about or understand the new PayTech industry's products and services. Nor whether their banking is enabled by open banking or not. Despite the General Data Protection Regulation and data security developments, the payments industry's role will be to make it possible to pay conveniently, securely and transparently, in real time and at near-zero cost.

A new payments scheme will be launched in Europe as others diversify

The European Central Bank recently lamented the disparate nature of Europe's payment schemes, despite the adoption of the second Payment Services Directive (PSD2) and SEPA direct debit and credit transfer. Many EU countries continue to use their own schemes or schemes owned by global companies. There is a case for having a regional payment scheme that is interoperable with global and other European payments schemes, giving favourable access to PayTech providers.

Meanwhile, the global payments schemes will continue to acquire PayTech companies to strengthen their hand and broaden their scope. What they lose in margins to bank-to-bank payments they will win in solving other problems around security, payments systems and digitalization.

Technology companies that become too dominant will be regulated

If Google, Amazon, Facebook and Apple (GAFA) overstep the mark and abuse their powerful market positions, EU regulators will be forced to act. If the UK is outside the EU, however, the possibility of using low taxation and/or regulatory arbitrage as a source of competitive advantage will not be lost on our politicians. As a result, regulation of GAFA-type companies will remain light in the UK.

Social networks will adopt PayTech to drive social inclusion

This will reduce the cost of moving money from developed to developing markets, thereby enabling the financially excluded, including the old and vulnerable, to benefit. Apple Card will compete aggressively with traditional credit cards from 2020 to show social networks how to adopt payments on their way to owning the whole customer experience, everywhere.

Open banking will be great, until it isn't

When consumers try to get refunds on their bank-to-bank payments, the liability for that refund is currently a grey area. Unless it is resolved soon, consumer groups will cry "foul" and open banking will lose credibility. As strong customer authentication becomes widely adopted, those consumers seeking a friction-free shopping experience will complain loudly, adding an extra customer service burden to merchants everywhere.

Non-card payments will increase their market share, but not for the expected reasons

Open banking and PSD2 enable consumers to move money between banks without using the scheme rails, and to access and repurpose their data with third-party providers (TPPs). But the growth in the use of such TPPs will not come about because consumers are encouraged to switch to using bank-to-bank instead of scheme card rails (with debit/credit cards).

This is partly because the user experience is clunky, despite the industry's best efforts, and partly because consumers using non-card rails when paying are not protected – and if they lose money as a result, they may revert to payments on the card rails.

The growth of non-card payments will come about, however, because of a flood of new use cases deployed by TPPs under PSD2 and then PSD3. Payment initiation service providers and account information service providers will solve problems for consumers – and especially small and medium enterprises – that enable a value exchange far richer than the transaction itself. And the payments component, quite rightly, will remain irrelevant and invisible.

Change is improving lives everywhere

These 15 ideas are not forecasts. They are themes for change in an industry that now thrives on change. Our community welcomes challenge, obstacles and problems, and people willing to collaborate to innovate and overcome them. In this way, by enabling the adoption of new ways of moving money, we can improve lives everywhere.

List of Contributors

All chapters are included in this book, all abstracts can be read online on http://fintechcircle.com/insights/.

Rami AlHasan
Senior Manager Digital Commerce Solutions, Etisalat
www.linkedin.com/in/ramialhasan/
See chapter:
PayTech in the Cloud

Imran Ali
Managing Principal, Answer Digital
www.linkedin.com/in/imranaliprofile/
See chapter:
How ACH and Real-Time Payments Clearing and Settlement Works

Tyler Anderson
Chief Operating Officer, FinTech Growth Syndicate
www.linkedin.com/in/tylerclanderson/
See chapter:
Payments Explained

Philip Atherton
Chief Risk Officer, SafeCharge
www.linkedin.com/in/phil-atherton-7b4ab918/
See chapter:
eKYC: The Next Mountain for e-Businesses to Climb

Christine Bailey
Chief Marketing Officer, Valitor
www.linkedin.com/in/drchristinebailey/
See chapter:
Reinventing the Customer Experience by Focusing on the After-Payment Emotional Experience

Omar Bairan
General Counsel, Banco Santa Cruz
www.linkedin.com/in/omar-bairan-cfa-frm-5735b64/

See chapter:
A New Law for Derivatives Markets and the Use of Smart Contracts

J.B. Beckett
Consultant, New Fund Order
www.linkedin.com/in/jonbeckett/
See chapter:
AML Systems After Madoff: Ponzi-Identification Using "Complexity"

Mohit Bhargava
Deputy General Manager, Product Marketing, Mobile Financial Solutions, Comviva
www.linkedin.com/in/mohitbhargava74/
See chapter:
Mobile Money: Creating a Cash-Light Africa to Solve the Financial Inclusion Problem

Michael Boevink
Founder, Boevink Group
www.linkedin.com/in/michael-boevink-布-纷-奇-232210/
See chapter:
How Decentralization Can Create a Customer-Centric Ecosystem

Mihaela Breg
Advisor – Risk and Regulatory Compliance, SmartBill FinTech Startup (Smarter Financial Ltd)
www.linkedin.com/in/mihaela-breg-profile/
See chapter:
The Hidden Value of Greater Standardization for the EU-Wide FinTech Market

Nicolette Brown
Marketing Manager, Napier
www.linkedin.com/in/nicolette-brown-54033920/
See chapter:
Refining the Collective Responsibility for Compliance

Andrew Burnie
PhD Student, Alan Turing Institute and University College London
www.linkedin.com/in/apburnie/
See chapter:
Blockchain, Cryptocurrencies and How They Fit Within Current Payments Regulation

230

James Burnie
Senior Associate, Eversheds-Sutherland (International) LLP
www.linkedin.com/in/james-burnie-889b09a5/

See chapter:
Blockchain, Cryptocurrencies and How They Fit Within Current Payments Regulation

Havva Canibek
Vice President Product Management, Card Payments at Bankalararası Kart Merkezi (Interbank Card Center of Turkey)
www.linkedin.com/in/havva-canibek-42a6442/

See chapter:
An Innovative Local Payments Method in an Ancient Land

Teresa Connors
Head of Market Engagement, RBS
www.linkedin.com/in/teresa-connors-56750b17/

See chapter:
Do We Still Need to Pay?

Robert Courtneidge
CEO, Moorwand Ltd
www.linkedin.com/in/robert-courtneidge-154727/

See chapter:
How Payments Regulation and Compliance Can Create a Better Future

Tony Craddock
Director General, Emerging Payments Association
www.linkedin.com/in/tonycraddock/

See chapter:
Fifteen Ways in Which Our Digital Future Will be Shaped by PayTech

Nigel Dean
Head of Marketing, MYPINPAD
www.linkedin.com/in/nigel-dean-a0386535/

See chapter:
PIN on Mobile – A Pivotal Moment for Payments

Julian Dixon
CEO, Napier
www.linkedin.com/in/julian-dixon-b2a19926/

See chapter:
Refining the Collective Responsibility for Compliance

Conny Dorrestijn
Founding Partner, BankiFi Ltd
www.linkedin.com/in/conny-dorrestijn-74b365/

See chapter:
Payments as Open Business Banking Enabler for the Gig Economy

Steven Dryall
CEO, Incipient Industries Inc.
www.linkedin.com/in/sdryall/

See chapter:
Cryptocommodities: An Essential Element of Decentralized Payments

Andrea Dunlop
Chairwomen of the Emerging Payments Association, Angel Investor and Non-Executive Director; formerly CEO, Merchant Acquiring (part of the Paysafe Group)
www.linkedin.com/in/andreadunlop/

See chapter:
The Perspective of a Passionate Payments CEO

Szilvia Egri
Founder, Femtechlab Ltd
www.linkedin.com/in/szilviaegri/

See chapter:
Why Personal Financial Management Will Be Embedded Into the Next Generation of Payments

Markus Eichinger
Executive Vice President Group Strategy, Wirecard
www.linkedin.com/in/markuseichinger/

See chapter:
From Barter to App – How Payments Have Changed

Alessia Falsarone
Managing Director, PineBridge Investments
www.linkedin.com/in/alessiafalsarone/

See chapter:
How Payment Agility and Cash-for-Carbon Can Solve a Global Problem for Mankind

Zhaoben Fang
Professor in Department of Statistics and Finance, USTC
www.linkedin.com/in/zhaoben-fang-a741b347/

See chapter:
How UnionPay Quick Pass is Beating Alipay and WeChat Pay in China

Rob Fernandes
Managing Director, Pay2Z Ltd
www.linkedin.com/in/robfernandes/

See abstract:
Indirect Disruption of Payments – The Strategists Dream

Eleftherios Jerry Floros
Entrepreneur and Investor, MoneyDrome Edge Ltd
www.linkedin.com/in/jerryfloros/

See chapter:
Web 3.0 – The Internet of Value

Rachel Gauci
Head of Legal & Compliance, Truevo Payments Ltd
www.linkedin.com/in/rachel-gauci-34a368ba/

See chapter:
Is Europe a Good Example of Open Banking?

Mark Gerban
Payment Industry Expert
www.linkedin.com/in/markgerban/

See chapter:
Why Distinctions Within Mobile Wallets and Tokenization Matter

Samiran Ghosh
Independent Consultant / Startup Advisor
www.linkedin.com/in/samiranbghosh/

See chapter:
Blockchain and Beyond

Daniel Gozman
Senior Lecturer, University of Sydney
www.linkedin.com/in/daniel-gozman-938a822/

See chapter:
The Future of Digital Payments Market Infrastructures

David Grenham
VP Marketing, MishiPay
www.linkedin.com/in/david-grenham/

See chapter:
Plugging the Data Black Hole: How Mobile Self-Checkout Can Help Revive the High Street

Suramya Gupta
Fund Manager, SBI Holdings – Japan
www.linkedin.com/in/suramya-gupta-3760b41/

See chapter:
Exploiting the Value of Data Embedded in Payments Systems

Vishal Gupta
Business Architect, Tata Consultancy Services
www.linkedin.com/in/vishalgupta6/

See chapter:
Taking PayTech to the Villages of India

David Gyori
CEO, Banking Reports
www.linkedin.com/in/davidgyoribankingreports/

See chapter:
Back to the Future: A Miraculous Time-Trip Through the Future, Present and Past of Payments

Jennifer Hanley-Giersch
CEO, Berlin Risk
www.linkedin.com/in/jennifer-hanley-giersch-5909a99/

See abstract:
Virtual Assets and Financial Crime Regulation

Simon Hanson
Head of Public Affairs, BACS
www.linkedin.com/in/simon-hanson-3a213212/

See chapter:
It's the Ecosystem, Stupid! Keeping Ahead in a Payments Ecosystem

Mark Hartley
Founding Partner BankiFi Ltd
www.linkedin.com/in/mark-hartley-038b38/

See chapter:
Payments as Open Business Banking Enabler for the Gig Economy

Andrew Henderson
Partner – Financial Services, Eversheds-Sutherland (International) LLP
www.linkedin.com/in/andrew-henderson-2587776/

See chapter:
Blockchain, Cryptocurrencies and How They Fit Within Current Payments Regulation

Dan Horne
Professor and Associate Dean, Providence College School of Business
www.linkedin.com/in/dan-horne-5b41634/

See chapter:
Accelerating the Adoption of PayTech Innovations

Bruna Jachemet Esin
Lawyer, Brazilian Bar Association
www.linkedin.com/in/brunajachemet/

See chapter:
PayTech Regulation Trends

Michael Kapilkov
Managing Director, mmviii [2008] Digital Asset Group
www.linkedin.com/in/michael-kapilkov/

See abstract:
Emergence of Cryptocurrency

Marion King
Director of Payments, NatWest
www.linkedin.com/in/marion-king-29b01b1b/

See chapter:
A Blueprint for Change

S. Elif Kocaoglu Ulbrich
FinTech Consultant and Author
www.linkedin.com/in/sebnemelifkocaoglu/

See chapter:
Revolutionizing the Retail Industry Through Integrated Payments Systems

Himanshu Kolhekar
FinTech Mentor, Coursera.com
www.linkedin.com/in/hkolhekar/

See abstract:
The Digital Smart Programmable Money

Bhagvan Kommadi
CEO, Quantica Computacao
www.linkedin.com/in/bhagvan-kommadi-b463a6/

See chapter:
Blockchain – An Elixir for Anti-Money Laundering?

Rajesh Krishnamoorthy
Vice Chairman, iFAST India Holdings Pte Ltd
www.linkedin.com/in/rajeshkmoorthy/

See chapter:
Asset Management and Payments in India – So Near and Yet So Far

Suneel Kumar Rathod
Head of Blockchain, Optimizia
www.linkedin.com/in/suneel-kumar-779a5539/

See chapter:
The Future is Already Here; It is Just Not Evenly Distributed

Anders la Cour
Co-Founder and Chief Executive Officer, Banking Circle
www.linkedin.com/in/anders-la-cour-48b6a53/

See chapter:
The Rise of a Super-Correspondent Banking Network

Frans Labuschagne
Country Manager UK & Ireland, Entersekt
www.linkedin.com/in/frans-labuschagne-40ab164/

See chapter:
Taking Back the Power: Regulations in the EU are Changing the Face of Banking

Israel Cedillo Lazcano
The University of Edinburgh
www.linkedin.com/in/israel-cedillo-lazcano-07966913/

See chapter:
Money: A History of Gods and Codes

Jonathan Liebenau
Reader in Technology Management, London School of Economics and Political Science
www.linkedin.com/in/jonathan-liebenau-548a418b/

See chapter:
The Future of Digital Payments Market Infrastructures

Dana Lunberry
PhD Candidate, London School of Economics and Political Science
www.linkedin.com/in/dana-lunberry/

See chapter:
The Future of Digital Payments Market Infrastructures

Ali Paterson

Editor in Chief, Fintech Finance
www.linkedin.com/in/alipaterson1/

See chapter:
The Payments Race

Gary Pine

Chief Product Officer, W2 Global Data
www.linkedin.com/in/garywpine/

See chapter:
Dynamic Regulation Readiness – Implementing the 5th Anti-Money Laundering Directive

Georgios Raikos

CEO, Talk on Strategy Ltd
www.linkedin.com/in/raikosg/

See chapter:
PayTech and Blockchain: Adjusting for Security and Risk

Naveed Rajput

Director Capital Markets – Associate & Strategic C-suite Advisor, KPMG
www.linkedin.com/in/naveedrajput/

See abstract:
Navigating Regulatory Maize – A Balancing Act or a Trigger for Strategic Innovation

Judie Rinearson

Partner, K&L Gates
www.linkedin.com/in/judithrinearson/

See chapter:
Regulation and the Future of Blockchain: Which Approach Will Succeed?

Mauro Fonseca Romaldini

Business Cosultant, M Romaldini
www.linkedin.com/in/maurofromaldini/

See abstract:
Blockchain Impact in the Future of Cross-Border Payments

John Ryan

Director General, Emerging Payments Association Asia
www.linkedin.com/in/jaryan1/

See chapter:
The New Emerging Banks and Their Role in Payments

Ekaterina Safonova

Director of Partnerships and Training, Technical Advisor, Cybertonica
www.linkedin.com/in/ekaterina-safonova-03959830/

See chapter:
The Financial Arms Race: The Game With No Rules

Julian Sawyer

Co-Founder and former COO, Starling Bank
www.linkedin.com/in/juliansawyer/

See chapter:
Payments as a Service

Ali Sohani

Founder and Chief Technology Advisor, Optimizia
www.linkedin.com/in/alisohani/

See chapter:
The Future is Already Here; It is Just Not Evenly Distributed

Vasyl Soloshchuk

CEO, INSART
www.linkedin.com/in/vsolo/

See chapter:
How to Build a Successful PayTech Product

Suresh Sood

Regional Director, Fanplayr
www.linkedin.com/in/sureshsood/

See abstract:
The New Era of Behavioural E-Commerce and Predictive Instant Payments

Udo Steger

Lawyer/Partner, PayTechLaw Blog
www.linkedin.com/in/usteger/

See abstract:
Moving to the Financial Cloud

Phil Toth

CEO, QueensGiant LLC
www.linkedin.com/in/phillip-toth-1a70871/

See abstract:
Moving Towards A Decentralized Payment System

Andréa Toucinho

Head of Studies, Prospective and Training, Partelya Consulting
www.linkedin.com/in/andr%C3%A9a-toucinho-95102597/

See chapter:

Instant Payments: A New Deal for the Payments Market?

Anna Tsyupko

CEO, Paybase
www.linkedin.com/in/atsyupko/

See chapter:

Can Operational Agility Grow Payments in the New Online Platform Marketplaces?

Isil Ugurlu

Head of Payment, Elumeo SE
www.linkedin.com/in/isilugurlu/

See abstract:

Acknowledging Customer Experience to Implement the Right Payment Solutions

Rafi Ullah Khan

Head of Data-Science, Optimizia
www.linkedin.com/in/rafi-ullah-368b1187/

See chapter:

The Future is Already Here; It is Just Not Evenly Distributed

Nadja van der Veer

Co-Founder, Payments Lawyer, PaymentCounsel
www.linkedin.com/in/paymentcounsel/

See chapter:

Money Laundering Laws, Technology and Keeping Up With Criminals

Ciske van Oosten

Global Manager – Intelligence, Verizon
www.linkedin.com/in/ciske/

See chapter:

Achieving Control Effectiveness and Sustainable Compliance Using Nine Factors

Andy White

CEO, AusPayNet
www.linkedin.com/in/amswhite/

See abstract:

Digital Identity: The Cornerstone of the Future of Payments

Junpeng Zhu

Doctor, Hefei iFlybank Financial Technology Co., Ltd

See chapter:

How UnionPay Quick Pass is Beating Alipay and WeChat Pay in China

Zeng Ziling

Fellow, Sichuan Association of FinTech, China
www.linkedin.com/in/zeng-ziling-3683663a/

See chapter:

How Network Paradigms Can Lead to New Payments Innovations

Dorota Zimnoch

Founder and Managing Director, ZING Business Consulting
www.linkedin.com/in/dorotazimnoch/

See abstract:

Future of Money and the Determinants of Consumer Choice Over Payment Methods, Globally

Index